D0269972

# The Mid-Tudor Polity
## *c.* 1540–1560

Each volume in the 'Problems in Focus' series is designed
to make available to students important new work on key
historical problems and periods that they encounter in their
courses. Each volume is devoted to a central topic or theme,
and the most important aspects of this are dealt with by
specially commissioned studies from scholars in the relevant
field. The editorial Introduction reviews the problem or period as a whole, and each chapter provides an assessment
of the particular aspect, pointing out the areas of development
and controversy, and indicating where conclusions can be
drawn or where further work is necessary. An annotated
bibliography serves as a guide to further reading.

# PROBLEMS IN FOCUS SERIES

FURTHER TITLES ARE IN PREPARATION

# The Mid-Tudor Polity
## *c.* 1540–1560

EDITED BY
JENNIFER LOACH
*Fellow and Tutor, Somerville College, Oxford*
AND
ROBERT TITTLER
*Associate Professor, Concordia University, Montreal*

© Lewis Abbott, C. S. L. Davies, Dale Hoak,
Jennifer Loach, Rex H. Pogson,
Paul Slack, Robert Tittler, Ann Weikel 1980

First published 1980 by
THE MACMILLAN PRESS LTD
London and Basingstoke
Associated companies in Delhi Dublin
Hong Kong Johannesburg Lagos
Melbourne New York Singapore and Tokyo

Printed and bound in Great Britain by
REDWOOD BURN LIMITED
Trowbridge & Esher

**British Library Cataloguing in Publication Data**

The mid-Tudor polity, c.1540–1560. – (Problems
in focus series).
  1.  Great Britain – Politics and government
  – 1485–1603
  I.  Loach, Jennifer  II.  Tittler, Robert
  III.  Series
  320.9′42′05     JN181

  ISBN 0–333–24526–1
  ISBN 0–333–24528–8 Pbk

# Contents

# Acknowledgements

No volume of this type could come to fruition without the co-operation and generous support of numerous people along the way. Our colleagues-in-print have made the task of editing run smoothly by their prompt and conscientious efforts in contributing. Derick Mirfin and Sarah Mahaffy of Macmillan Press Ltd have been enormously helpful in guiding the work through the publication process from beginning to end, and in introducing to two novices the strategies of editing. We have also benefited from the patience and expertise of Paul Slack, and of Susan Dickinson of Macmillan Press Ltd, at several points along the way. Although they should bear none of the responsibility for our efforts, the volume would be poorer without their help. The skilful and intelligent typing of Beverley Cobb was an invaluable asset in preparing the final manuscript, as was the support of the Arts and Science Faculty of Concordia University, which placed her talents at our service. Finally, we are grateful to Angela Britton for her assistance with the proofs and index.

S. J. L.
R. T.

# Introduction

JENNIFER LOACH and
ROBERT TITTLER

No period of early modern English history is more over-shadowed by the liberal and Protestant shibboleths of the Asquithean era than the mid-sixteenth century. In the opening years of our own century the magisterial tomes of Professor A. F. Pollard brought to a climax the work of the great Victorian historians and confirmed a concept of Tudor government which has endured ever since.[1] Pollard saw the sixteenth century, and, indeed, the whole cloth of history, as the story of conflict between opposites – Crown and Parliament, Catholic and Protestant, feudalism and modernity – from which emerged a national will, forging onward to some liberal empyrean. By his emphasis on the achievements of the Henrician and Elizabethan eras, moreover, Pollard implied that little of worth occurred in the decades in between, save for the brief rule of the 'good duke' of Somerset. His verdict on the reign of Mary, that 'sterility was the conclusive note', is particularly damning. So serious has been the impact of this judgement on subsequent scholarship that it is worth recalling, if only in part:

> In default of royal or ministerial leadership there could be only stagnation. Lords and Commons could do no more than resist, and the statute book bears witness to the consequent deadlock. Nor was resistance limited to the houses of Parliament; the whole nation malingered in diverse degrees. Debarred from the paths it wished to pursue, it would not follow in Mary's wake. A blight had fallen on the national health and confidence, and Israel took to her tents.[2]

These statements have, of course, been much qualified since Pollard issued them, but his priorities remain. Only in the past decade or so have historians begun to scrape the lamp-black from the bust of Northumberland, whilst the golden legacy of proto-liberalism which Pollard saw in Somerset still shines for legions of undergraduates. Sir John Neale, Pollard's successor at University College, London, so eulogised the person and reign of Elizabeth as to obscure further the years prior to her accession, and he elaborated even more than his mentor on the theme of conflict between Crown and Parliament in that era.[3] In 1950 a pupil of both Pollard and Neale, S. T. Bindoff, pronounced Marian England 'politically bankrupt, spiritually impoverished, economically archaic, and intellectually enervated',[4] although he did presciently suggest that there was more in the years from 1540 to 1558 than met the eye.[5] Unfortunately, this invitation to a more balanced view of the period was cast into the shadows by the publication in 1953 of Geoffrey Elton's provocative work, *The Tudor Revolution in Government*.[6] The stress laid in this book, and in Elton's subsequent writings on the achievement or significance of the 1530s, did for the beginning of the mid-Tudor period what Neale had done for the end: it produced a contrast between, on the one hand, a forward-looking and formative period under Cromwell, and, on the other, what Elton saw as a period of administrative collapse and legislative decline in the two decades which followed.[7]

Elton's thesis of 'the Tudor Revolution' produced much controversy in ensuing years, but, as its opponents dealt with the lack of novelty in Cromwell's achievements as seen against *mediaeval* precedents, such controversy did not prompt the active research into the 1540s and 1550s which it might have done.[8] Indeed, Pollard's views were then given a further airing by the publication of Professor W. K. Jordan's two volumes on the period 1547 to 1553, *Edward VI: The Young King* and *Edward VI: The Threshold of Power*. Here we find Somerset described as a man of moderation and tolerance, whose 'stubborn and high minded devotion to a programme of revolutionary reform was the prime cause for the gathering of a successful conspiracy against him'.[9] Once again, moreover, the duke of Northumberland is described as a man of 'dour and frightful ruthlessness'.[10] The only recent general survey of this period, Whitney D. Jones's *The Mid-Tudor Crisis, 1539–1563*, published in 1973, perpetuated even by its very title the notion of a hard winter between the golden summers of Henry's reign and Elizabeth's.

None the less, the thaw has begun. Some of Pollard's assertions about the reign of Edward VI are under attack. M. L. Bush has suggested, in his study of *The Government Policy of Protector Somerset* (1975), that 'the good duke' was ready to sacrifice the well-being of the poor in his desire to win the war in Scotland. R. W. Heinze has joined the fray to reveal, in *The Proclamations of the Tudor Kings* (1976), that Somerset doubled the use of proclamations and relied on severe penalties more often than his predecessors, not only in response to the exceptional circumstances of 1549, but also for such relatively trivial matters as the deforestation of Waltham.[11] In a study of *The King's Council in the Reign of Edward VI*, published in the same year, Dale Hoak argued that the government in the reign of the Protector was more autocratic and less 'conciliar' than it was to be during the remainder of the reign.[12] In his essay in this volume (chapter 2), Hoak takes the rehabilitation of Northumberland one stage further, and shows that the duke used the office of Lord President of the Council to re-establish the executive, administrative, and quasi-judicial competence of the Privy Council: these reforms, he suggests, enabled Mary and Elizabeth 'to inherit a type of government-by-council more efficient than any of those which served Continental kings'.

Such a reassessment of Northumberland's work as Lord President could easily have perpetuated the myth of the Marian Privy Council as, by contrast, unwieldy, inefficient and faction-ridden. However, the researches of Ann Weikel and G. A. Lemasters have revealed a different picture.[13] Ann Weikel's dissection of the composition and working of the Council during the early years of Mary's reign (see chapter 3) shows it to have operated more regularly in the conduct of administration, and more decisively in the formulation of policy, than has generally been supposed. What many observers have seen as factionalism centring on the figures of Stephen Gardiner and William Paget is shown to have been more of a creative rivalry: even at the worst of times, it precluded neither the co-operation nor the collaboration of both groups.

We may now hope that, as a result of these efforts, further attempts will be made to assess the relative efficiency and success of conciliar government in various spheres of activity during this period. One area that has recently been explored in this manner is that of finance, for, although controversy continues to rage about the impact of debasement on the national economy, the work of C. E. Challis and J. D. Gould has illuminated its function in the funding of government.[14] In the course of *The Tudor Coinage* (1978), Mr Challis illustrates many aspects of conciliar activity, and makes a particularly interesting contribution by pointing out the workmanlike preparations made by the Marian Council for a reform of the coinage.[15] Though in the end this scheme lapsed through a sheer failure of nerve, it tells us much about the creative ability of Mary's councillors, and served as a blueprint for the completion of recoinage under Elizabeth. In a more successful Marian scheme for financial reform, a committee was set up in 1557 to inquire 'why customs and subsidies be greatly diminished and decayed'. The result of the committee's deliberations was the appointment of a Privy Councillor, Sir Francis Englefield, as Surveyor General of the Customs, and the issue, in May 1558, of a new Book of Rates.[16] The new Book increased customs revenue by over 75 percent, and has been described by George Ramsay as 'a major achievement in Tudor fiscal administration, making the recovery of a large, expanding, and virtually permanent source of revenue for the Exchequer'.[17]

In other areas of activity the Council had to formulate and implement policy with the assent of Parliament. Once again, the theme of conflict in government–Parliament relations so emphasised by Pollard, Wallace Notestein and Neale has been misleading.[18] The work of Professor S. E. Lehmberg on the parliaments of Henry VIII has done something to correct this tendency to see sixteenth-century parliaments simply as an overture to the constitutional clashes of the early Stuart era, while Professor Elton's discussion of meetings of Parliament as a 'point of contact' has also been a valuable corrective.[19] Study of parliamentary opposition under Mary has led to a questioning of the reality of the organised factional strife described by Neale and others. What emerges in its place is consensus: a sensitive give and take in which conflict was usually circumvented by the design either of those who sat in Parliament or of the Crown and Council.[20]

The results of conciliar vitality and the relatively harmonious behaviour of Parliament are most clearly visible in the initiation of policy in the social and economic sphere. Robert Tittler and Paul Slack suggest in their essays in this volume (chapters 4 and 5) that the recognition by Parliament of local initiative in the solution of domestic problems, and the subsequent incorporation of such initiatives into official government policy, are important and generally consistent themes. For Paul Slack this conclusion arises in the context of charitable institutions and their relation to the government. He finds, as did Ann Weikel in her study of the Council, that government worked most effectively when the perception of crises was at its height. This is most convincingly illustrated by the great interest displayed in the foundation of charitable institutions in London after 1547, at a time when harvest failures, epidemics and inflation intensified an already serious problem of poverty and vagrancy.

Robert Tittler also finds ample evidence of government responsiveness to domestic problems in the emergence of a definable and coherent set of official attitudes towards the troubled urban areas of the realm. Here he notes that the governments of the mid-Tudor period, often guided by local initiative, formulated and implemented clear strategies of support for economically and politically beleagured towns, and established the foundations of municipal government for the post-mediaeval era.

Consensus in government is, then, a theme which emerges out of many of the essays in this volume. Although the stress here placed on agreement and concord makes a break with earlier traditions, it is perhaps less remarkable if the economic and social background of the period is kept constantly in mind. In a period of social stress and economic difficulties it is not surprising that the Crown and the governing classes closed ranks: it is interesting to note, for example, how much stronger were denunciations of rebellion after 1549, even amongst those clerics and reformers who believed that the lot of the lower classes was unnecessarily miserable.[21] Recent work on the rebellions of 1549 has suggested that the risings in the West and in East Anglia became full-scale revolts not because economic distress was any greater there than elsewhere, but because the gentry of these areas were less united and less directed by the leadership of local nobility.[22] Further consideration of the abortive risings is probably necessary before this theory can be substantiated, but it does seem as if political stability was prized above all else in the 1550s.

The same theme of respect for stability is elaborated in the essay in this volume by Lewis Abbott (chapter 7), who shows how the legal profession, after the debacle of Lady Jane Grey's reign, sought through ostentatious loyalty and unswerving conformity to the Church of Rome to secure those goals which it most desired: personal advancement, private profit, and social conservatism. Similarly, C. S. L. Davies argues (chapter 8) that, despite its ill success, the Anglo-French War united the upper classes to a remarkable extent: even those families who had challenged the Spanish marriage were prepared to fight for the Imperial alliance.

In the light of these historical revisions many elements of Jones's 'mid-Tudor crisis' may be dismissed. The 'crisis of governance' which he discusses has been reduced by new work on the Privy Council and by an increasing realisation that, although many of Thomas Cromwell's creations underwent change in the decades after his fall, such change was not necessarily for the worse.[23] The standards of Cromwellian administration amply survived the fall of their alleged architect, and government remained resourceful and responsive in the face of changing and difficult circumstances.

One ingredient of crisis, however, remains. It would be difficult to deny that the religious life of the realm underwent considerable strain with the establishment of Edwardian Protestantism, the Marian reaction, and the Elizabethan settlement.[24] Yet Rex Pogson is able to suggest in this volume (chapter 6) a counterweight to the idea of relentless conflict between Catholic and Protestant which was first proposed by John Foxe and which has been echoed by Pollard and others virtually to the present. His study of parochial clergy reveals that Mary and Cardinal Pole were compelled to accept schismatics because the Church lacked manpower; this in its turn suggests that the average English cleric was less driven by conscience and more open to compromise than tradition has permitted us to accept. Mary's policies might even, given more time, have resulted in the peaceful return of the clergy to their old familiar beliefs: as it was, Mary and Pole appear to have produced a clergy distinguished for its integrity and level of education. Far from failing to discover the Counter-Reformation, Mary and Pole anticipated the most forward-looking of the Tridentine decrees in their emphasis on the educational attainments of the clergy and on the pastoral duties of the episcopacy.[25] The strength of the Catholic revival can be seen, as Jennifer Loach argues in this volume, in the united front presented by the Marian bishops in 1559.

It is most important that, in seeking to revise the emphasis laid by earlier historians on conflict and sterility, we do not create a view of equal distortion on the other side. There was indeed concord and creativity in this period, but there were also some 300 deaths by burning and numerous executions in the aftermath of the 1549 risings. Yet the notion of crisis must not even here be too lightly assumed. Professor Bellamy has recently pointed out that neither the reign of Edward nor that of Mary was a time of great repression in so far as the law of treason was concerned:[26] measured by that yardstick, contemporary governments do not seem to have felt as besieged as, for example, Thomas Cromwell did in the 1530s.

The editors are well aware of the gaps and limitations of this volume. Until a number of important themes and issues have been further explored, a revisionist approach to the middle years of the Tudor century cannot be complete. The table of contents reveals an imbalance of the essays in favour of the reign of Mary: this was not entirely the conscious design of the editors, but it does help to correct a longstanding bias against that reign, which has provoked less study than perhaps any comparable period of the whole century.[27]

Perhaps the most serious hiatus is in the realm of ideas. The exploration of the intellectual underpinnings of the post-Reformation era, from the pioneering efforts of Gordon Zeeveld to the later publications of J. K. McConica, A. B. Ferguson, W. R. D. Jones and Geoffrey Elton, have illuminated contemporary perceptions of the social and economic problems of the 1540s and, to a lesser extent, the 1550s, and has illustrated the links between political analysis and government action.[28] A great deal more work needs to be done, however, before the initiation of ideas in government and their implementation at the level of the Privy Council and the courts of law can be fully understood. This work, moreover, needs to be undertaken in the light of Professor Elton's warning that a careful distinction must be made between ideas expounded in material spontaneously offered to the government and those concepts contained in material put out by the government on its own initiative.[29] Our understanding of these problems would undoubtedly have been much deepened by the study on which J. P. Cooper was engaged at the time of his death: the loss to this volume is a reminder of how great is the void now left in sixteenth- and seventeenth-century historical scholarship.

Despite all these gaps and imperfections, this volume suggests that the ground-work for a more subtle and more positive approach to the mid-Tudor period has been established. Pollard's sterile interlude has been found teeming with life, and the distance between the Cromwellian achievement on the one hand and the reign of Gloriana on the other seems rather shorter than has been supposed.

# 1. Conservatism and Consent in Parliament, 1547–59

## JENNIFER LOACH

I

HISTORIANS differ in their interpretation of the parliamentary history of the reigns of Henry VIII and of Elizabeth – did concord prevail or conflict, how much did initiative lie with private members, how significant was aristocratic patronage? – but they are agreed on the importance of the two periods for the development of the institution itself. No such consensus exists about the parliamentary history of the 1540s and the 1550s. For these years commentators have followed Sir John Neale, who saw them simply as an essential prelude to his explanation of Elizabethan developments and, in particular, to his interpretation of the events of the parliament of 1559.[1] Neale laid particular stress on opposition in the House of Commons during Mary's reign and on the part Protestantism played in the creation of that opposition. As a result, those writers who do not simply dismiss the period as one of hiatus generally distinguish between the co-operation which they regard as characteristic of the relations between Crown and Parliament in the reign of Edward VI and the conflict which they consider endemic in Mary's reign.[2] Thus they imply that Crown and Parliament worked in harmony when they aimed at the advancement of Protestantism but fell into disagreement when they faced the restoration of Catholicism.

This interpretation is open to attack on four fronts. It stems from a narrow concentration on events in the House of Commons and largely ignores the House of Lords, where there was in fact considerable resistance to the introduction of Protestant doctrine during the reign of Edward VI and at the beginning of Elizabeth's reign. It exaggerates both the extent to which members of the Lower House opposed Catholic policies in the reign of Mary and the extent to which they urged radical Protestantism on her sister in the parliament of 1559. It assumes, on inadequate evidence, that opposition to Mary's policies was based on principle rather than on material considerations. Finally, it places too much emphasis on religious legislation as a gauge of Crown–Parliament relations.

Neither the Crown, whose prerogative it was to decide when Parliament should be assembled, nor those who sat in Parliament, regarded the settlement of the Church as the sole or even the most important justification for meeting. The Crown's need of money, for instance, was a factor of immense and growing importance. This need had prompted the calling of Parliament in 1545[3] and brought about the second session of Edward's first parliament, in 1548. Indeed, Lord Paget reminded Protector Somerset in the course of that session that taxation was 'the only cause why the Parliament was called before Christmas'; the Commons, he went on, knew this and had expected that the subsidy bill would be 'the first thing that should have come in Parliament'.[4] Edward's parliament of March 1553 was also summoned specifically to grant taxation, as the duke of Northumberland made clear when he tried, unsuccessfully, to persuade the Council to postpone the meeting until after the harvest was in, when, he believed, the King's subjects might be more willing to assist.[5] Although Mary did not seek taxation in the first three of her parliaments, financial necessity was amongst the most pressing of the reasons for summoning a meeting in 1555,[6] and in the wartime circumstances of 1558 it was the most important. Elizabeth was the first of the Tudors to ask for a grant of taxation in the opening parliament of a reign, and only one of her subsequent parliaments, that of 1572, was to pass without any grant being made. Other reasons prompting the assembly of Parliament during these years included the ratification in 1554 of the marriage treaty with Spain and the confirmation, however indirectly, of the title to the throne of both Mary and Elizabeth.

The settlement of the Church was not, then, the most important reason for which the Crown in this period decided to summon Parliament. After all, statute was not the only method by which the Crown sought to direct religious affairs. All Henry VIII's children used proclamations at the beginning of their reigns to regulate and often to alter the teaching and ceremonial of the Church;[7] indeed, ten months elapsed between Henry VIII's death and the opening of his son's first parliament, and during that time injunctions were issued on the royal authority alone that substantially altered the doctrines of the English Church.[8] There is, moreover, evidence to suggest that in 1548 Somerset seriously considered further implementing his religious policy by means of proclamation rather than statute.[9] Throughout the sixteenth century, statute remained only one among many methods of controlling the Church.

Those who sat in Parliament and those who had elected them were also more interested in legislation that affected their localities, their trades, professions and even their personal affairs than they were in changes in the Church. If we examine, for example, the instructions given by the city of York to its representatives during this period, we find that, although the city attached much importance to 'the parliament time' as an occasion on which all sorts of business might be done in the capital – the members were told to discover what was happening to cases pending in various courts, to seek reductions in the city's tax assessment and to ask for confirmation of various charters – it showed little interest in general legislation.[10] The city records mention very few statutes of anything other than local interest, save the subsidy acts: they are silent about religious legislation. York's example could be paralleled elsewhere: the interest taken by the city of London in the problems of the leather trade,[11] for instance, or the constant concern of Norwich with the regulation of the cloth trade.[12]

These preoccupations are reflected both in the statute book and the Journals of the House of Commons and House of Lords. A glance at any day's business as recorded in the Journals shows that an enormous amount of time was taken up in the discussion of bills that were of interest only to small sections of the community. Over one-fifth of the statutes passed in the reigns of Edward and Mary dealt with the affairs of named private individuals: acts of attainder and restitution, land settlements, divorces and acts of naturalisation.

If, therefore, religion was not the sole or even the main reason for which parliaments were summoned at this period, if it was not the most pressing concern of those who assembled in response to the royal writ, if, indeed, large stretches of parliamentary time elapsed without any mention of religion, then the link between harmony in Crown–Parliament relations and periods of Protestant ascendancy begins to look less secure. But is it in any case correct to assume that Parliament was full of men of Reformed tendencies who co-operated with the Crown under Edward VI and opposed it under Mary?

II

Let us begin by examining the House of Commons. There does indeed appear to have been support for, or rather – and the distinction is a crucial one – little opposition to, the ascent of Protestantism. Only on two occasions did government religious policy run into difficulties, and in neither instance was the issue purely doctrinal. The passage of a bill in 1547 to dissolve the chantries was not easy, but the problems probably arose from the use to which some boroughs put chantry revenues rather than from religious zeal.[13] In 1552 it was the action of the Commons that led to the loss of a bill that would have deprived Tunstall of the bishopric of Durham on the grounds of misprision of treason, but, as the bill had also been opposed in the Upper House by Cranmer himself, it would be an error to see in this move genuine sympathy for the conservative cause. Opposition probably arose from a dislike of fudged evidence and unprecedented procedure rather than from any Catholic enthusiasm. Although the Journal of the House of Commons for Edward's reign is extremely terse and there is not much other evidence about what went on in the Chamber, it is probably correct to assume that little dissent was expressed.

At first sight things look very different in the reign of Mary. Indeed, the parliament of 1555 is notorious for what Neale described as its 'critical spirit'. There was, it is true, considerable controversy over two government bills with religious implications. One of these was the bill whereby the Queen restored first fruits and tenths to the Church.[15] This bill was passed only by keeping the House sitting until the unusually late hour of 3 p.m., by which time many hostile members, anxious to get their lunch, had departed.[16] The second controversial bill was the exiles bill, which permitted the Crown to sieze the lands of those who had gone abroad and refused to return. When this came to the vote, those who opposed it, fearing a repetition of the government's earlier tactic, locked the door of the chamber and forced the Speaker to put the question before Councillors and others who wanted the bill to succeed could go and find reinforcements.[17] The bill was then rejected.

This was certainly a triumph for opposition. Was it, however, a triumph for Protestantism? We can try to answer this question in two ways: first, by looking at the religious views of those we know to have opposed it, and, secondly, by looking at the content of the bill itself. The most violent opposition to the bill came from a West Country gentleman, Sir Anthony Kingston, who seized the key from the Sergeant-at-Arms and locked the door of the Chamber. Kingston's religious views are not known: he struck Hooper in 1551 when the bishop attempted to reprimand him for adultery, but Foxe records that the two were reconciled before Hooper's burning in 1555.[18] Kingston's dislike of the bill was shared by Sir George Howard, who nearly came to blows with Sir Edward Hastings in the Chamber itself.[19] Howard's religious inclinations are again a matter of speculation; he served against Wyatt and was also in receipt of a Spanish pension.[20] The only other man who can be identified with certainty as opposed to the exiles bill was an influential

Pembrokeshire gentleman, Sir John Perrott,[21] whose sympathies may indeed have been Protestant.[22] We know the names, then, of only three of the men who opposed the exiles bill. Of these only one may be identified as having Reformed ideas and even here the evidence is fairly tentative.

In addition, William Cecil is known to have disliked some major piece of government legislation in this Parliament, probably either the exiles or the first-fruits bill.[23] Cecil was to be, of course, a Puritan sympathiser in the reign of Elizabeth. He identified Sir John Pollard and Sir William Courtenay as dissidents,[24] and Courtenay is known to have complained of the first-fruits bill to the French ambassador.[25] Nothing definite can be said about the religious views of either of these men. The investigations into the Treasury plot were later to include Pollard and Courtenay among the six members of the House of Commons who were said to have met in Arundel's Tavern during the session, complaining about 'such Catholic proceedings as they perceived the Queen and all Catholic men went about' and declaring that 'they intended to resist such matters as should be spoken of other than liked them'. The other names mentioned were those of Arthur Champernowne, John Young, Henry Peckham and Sir John Perrott.[26] Champernowne and Young are shadowy figures, whilst Peckham, whose father and brother were both Marian Privy Councillors, appears to have been an extravagant young man whose actions were prompted by his need for ready cash rather than by any stirrings of conscience.[27] Another man who offended the Queen by his behaviour at some juncture during the parliament was Sir Thomas Gargrave, who was Speaker of the House of Commons in Elizabeth's first parliament;[28] Gargrave was described in 1564 as 'a favourer' of the Protestant settlement, but he was a client of the conservative earl of Shrewsbury and certainly no zealot.[29]

We know, therefore, very little of the religious views of those few men who can be identified as hostile to the first-fruits bill and the exiles bill. Moreover, we do not even know the names of the major part of those who voted against the first-fruits bill and were responsible for the defeat of the exiles bill.[30]

The intentions of the government in proposing the exiles bill are, however, clearer than the motives of those who opposed it. The law relating to the confiscation of the property of Englishmen who had taken up residence abroad was uncertain and a poverty-stricken government was anxious to clarify the position to its own advantage. However, the proposal put forward dangerously undermined property rights. Without having any sympathy for those who had fled for religion or for their beliefs, a landowner might regard the measure with suspicion.[31] When a similar measure was passed in 1571, permitting the Crown to confiscate the property of Catholic exiles, it also ran into difficulties and was passed only after various amendments and with the addition of a number of clauses safeguarding the interests of the exiles' families and descendants.[32] But no one has yet suggested that the House of Commons of 1571 was dominated by crypto-Catholics.

Hostility to the exiles bill could be based on entirely secular considerations, and so too could dislike of the first-fruits bill, since reduction in the Crown's permanent revenues would almost certainly lead to an increase in taxation. Indeed, there was much resentment that the proposal to restore these revenues was made at the same time as a request for taxation,[33] and the grant finally offered was for a sum lower than that initially proposed.[34] In a worsening economic climate, property owners were worried about taxation and the effect it might have on the poor, about the invasion of property rights implicit in the exiles bill and about the threat to their tenure of former ecclesiastical property offered by the Queen's restoration of first fruits, which some regarded as the 'thin end of the wedge'. The prevailing atmosphere of the 1555 parliament was one not of Protestant enthusiasm but, rather, of concern for material things.

If we look at events in Mary's parliaments as a whole, it becomes obvious that, as in the previous reign, there was little active opposition in the House of Commons to the Crown's religious proposals. Some part of the Commons – one report says eighty out of 350 – opposed the bill in the first parliament whereby all Edwardian religious legislation was repealed.[35] Given that many of these men were members of the parliaments that had passed the statutes now being revoked – an average rate of re-election of about one-third can be assumed from parliament to parliament – the small scale of this opposition is remarkable. There was, moreover, no hostility in the Commons to Gardiner's proposal of April 1554 to revive the heresy laws. The great bill of repeal which reunited England with Rome took, it is true, nearly a fortnight to pass the Commons in December 1554, but the reason for the delay was not opposition to the reunion itself but, rather, general anxiety about former ecclesiastical property. The problem was that, whereas Cardinal Pole considered it simoniacal to include in the bill the Pope's dispensation to holders of such property, those who possessed former Church land believed only statute would give them security of tenure.[36] Although the matter was discussed in Parliament, it was finally resolved elsewhere, in a meeting that took place on 21 and 22 December between the Queen, the Cardinal, members of the Privy Council and the Crown's legal advisers.[37] Pole was then forced to agree that the dispensation should be part of the bill – this clause of the act has clearly been inserted into the main body of the manuscript – although he did win some concessions on mortmain.[38] There is no evidence to suggest that this highly important proposal was opposed in the Commons on any ground other than that of anxiety about property. Only one man, Sir Ralph Bagnall, spoke against it, and the burden of his speech was loyalty to the memory of Henry VIII and his anti-papal legislation.[39] The rest of the House, kneeling and in tears, cared only for the Cardinal's forgiveness and their property rights.

Under Mary, then, the House of Commons displayed little of the Protestant fervour so often attributed to it. It was an overestimation of such fervour that led Sir John Neale to misinterpret the events of the parliament of 1559. An understanding of the events of this, the first of Elizabeth's parliaments, is, as Neale appreciated, crucial to our understanding of the parliamentary history of the whole mid-Tudor period; unfortunately, his own interpretation not only rests, as we have seen, on an exaggerated estimate of the strength of Protestant opposition to the Crown in the Marian Commons but also suffers as a result of his neglect of the House of Lords.

### III

Although nineteenth- and twentieth-century historians have tended to concentrate on events in the House of Commons at the expense of those in the Lords, contemporaries were well aware of the enormous potential for disruption presented by the Upper Chamber. It is revealing to find that the duke of Northumberland, an astute and wary politician who devoted considerable energies to the task of management in the House of Commons, was also very conscious of the danger of opposition in the Lords. In January 1553, for instance, he suggested that certain heirs apparent of noble families be allowed to sit and even to vote in the Chamber, in theory to give them experience of public affairs but in reality to strengthen his own position.[40] Northumberland's caution was doubtless provoked by recent events. Thomas Seymour, Lord Sudeley, had attempted in late 1548 to build up a party in the Upper House against his brother, the Protector. Seymour had told the earl of Rutland that he hoped the earl would take his seat in the House, as 'he trusted to have [his] voice with him', and asked Lord Clinton and the earl of Dorset not only to give their consent to a bill that he proposed to introduce, but also to gain for him the votes of as many of their 'friends in the House' as they could.[41] Somerset himself later thought of using Parliament against Northumberland.[42]

But it was not only as a platform for the grievances of discontented peers that the Upper House presented Northumberland with a challenge. It was manifest by the time Northumberland rose to power that there existed in the Lords a substantial and articulate body of conservative feeling opposed to the Protestant policies pursued by Edward's governments.

During this time there was, as has been shown, little opposition in the House of Commons to the government's religious policies. In the House of Lords, however, things were not so easy. There a substantial minority opposed all the Edwardian religious changes. Sometimes this minority succeeded in defeating a measure which it disliked – a bill permitting the marriage of priests had to be abandoned in 1547, for example[43] – but more often it managed to hold up and modify legislation and frequently it protested against those bills that were successful. Peers who disapproved of royal policy had one weapon in their armoury that was denied to members of the Lower House: the formal protest. When a bill was passed which they disliked, peers had the right to register a formal protest in the Journal, and they were liberal in their use of this privilege. Thus, although the bill for the administration of the sacrament in both kinds was passed by the Upper House on 10 December 1547, the bishops of London, Norwich, Hereford, Worcester and Chichester found relief for their feelings in a formal protest. Indeed, formal protests were registered against almost all the religious bills passed in Edward's reign. These protests cannot be dismissed as futile: they appear in the Journal too frequently to be regarded simply as gestures of pique. Rather they were a constant warning to the government of the strength of conservatism.

Of course, once Northumberland had triumphed over the conservatives, the Henrician bishops who had played a promi-nent part in the opposition to radical Protestantism were replaced by men such as John Ponet. But this did not end the problem, for the bishops had not fought alone. A number of lay peers, including the earl of Derby and Lords Dacre, Wharton, Stourton and Windsor, had also registered protests against the Crown's Protestant policies. Other peers also pro-tested from time to time: Lord Morley, for example, added his name on 19 February 1549 to that of Dacre, Windsor, Wharton and eight bishops in a protest against the bill that sanctioned the marriage of priests, a bill that had run into such difficulties in the Upper House that it took two months to pass. Clerical marriage was clearly an unpopular thing with many peers, since the earls of Shrewsbury, Derby, Rut-land and Bath, with Lords Stourton, Mounteagle, Sandys, Windsor and Wharton, all protested against another such bill on 10 February 1552.

To see the parliamentary history of Edward's reign as one of effortless harmony in religious matter is, therefore, to concentrate too narrowly on events in the House of Commons. The Upper House contained many who did not care for the doctrines put forward by Edward's governments, either because they were attached to the old faith or because they feared that innovation might break the bonds that held society together. Although there were in the House men of Reformed ideas, men such as the patron of Protestant scholars Henry Grey, marquis of Dorset and later duke of Suffolk, it was a fundamentally conservative body.

This conservatism has sometimes been obscured by the misinterpretation of an episode in the second of Mary's parliaments, that of April and May 1554. This parliament was called in the aftermath of Wyatt's rebellion, which had left an atmosphere of suspicion and mistrust at court. Politicians jockeyed for position and sought to make capital out of the Queen's own doubts and fears. In particular the Lord Chancellor, Stephen Gardiner, whose position had been weakened by his known opposition to the Spanish marriage, tried to recover favour with the Queen by expressions of religious fervour. His desire to push forward the restoration of Catholic drama and ceremony was not shared by all his fellow Privy Councillors and, in particular, alarmed William Paget.[44] Paget, the most consistent advocate of the alliance with Philip, not only feared the consequences of over-hasty action in religious matters, but also saw that Gardiner might oust him from the royal favour. Unable to block Gardiner's plans in the Privy Council, Paget carried the quarrel to the House of Lords, where he persuaded the secular peers that the bishop's bill for the revival of the mediaeval heresy laws posed a threat to those who held former ecclesiastical property.[45] The bill was rejected.[46]

This caused the government great embarrassment, for preparations had already been made in Oxford for the trials of Cranmer, Latimer and Ridley in the expectation that the necessary legislation would be implemented. The trials had to wait until, six months later, a House almost entirely unchanged in composition passed without demur an apparently identical bill.[47] The loss of the heresy bill in the spring of 1554 should not, therefore, be seen as an expression of sympathy for the Protestant bishops and their fellows: it seems rather that the peers who told the Chancellor that they had rejected the bill only to safeguard their property and not to favour heresy were speaking the truth.[48] The spectre of a threat to secularised property loomed large in Mary's parliaments.

Paget's activities were not confined to blocking the heresy bill.[49] He also brought about the loss of a bill that would have extended to Philip the protection of the treason laws, a measure that was, like the heresy bill, passed in the next meeting.[50] Given Paget's position, both before and after this incident, as leader of the pro-Philip faction in the Council, his behaviour cannot have been based on principle but must rather have been based on a desire to prove to Mary his strength. Much is made of the trend during this period for Privy Councillors to find seats in the House of Commons, and it is true that the most unruly House of Commons of the reign, that of 1555, contained the fewest Privy Councillors. Yet it is also important to remember that a large number, often a majority, of the Council were members of the Upper House and that conciliar squabbles and jostling for position could have a considerable impact on that smaller and more intimate body. Moreover, the fact that most of the more active and articulate members of the House of Lords were also members of the Privy Council meant that many of their criticisms of policy or particular measures had already been acted upon before they were discussed in the House: it was because Paget had failed in the Council that he needed to fight Gardiner's measures in the Chamber. In general, however, the existence of a bench of bishops firmly committed to the old faith and of a number of lay peers who shared their views meant that relations between the Crown and the House of Lords were more cordial in Mary's reign than they had been in that of her Protestant predecessor. But the result of this conservatism was to be, paradoxically, the creation in the next reign of a more radical Church settlement than that for which the new queen had herself hoped.

IV

To understand this paradox we must look closely at the

events of the parliament of 1559, and, in particular, at the passage of the bills of uniformity and supremacy. We may accept the outline of events set out by Sir John Neale.[51] Initially, as Neale demonstrated, the Queen intended only 'to restore religion as her father left it', with a sop to the Protestants in the form of the administration to the laity of the sacrament in both kinds. Thus, the supremacy bill first read in the Commons on 9 February 1559, which included a permissive clause about communion in both kinds, was intended to be the only doctrinal measure of the Parliament. But there were radicals in the Lower House – although far fewer than Neale thought – whom this measure left dissatisfied. Other bills were introduced on their initiative, 'for the order of service and ministers in the Church' and 'for common prayer and ministration of the sacrament'. These bills, which almost certainly represented an attempt to revive the Edwardian religious statutes and in particular the use of the 1552 Prayer Book, were read only once but seem to have been amalgamated into a second supremacy bill drafted within the House itself.[52]

This bill, more radical than that proposed by the Crown, ran into problems in the Lords, where, according to the Venetian ambassador, there was 'very great altercation and disputes on the part of the bishops and of other good and pious peers'.[53] The conservatives struck out various clauses that offended them, which led the Commons to pass a bill 'that no persons shall be punished for using the religion used in King Edward's last year'.[54] The Venetian ambassador noted that

the Earl of Pembroke, the Earl of Shrewsbury, Viscount Montagu and Lord Hastings did not fail in their duty like true soldiers of Christ to resist the Commons, whom they have compelled to modify a book passed by the Commons forbidding the Mass to be said or the communion administered except . . . in the manner of Edward VI.[55]

Anthony Browne, Viscount Montagu, was indeed a devoted Catholic who spoke eloquently of the 'great dishonour to England, if it again so soon revolted from the apostolic see,

to which it had of late humbly reconciled itself'.[56] It took
the Upper House three weeks to consider the supremacy
bill, and, when the purged and less radical measure was
finally passed, on 18 March, Shrewsbury and Montagu joined
the spiritual peers in their protest against it.

Elizabeth was in a dilemma. The bishops had shown by
their words and actions in the Lords that they would not
accept the restoration of the royal supremacy. In order to
secure the supremacy, the cornerstone of the Henrician settlement, she would be forced to change her bishops, and this
would thrust her into the bosom of more radical churchmen.
In the process she would alienate conservative laymen and
be driven, much against her will, to rely on the support
of determined Protestants. Thus, during the parliamentary
recess, Elizabeth found herself vulnerable to the ideas of
men in her intimate circle who sympathised with the radicals:
men such as Cecil, who was later to say of the 1559 settlement
'I must confess I am thereof guilty',[57] and the Lord Keeper,
Nicholas Bacon, whose outburst against the conservatives
at the Westminster synod, which took place during the recess,
forced his fellow Councillors to support him by the arrest
of the bishops of Winchester and Lincoln.[58] When Parliament
reconvened, the idea of confining religious legislation to a
measure restoring the royal supremacy had to be abandoned,
and in its place a bill was introduced that authorised the
use of the second Edwardian Prayer Book.

The stand taken by the Marian bishops against the supremacy bill was therefore crucial. Had they been willing to
accept the royal supremacy they would almost certainly,
given Elizabeth's own inclinations, have presided over a
Church different in few respects from that of the early 1540s:
There was considerable support for such a policy in the
House of Lords: nine temporal peers (the marquis of Winchester, the earl of Shrewsbury, Lords Montagu, Morley, Stafford,
Dudley, Wharton, Rich and North) protested against the
uniformity bill,[59] although only Montagu doggedly joined
the bishops in registering a protest against the supremacy
bill that was passed on 26 April. The abbot of Westminster,
John Feckenham, was harping on a theme dear to the hearts
of many secular lords when he argued that Catholicism pro-

duced loyal and obedient subjects.[60] There can be little doubt that acceptance of the supremacy by the bishops would have created a strong conservative party in the Lords, a party that might well have reanimated Henrician Catholicism.

This is, of course, to argue that the House of Lords was more important in 1559 than Neale suggested, the House of Commons less so. Neale found little need to examine closely what went on in the Lords, because he believed that in the House of Commons there was a substantial number of radical Protestants, whose views were made explicit and orchestrated by what he called 'a Puritan choir' of returned Marian exiles, and who put irresistible pressure on the Queen.[61] Undoubtedly he overestimated the number of such exiles who were present in the House: there were probably only eight or nine of them, rather than the 'twelve and probably sixteen' that he mentions, and some even of these, such as Sir Ralph Bagnall, seem to have gone abroad to escape their creditors rather than the tyranny of the bishop of Rome. Neale went on to argue that 'in addition to the vital core of émigrés in the House of Commons there were at least 64 other members who had sat in Mary's obstreperous Parliament of 1555, most of whom might, with due caution, be reckoned along with this radical core'.

His interpretation of the mood of the Commons in 1559 thus rests largely on his interpretation of the mood of the House of Commons in 1555, and on his belief that anyone who sat in that Parliament may be assumed to have been opposed to Mary's Catholic proposals. This, of course, was not the case. Moreover, although in 1555 some Members of Parliament were opposed to the policies of the Crown, they cannot be identified; it is as likely that the sixty-four men whom Neale described as being sympathetic to Protestantism in 1559 had been amongst those who voted in 1555 in favour of Mary's Catholic proposals as it is that they had been amongst those opposing them.

In giving the House of Commons so central a role in the creation of the Elizabethan Church settlement Neale misread two decades of parliamentary history. The remarkable thing about the Lower House throughout this period, and here we may include the last years of Henry VIII's reign, is the readiness with which it acquiesced in the royal religious policy, regardless of what that policy was.

It is, of course, possible to argue that this acquiescence was not natural, and that it arose from fear, resulted from government intervention in elections or sprang from Crown management in the House. However, during this period it seems that government intervention in elections in areas other than those in which it had direct local influence (such as the stannery towns) was rarely successsful. An attempt to secure the return of Sir John Baker as Knight of the Shire for Kent in 1547 alienated the electors, who seem to have felt that their independence was being eroded.[62] Before the parliament of March 1553, a systematic attempt was made to secure the return of named individuals as Knights of the Shire, but it was only partially successful.[63] General letters were also sent out then asking for the return of 'men of gravity and knowledge in their own countries [i.e. counties] and towns fit for their understanding to be in such a great council'.[64] In like fashion electors were instructed before Mary's third parliament to choose men of 'the wise, grave and Catholic sort, such as indeed mean the true honour of God with the prosperity of the commonwealth'.[65] No letters appear to have been sent before Mary's fourth parliament, but before the last one instructions were circulated asking for the election of men of 'gravity and knowledge in their own countries and towns'.[66] Elizabeth did not use circular letters until 1571. It is impossible to tell how much impact letters of this kind had. Some returns in 1554 explicitly state that men of 'the wise, grave and Catholic sort' had been elected,[67] but a study of areas sending in such returns suggests no break in electoral patterns; it appears, in short, as if constituencies were claiming credit for doing what they were going to do anyway.

Another way in which the Crown could affect the composition of the Lower House was through the enfranchisement of boroughs. Under Edward VI membership of the Commons grew from 341 to 375, and under Mary the number of members increased to 400. These new enfranchisements added to the number of seats in which the Crown had some influence – six of the constituencies thus created were under the sway of the Chancellor of the Duchy of Lancaster and others were controlled by the Council of the North – but this does not seem to have been their sole purpose. Indeed, if 'packing' were the object, it is hard to understand why Mary created three single-member constituencies, thereby voluntarily reducing the amount of patronage at her disposal.[68] Enfranchisement was a royal favour, a reward for loyalty on the part of some magnate with an interest in the area or by the borough itself. Mary thus rewarded towns in the Thames Valley which had supported her during the succession crisis but stripped Maidstone of its representatives after it had served as the focus for Wyatt's rebellion.[69]

During the session itself the Crown could of course smooth the path of its legislation by careful use of Speaker and Privy Councillors; in 1555 when the first-fruits bill met opposition, Pole summoned the Councillors sitting in the House, and each 'promised him his individual vote and also to exert themselves with the others for the approval of the measure with less difficulty both by the Lords and the Commons'.[70] But criticism could not be entirely stifled in this way. If during this period there was relatively little overt opposition in the Commons to the Crown's religious policies, the explanation does not lie in the Crown's greater tactical strength. There were, after all, other areas of policy in which the Crown suffered far more reverses than it did over the Church.

An obvious example here is treason legislation and related matters. (It seems reasonable to assume that all treason legislation – except that later aimed at Mary Queen of Scots – was government inspired.) Here the Commons felt free to criticise, amend and alter. M. L. Bush has shown that of the twenty-two sections in the 1547 Treasons Act only 'the preamble and the first eight and a half sections express with any certainty the government's original aims'; many of the act's more 'liberal' provisions were the result of redrafting by the Commons.[71] The act of 1549 which made it high treason for twelve persons to assemble for certain purposes, including that of planning to murder a Privy Councillor, completely redrawn by the Commons, was still debated at great length. It received six formal readings and was discussed on a number of other days.[72] When the offence of treason by words was reintroduced in 1552, the bill was rewritten in the Commons, although the Lords had already passed one version, whilst in the same session, as we have seen, the Commons refused to pass a bill condemning Tunstall without giving him a chance to defend himself before the House.[73] In 1553 the Commons were slow to pass a bill confirming the attainder of the duke-of Northumberland and his confederates and added to it a proviso limiting the Crown's right of confiscation.[74] In 1554 the Commons considered at great length the question of whether or not Philip should be protected by the treason laws: one of the main objections to crowning him was the idea that those who attacked him might then be prosecuted under the treason laws.[75] The Commons also moderated the harsh physical penalties of an act against seditious words and rumours.[76] The whole pattern of this legislation is of the House of Commons examining government proposals with great caution, of the House modifying and moderating, of the House limiting the rights of the Crown and carefully delineating the area within which it could act. These are not the actions of men reluctant to utter a word critical of the Crown or the actions of men who were afraid.

The relative ease with which the Crown got its religious legislation through the House of Commons during these years should not, therefore, be explained entirely in terms of either management or bullying. Rather it would seem that most members were willing to leave matters of conscience to the monarch and to the clergy. It was Puritanism that in later parliaments disturbed this happy belief.

The House of Commons of this period could, if it so wished, resist the Crown. Over questions of conscience it did not choose to do so in the reign of Edward VI and did so only to a very limited extent in the parliaments of Mary's reign and in 1559. In such matters the House of Lords was much more likely to create difficulties. Historians often imply that the Upper House in the sixteenth century was little more than a rubber stamp for government policies: bishops were, after all, royal nominees and new secular peers could be created at the royal pleasure. However, the House of Lords was in practice more difficult for the Crown to control than this analysis of its composition would suggest. Bishops were, it is true, royal nominees, but they could not be relied upon to support royal policies, since changes in government thinking on religious matters could leave earlier episcopal creations marooned on islands of outmoded doctrine. Mary solved this problem by imprisoning the Protestant bishops at the beginning of her reign, thereby preventing them from attending Parliament. The Crown's control of the Upper House had also been reduced by the early-sixteenth-century standardisation of the list of writs of summons sent to peers: the holder of a particular title was now summoned consistently or not at all, regardless of any individual's personal political or religious views.[77] New creations were few, and do not appear to have been made with any eye to management of the Upper Chamber. It has been argued that the Crown could none the less control the House through the institution of proxies.[78] (Peers who obtained a royal licence excusing them from attendance at a parliamentary session had the right to name proxies in their place.) Very often the government appears to have suggested the names of peers who would be suitable proxies; these suggestions were usually accepted and Privy Councillors therefore held a large number of proxies. However, the significance of this should not be overestimated, as there is no evidence that proxy *votes* were ever cast at this time or that proxies had any practical function.[79] When Stephen Gardiner died in the course of the 1555 parliament he held five proxies; no attempt was made to provide a replacement and no problems seem to have arisen. It was not through proxies that the Crown controlled the House of Lords. Indeed, the evidence all suggests that it was much more difficult for the Crown to control the Lords than to control the Commons. The House of Lords was, after all, a body composed of men who regarded themselves as the Crown's natural advisers, men of great power in the localities whose views on many questions were of more importance than those of the civil servants who formed the other group of royal councillors.

V

The concentration of twentieth-century historians on the House of Commons, which has led them virtually to ignore the House of Lords, stemmed from their desire to push back the origins of conflict in the Stuart parliaments. This same desire produced an interpretation of sixteenth-century parliaments in terms of ever-increasing tension, tension that was ultimately kept in check only by the force of Elizabeth's personality. By concentrating on certain issues and ignoring others, a very misleading impression has been created by historians such as Notestein and Neale:[80] on matters such as social and economic policy, Crown and Parliament were, as Paul Slack shows in chapter 5 of this volume, in broad agreement. Even in areas as controversial as those of the doctrine and organisation of the Church, there was little criticism of the Crown's proceedings. Most of what little there was came from the Lords and not from members of the Lower House, who seem at this period to have been interested chiefly in questions of local interest and those that affected the circumstances of their material existence.

# 2. Rehabilitating the Duke of Northumberland: Politics and Political Control, 1549–53

DALE HOAK

To students of the mid-Tudor crisis, the brief reign of Edward VI (1547–1553) presents the extraordinary spectacle of both a government and a society on the point of collapse. In October 1549 the machinery of monarchical government actually broke down, one consequence of an internecine war among Privy Councillors collectively unable to exercise the powers of kingship delegated to them by Henry VIII during his son's minority. In this narrow sense, the political crisis was a predictable one, the result of a fierce competition at court to bestow the pensions, grants and offices in the gift of the Crown. But the *coups* and state trials of the period reflect more than an exaggerated rivalry for control of the royal powers of patronage. The *coup d'état* of October 1549, for example, signalled the failure of the duke of Somerset to surmount the simultaneous shock-waves of inflation, rebellion and war on two fronts. The crises which filled Somerset's protectorate were not resolved by that event; Somerset's successor, the duke of Northumberland, inherited many of the same problems and more. Indeed, he and his colleagues confronted a permanent crisis of domestic security: in the name of their sovereign lord, the King, they ruled a people whose loyalty they knew they did not command. Contemporary ballads, broadsheets and alehouse songs consistently expressed the raging disaffection of the commons, and poverty and hunger threatened to spark this disrespect and unrest into rebellion after 1549.

Perhaps no Tudor government ever stood in greater fear of a rebellious commons than did that of the duke of Northumberland in the period 1550–3; this is one of the important facts of the political history of that time, and it explains why Northumberland's government, even more than Somerset's, exhibited a practical concern for social justice.[1]

The maintenance of order and stability provided but one test of Northumberland's ability to govern. The financial debacle of Somerset's failed administration also threatened to undermine his newly-won power. The severity of the financial crisis in 1549 can be gauged by the fact that the soldiers engaging the West Country rebels had awaited payment in coins rushed fresh from the mints to the fields of battle: payment in debased coins struck from the melted-down plate of a Church whose further reformation Somerset's impoverished government had only recently decreed. The crisis was viciously circular: the Edwardian reformation itself had helped precipitate the Western Rebellion; its supression had pushed the King deeper into debt. However, Northumberland advanced the Reformation after 1549 and not simply in order to justify further seizures of ecclesiastical property. Given his fear of rebellion and his religious indifference, the question of why he adopted a more radical liturgy obviously warrants investigation.

This essay will argue that after 1549 Northumberland's religious policy as well as his financial programmes were geared closely to his personal political objectives. At first – that is, in October 1549, when he and his colleagues assumed Somerset's authority – Northumberland possessed no readily discernible goal beyond a share of the ex-protector's power. In the months following the *coup*, however, he developed a set of recognisable, legitimate political objectives. He did so in order to create administrative stability and efficiency, the lack of which had so visibly destroyed Somerset. Northumberland's ultimate political failure should not obscure his success in this regard. He restored and reorganised methods of government-by-council in England, and in so doing set administrative precedents to be followed by Elizabeth I's Privy Councillors. Whether this conclusion compels agreement or not, the purpose of the following reassessment should be self-evident: it allows one to consider the nature and significance of the mid-Tudor crisis of government.

Another good reason for examining the period of Northumberland's ascendancy is the duke himself. Traitor, schemer, arch-deceiver: such is the reputation of the man who for three and a half years governed the King's realms and dominions. Evil fascinates us in a way that goodness will never do and Northumberland's later career seems to exhibit in full measure the sort of evil we expect of the true 'Machiavel'. Certainly one cannot sensibly write a history of politics and government in his time without taking into account his reputedly devious character. Three episodes are said to have revealed Northumberland's duplicity and cunning: the *coup* which he engineered against Somerset (October 1549), the trial (December 1551) which resulted in Somerset's execution (22 January 1552), and the well known scheme (1553) to alter the succession in favour of his daughter-in-law, Jane. The appearance of a sham religiosity and piratical greed have deepened the suspicion that while in office he practised the politics of expediency.

On the face of it, the facts in these matters appear overwhelmingly to confirm the legend of the duke's opportunism and treachery. There is no denying his complicity in the plot to overthrow Somerset. After the *coup*, he gained control of the Privy Council by purging it of the very men who with him had headed the conspiracy. In 1551 he arbitrarily ordered Somerset's arrest and then manufactured enough evidence against him to secure a sentence of death, all of which he later confessed. In 1553, when Edward VI lay dying, Northumberland knowingly committed himself to treason by attempting to block Mary Tudor's rightful accession to the throne. In respect of his religion and landed fortune, the facts once again seem to corroborate his apparently two-faced behaviour. It was said that in order to win conservative support for the *coup* he had posed as a Henrician Catholic. A few months later he certainly became officially Protestant, rewarding himself thereafter with the goods of the Church his government had reformed. On the scaffold he pronounced his 'conversion' to Catholicism, no doubt hoping thereby to win Mary's pardon.

Apart from the facts, two things may be said about the reputation based upon them. First, it is posthumous: fixed upon him by his enemies in order to explain his otherwise obscure motives during the three years before Edward VI's death. Secondly, it is based uncritically upon appearances. Legally, of course, his handling of Somerset in 1551–2 and his part in the plot against Mary constituted criminal behaviour, but, in the absence of hard evidence explaining these actions, merely the appearance of cunning, the appearance of perversity, began to generate the now familiar assumptions about him: because he had reached the top and tried to stay there by often subtle and deliberate manoeuvring, he was thought inherently crooked. Thus, only one week after his beheading on Tower Hill, Lady Jane, never his admirer, is reported to have said from *her* Tower cell: 'Woe worth him! . . . his life was wicked and full of dissimulation. . . . He hath brought me and our stock into most miserable calamity and misery by his exceeding ambition.'[2] In an attempt to explain his conduct, latter-day historians have repeated the contemporary judgement that he possessed an evil ambition. The point is, however, that we can understand neither his character nor his regime by assuming that 'a fatal taint of crooked self-seeking' in his family's blood had naturally disposed him to a life of dissembling and crime.[3] To call him a member of 'the most unprincipled gang of political adventurers and predators that England had seen for many centuries'[4] does nothing to advance our understanding of his political motives or the nature of his political control. At the very least it can be said that no one has systematically examined his political activities, 1549–53, in light of the available evidence.[5] The following discussion certainly does not attempt to do so comprehensively, but it does suggest how such an analysis might proceed. What is at issue here is not the ethics of Northumberland's behaviour, but the historical accuracy of the accepted versions of his behaviour.

I propose to examine Northumberland's political activities in the context of the institutional history of his regime. This approach is dictated by two considerations: that Northumber-land exercised his authority legitimately as the royally appointed President of Edward VI's Privy Council, and that as President he supervised the Council's administration of Edward's affairs in response to Somerset's failure to do so as Lord Protector of the realm and Governor of the King's person. Since Somerset's Protectorate was overthrown not merely by Northumberland, but by eighteen Privy Councillors whom Somerset himself had appointed, the analysis of North-umberland's government may be introduced by saying something about the motives of those who abolished the Protector's title and office.

In *England under Protector Somerset* (1900) A. F. Pollard formu-lated what was until very recently the accepted version of the Council's *coup d'état* of October 1549. Pollard pictured Somerset as a generous, great-hearted man pulled down by colleagues unwilling to accept his allegedly 'liberal' pro-gramme of social reform. The 'good duke' had idealistically sought to champion the cause of the oppressed, especially those who could be identified as the victims of illegal enclo-sures. Such an attitude explained why the Protector, himself the author of momentous religious reform, was personally reluctant in 1549 to suppress a rebellious commons who loved him. In Pollard's view, the conspirators (some of whose parks the rebels were ploughing under) could not stomach Somerset's superior sense of social justice or his dilatory re-sponse to rebellion, and so they forced him out of office.

Professor W. K. Jordan amplified this interpretation in his narrative study *Edward VI: The Young King* (1968). Although he based his account on a range of manuscript materials unavailable to Pollard (who had used chiefly printed sources), Jordan preserved with only slight modifications Pol-lard's assumptions about Somerset's idealism and magna-nimity. He therefore followed his predecessor's lead in explain-ing the *coup* essentially as the Council's reaction to Somerset's misplaced attempts to promote a more liberal 'common-wealth'.

The suspicion that the Protector's allegedly attractive social conscience belonged more to the nineteenth and twentieth

centuries than the sixteenth was revealed by Dr M. L. Bush
in his reappraisal *The Government Policy of Protector Somerset*
(1975). By analysing the changing circumstances in which
Somerset framed his policies, Bush exploded the myth of
the duke's famed 'liberality'. Although Somerset may have
wished to be remembered as a fair-minded arbiter of peasant
complaints, both his own attitudes and his government's policies reflected the social conservatism of his class: the Lord
Protector's outlook and political objectives were unremarka-
bly those of the landed elite. Hence, Somerset's colleagues
did not overthrow him because they opposed a (non-existent)
social programme or his (mythical) liberalism. Quite the
contrary: according to Bush, the Council approved of Somerset's historically conventional objectives in Scotland and England and in fact had helped devise the policies in question.
To be sure, the invasion of Scotland misfired, but this indicated ' Miscalculation as well as misfortune, . . . a miscalculation for which a group of men was responsible'. Since policy
could not explain the *coup d'état* of 1549, Bush modified the
Pollard–Jordan thesis by combining fact (what is known about
Somerset's personality) with assumption (how the Council
may have interpreted Somerset's popular reputation). Somerset's abrasive arrogance annoyed his colleagues. By October
1549, beset by domestic rebellions and war with the French
and the Scots, his testy hauteur had become too much for
them to bear. As his reputation among the peasantry made
him *appear* too socially radical, the Council found a convenient
cause to topple him.[6]

The trouble with this interpretation is that, while it plausi-
bly suggests how the Council may have exploited popular
notions of Somerset's 'leniency', it ignores the institutional
setting in which policy-making and administration took place.
We find, for example, little treatment of conciliar operation
in an age where the Council had become the chief instrument
of Tudor government. Yet Sir William Paget, the duke's
nominal chief adviser, thought that Somerset's *methods* of
government, as much as his ill-calculated Scottish policy,
had precipitated the crises of his regime.[7] Had Paget provided
a clue here to the meaning of the Council's *coup*?

On the eve of his arrest Somerset ordered his household

officials to disperse and destroy the records of the protectorate. Some papers survived, including a rough copy of the book of the Council's own proceedings, and these provide ample proof of the procedural irregularities of the duke's personal rule. The unwitting evidence of these sources describes Somerset's attempt to govern without the Council, attending in his own household to business which his colleagues expected him to transact in the Council chamber at court.[8] Contemporaries pointed to Somerset's use of a so-called 'new council' of confidants: men such as Sir Thomas Smith, one of his servants, Sir Michael Stanhope and Edward Wolf of the King's Privy Chamber, Sir John Thynne, his steward, and one William Gray of Reading, none of them Privy Councillors (except Smith, who was the King's Secretary after 17 April 1548). Although Somerset's circumvention of the Council was not illegal – his royal commission as Protector allowed him to consult its members irregularly, at his pleasure – such action isolated him politically. Thus when, as in 1549, he needed political support on the Council, he found himself opposed by several of its key members, in particular Lord John Russell, Sir William Herbert and Northumberland, all of them commanders of mercenary troops. Somerset finally surrendered to them, unable to resist their combined military strength.[9]

Somerset also courted disaster by failing to exploit the administrative experience and expertise of these same men. In Paget's view, this was particularly true in perhaps the most important area of government service: royal finance. Somerset's personality and high-minded pride may explain why he found it difficult to delegate financial tasks to the Council, but in the eyes of contemporaries this did not excuse him of the responsibility for doing so himself. The Privy Council pulled Somerset down not because of how it interpreted his public (and historically ill founded) reputation, but because its members privately knew him to be an incompetent administrator.[10]

In retrospect, it is clear that the lessons of Somerset's failure were not lost on Northumberland. As an organiser of the *coup*, Northumberland could lay open claim to Somerset's seat in government; there is certainly no denying his quest for the Protector's power. But another protectorate was politically out of the question, and Somerset's discredited title had become a political liability to anyone seeking a similar climb to authority. Politically, the future lay with the Council, a Council whose members would in reality share the authority to govern England during the remainder of Edward's minority. It was Northumberland's genius to see that his political ambition depended on procedural control of such a Council. However, the fact that he achieved this administrative control by February 1550 was the accidental result of the fiercest struggle for the powers of the Crown since the Wars of the Roses. In this struggle (October 1549 to February 1550) Northumberland simply aimed to avoid political destruction. In the end he survived, and in surviving found the means to neutralise factious politics at court. As a consequence, he was able to create the conditions of political stability necessary for the efficient administration of state business.

The complicated story of the intrigues of October 1549 to February 1550 has been related elsewhere.[11] What must be emphasised here is the defensive nature of Northumberland's political behaviour during this period. So far from being the scheming, Machiavellian plotter of legend, he found himself to be the target of a second *coup*, organised by Thomas Wriothesley, earl of Southampton, the nominal leader of a group of 'Catholic' (i.e. conservative) lords who, by slanting their interrogation of the imprisoned Protector, were attempting to extract the 'confession' that in the commission of Somerset's wrongs Northumberland had played the part of adviser and accomplice. When Northumberland discovered their aim, he rallied his forces in a desperate attempt to avoid almost certain attainder and execution. In defeating Wriothesley, Northumberland revealed his mastery of the art of political manoeuvring, but his eventual triumph was not the result of a clever plan that he had somehow worked out himself beforehand. Along the way he sought the assistance of others, such as the archbishop of Canterbury, who in early October were better placed than he to influence the course of events. At the moment of Somerset's arrest and removal from court (13 October 1549), Cranmer, probably fearing the Catholic reaction that Wriothesley's victory would bring, persuaded Edward VI to appoint some of Northumberland's friends to key positions in the Privy Chamber. With these men (including his son, Sir Andrew Dudley) in the Household, Northumberland found it easier to win the King's formal approval for the addition of four other adherents to the Privy Council. With a majority of the Council behind him, Northumberland proceeded to vote Wriothesley and the conservatives out of office (2 February 1550).

This brief outline of events during the autumn of 1549 obscures the fact that Northumberland's rivalry with Wriothesley really passed through two distinct phases. During the first phase, before he learned of Wriothesley's ultimate purpose, Northumberland's only apparent political objective was to establish himself and his followers in the Household, so as to secure regular access to the King and to the royal favour. In this sense, the contest with Wriothesley was a conventional one, the prize being, as noted before, a share of the fruits of royal patronage. By 15 October Northumberland had with Cranmer's help won this contest. It was during the second phase, however, when Wriothesley's true aim became clear, that Northumberland sought to extend his indirect control of the Household to the Council. He saw that in future, to thwart other, potential opponents, he would need to be able to do more than merely add a few of his own men to the board. He must be able to control the Council's consideration of every item of business, every issue, every political question. He might indirectly have achieved political control of the Council, and even the ability to purge his opponents by way of the influence he could wield through his 'great friends about the King'. But to guarantee his use of the royal power of appointment (or removal), to assure his control of the Council's administrative staff and, through them, the machinery of the central government, and to dominate the Council and the Council's government of the realm Northumberland really needed the recognised authority which came with office.

During the autumn of 1549 Northumberland saw that such procedural authority lay potentially at hand in the office of Lord President of the Council, a position doubly advantageous for the realisation of his political ambition since the presidency, as he knew, fell automatically (by tradition) to the Great Master (or Great Steward) of the King's Household. At the time (November–December 1549), Lord William St John was Great Master, but by February 1550 St John had relinquished the office to Northumberland in exchange for an earldom and the high-treasurership of England: rewards almost certainly promised him in December for his support against Wriothesley and the conservatives. (It was St John who had tipped the scales against the Catholics by leaking the news of Wriothesley's intentions to Northumberland.) As President under Somerset, St John nominally was responsible for organising the Council's work; as Great Master he supervised the personnel and operations of Edward VI's Household. Thanks to Cranmer, Northumberland's already well established influence in the Household made him the obvious candidate to succeed St John as Great Master. How convenient it was that in the reign of a child king the great mastership also conveyed to the holder of that office the headship of the King's government in Council! When Northumberland realised that the path to power in Council ran officially through the royal apartments, he persuaded Edward VI to grant him verbally (on 2 February 1550) the great-mastership and presidency. On 20 February 1550 the King's letters patent formalised the appointment.

Thus, an early-Tudor President sat as the 'lieutenant' of the Crown in Council. In other words, in the absence of the King, the President presided at meetings, summoned Councillors to meetings, set times of meeting, dissolved meetings, and otherwise fixed schedules of attendance at court.[12] The registers of the Privy Council and the extant state papers reveal Northumberland doing all of these things or ordering them done. As President, Northumberland could also 'disbar' Councillors at will: his first official act on the day of his appointment (2 February 1550) was to banish the leaders of the conservative opposition from court and their seats on the Council. In more extraordinary fashion, Northumberland also modified the very terms of a Councillor's oath of office: he once ordered the earls of Derby and Shrewsbury sworn in to serve for one day only (9 August 1551). Finally,

Northumberland assumed the King's power to create new Councillors: as President he added twelve men to the board after February 1550. If 'the source of his dominance over his fellow Councillors has never been explained',[13] it is perhaps because Northumberland's powers as Great Master and President have never been fully appreciated.

On the face of it, Northumberland's ability to appoint the King's Councillors explains his political strength after February 1550. On the other hand, it has been argued that his packing really reflects his political weakness, that in a faction-ridden reign he could ill afford to alienate powerful nobles whose acquiescence or neutrality he won only by granting them the honour of a place in the highest counsels of government.[14] There may be another explanation, that the new appointees were expected to strengthen Northumberland's hand against Somerset, whom he had been compelled to save from attainder for fear of Wriothesley. Ironically, Somerset was the one man whose membership of the Council after February 1550 he could not deny, and Somerset remained a genuine rival as long as he lived. Almost from the moment of his release from the Tower (6 February 1550), Somerset began collecting adherents against the day when he should be able to gain parliamentary approval for Northumberland's removal.

Nothumberland sensed the danger early on, and this probably explains why ten of the twelve Councillors he appointed during his presidency were sworn in during the eighteen months when Somerset once again sat in the Council chamber (April 1550 through September 1551). The majority of the new men were experienced soldiers; four of them were powerful peers; all of them owed their office and title to Northumberland's favour and so could be expected to give their voices to his policies of state as well as his political designs. Since Northumberland could not discount the possibility of a popular rising in Somerset's behalf – he seems to have been obsessed by the idea of one in the North – he allowed those Councillors with military training to retain bands of fifty and a hundred horses, or 'gendarmes, at the King's expense. This extraordinary force, totalling about 900 cavalry, stood ready to repulse anyone, such as Somerset, who might attempt a counter-*coup*. This also suggests that Northumberland had learned the lessons of 1549. The military commands of some of the Councillors were also distributed geographically, since their estates placed them strategically near areas that Northumberland supposed to be potentially rebellious. The earls of Huntingdon and Westmorland, for example, almost never came to court to attend meetings of the Council; as specially commissioned lords lieutenant in their own 'countries', they were ordered to hold their retainers in readiness to smash any local revolts. The fact that they were Privy Councillors testifies to Northumberland's preoccupation with domestic order: their newly official tie to London enhanced their standing as royal commissioners.

Northumberland's ability to appoint new Councillors only partially explains the nature of his political control. Less dramatic but equally important was his procedural authority as President to supervise the handling of all business of state. Since illness (probably an ulcerous stomach) or duty (military tours of the North) often prevented his attendance at meetings, he relied on several of his appointees to represent him at court and in Council. Northumberland admitted to William Cecil, the junior Secretary of State after 5 September 1550, that, as Cecil could speak and write well, he (Northumberland) was necessarily 'laying part of my burden upon your shoulders'.[15] Cecil prepared agendas for meetings, but Northumberland frequently dictated their contents. Cecil's staff prepared the Council's letters, but Cecil's drafts of these letters frequently incorporated Northumberland's *verbatim* dictation. Nominally, all decisions of state were made by the whole Council, but these were almost invariably decisions towards which Northumberland had asked Cecil to guide the Council. With good reason did the Imperial ambassador describe Cecil most fully as 'the duke of Northumberland's man'.[16]

Within two months of his rise to the presidency, Northumberland had accepted a plan advanced by Lord Paget (awarded a barony for his help against Wriothesley) for the reorganisation and reform of the procedures governing the conduct and administration of Council business. By the date of Cecil's appointment, therefore, Northumberland could be sure that even in his own absence the Council would adhere to a prescribed routine. The internal evidence of the state papers for the period after Cecil's appointment corroborates Northumberland's decision (made early in 1550) to rationalise the Privy Council's government of the realm. The effect of the decision was to re-establish the Council's recognised executive, administrative and quasi-judicial competence.[17] The administrative history of his regime thus marks what might be called the Edwardian 'revival' of government by Council.

Administratively, Northumberland's chief purpose in re-establishing the Council was to resolve the financial crisis Somerset had precipitated. Somerset's war policy had contributed to an inflation of prices in England and his policy of debasing English coins had only worsened the problem. Northumberland brought the war against France and Scotland to a close, abandoned debasement (but not before briefly succumbing to its temptations) and adopted, probably on Cecil's recommendation, a deflationary monetary policy.[18] Unlike Somerset, Northumberland was capable of admitting to his colleagues that 'my capacity be not able to reach so far in this matter [of finance] as some of your lords doth', but as Lord President he reserved for himself final judgement in this, the most important of his government's policies. Since indebtedness had ruined Somerset, Northumberland himself determined on 16 June 1551 that the Council would reorder royal finance in such a way as to allow the King to 'live of his own'. 'To have His Majesty out of debt' was the duke's personally stated goal.[19]

Having set the priorities, he proceeded to act on his word. He called in Sir Walter Mildmay to advise Cecil, who was now given the responsibility for overall financial planning. Cecil's memoranda describe Northumberland's aims after 1551: to raise as much cash as possible from already identified sources (the Church, the mints, the King's debtors, and so on); to force a stricter accounting of income in the courts of revenue, so as to provide the Council with up-to-date reports of receipts and expenditures; and to establish in the Household an emergency fund of about £40,000 to be spent in the King's 'special affairs' (repayment of short-term loans,

rewards, the newly organised gendarmes, and so forth). Northumberland did not live long enough to realise his ultimate
goal, a reformed financial system allowing the King to charge
up expenses against a single, sufficient fund, but in the short
run he achieved most of his aims. He liquidated the whole
of the overseas debt; he enforced economies in government
spending; he established an extraordinary 'privy coffer', in
effect the Council's own treasury, allowing him a measure
of flexibility while the slower work of reform went forward.
Finally, he stunned his critics by driving down the price
of some basic foodstuffs.[20] Northumberland's methods once
again reveal the man's innate and very considerable executive
abilities: he clearly defined a realistic policy; he delegated
responsibilities to others more experienced or capable than
he; he insisted that his colleagues produce the desired results
on time.

He also preferred to do business secretly, which created
the impression that his government's policies promoted his
private gain. Thus, when the Council laid up gold and silver
coin in the Tower, it was thought that Northumberland
was robbing the King. In fact, such hoarding crudely served
Thomas Gresham's officially sponsored attempts to raise the
price of English money on the Antwerp exchange.[21] It would
be inaccurate to claim that Northumberland did not use
the King's money either for his own gain or for his political
ends, but, rather than assuming him to have been the slave
of an unbridled greed or a gangster bent on throttling the
King, one should try to fit the pattern of his actions into
a context which explains him historically. The administrative
history of his regime presents such a context. My thesis is
that he meant to restore efficient administration by conciliar
government. In particular, he meant to resolve the King's
financial difficulties, and he knew that he could not survive
politically without a sound financial policy. Ironically, in
order to accomplish this, he was forced to disband the expens-
ively maintained gendarmes, whom he might have used to
crush Mary in 1553. That he disarmed himself in 1552 should
tell us something about his official priorities: however one
explains his criminal behaviour, there can be no denying
the consistency and realism of his efforts to put right the

administration of royal finance.

It remains to say something of the duke's relations with the King, and of his use of the King's favour. Edward VI turned twelve at the time of the *coup d'état* and as the months passed it became clear that Northumberland could not safely ignore a bright, even precocious lad whose princely training had evidently equipped him to do more than converse ceremoniously with foreign diplomats. How did Northumberland accommodate the boy's intelligence? Edward's so-called 'state papers' and his speeches in Council seemingly bespeak a king on, as Professor Jordan has put it, the 'threshold of power': an extraordinarily capable young man who by his fourteenth year had actually begun dictating business to his Councillors and even reorganising them and their work.[22] In fact, the boy's notes, 'agendas' and memoranda, when properly read in the context of the Council's procedures, reveal a student merely following the course of state business, not directing it: this is manifestly clear from what we know of the secretaries' management of the items of business which the King copied out from lists provided him by the Council's staff. On Northumberland's orders, Cecil and Sir William Petre (the senior Secretary) not only kept Edward well informed of current affairs, but also persuaded the boy of the wisdom of decisions already taken, *as if these were recommendations the King himself should propose to his men in Council.* In short, Edward VI's 'speeches' and papers really present the somewhat pathetic figure of an articulate puppet far removed from the realities of government.[23]

Priming the King for a Council meeting was one thing, manipulating his thinking about politics generally was quite another matter, and yet Northumberland's political control is ultimately to be explained by just this sort of manipulation. How did he really accomplish it? In his capacity as Great Master he staffed the Household and especially the Privy Chamber with men who controlled all access to the King as well as all news and information, spoken and written, which might reach him. Sir John Gates, a former gentleman of Henry VIII's Chamber, and after Cecil the man most closely associated with Northumberland, policed the precincts of the court as the King's Vice-Chamberlain. Gates commanded the King's guard and, in more extraordinary fashion, retained possession of the dry stamp of Edward VI's signature.[24] Northumberland's correspondence shows that his instructions went directly to Cecil or Gates, and if not Gates, to another of the duke's men at court, the King's Chamberlain, Thomas Lord Darcy (Vice-Chamberlain before Gates). Gates reported to Northumberland all comings and goings about the King; Darcy took over this duty whenever Gates was otherwise occupied. Few had served longer than Darcy in Northumberland's cause. Darcy had entered the Privy Chamber the moment Northumberland's men replaced Somerset's there (15 October 1549); for his work in the Household during the struggle with Wriothesley, Northumberland raised him to the Council (16 January 1550). In Council both Darcy and Gates ('my special friends,' as Northumberland described them to Cecil) spoke for the duke. In the Household a clerk of the Council, William Thomas, schooled the King in the maxims of the studious prince; Thomas's earlier *Historie of Italy* (1548) had been dedicated to Northumberland. The King's tutor, Sir John Cheke, almost certainly spoke for the duke too; his experience with the King probably explains his appointment to the Council during the last month of the reign. In the Chamber, however, it was Northumberland's son-in-law and one of the King's closest boyhood friends, Sir Henry Sidney, who 'had acquired so great an influence next to the King that he was able to make all of his notions conform to those of the duke'.[25]

This same observer, probably a member of the French embassy, whose head, Boisdauphin, Northumberland regularly entertained, also said that Edward VI 'revered' Northumberland so much that the King willingly decreed the duke's wishes as his own in order 'to prevent the envy which would have been produced had it been known that it was he [Northumberland] who had suggested these things to the King'.[26] The accuracy of this statement may be questioned, though the fact of the King's admiration for Northumberland is also suggested by the impression the duke's voice, manner and bearing made on this eyewitness. Northumberland disarmed everyone with his 'liberality', a noble courtesy difficult to resist or surpass. Affable and unusually graceful for a soldier, he commanded a 'great presence' and knew it. Perhaps his consciousness of this quality made him appear to be acting a part at times, but even his detractors spoke respectfully of his 'great courage', a force of character that suggested superior political nerves. In contemporary fashion he was said to be 'proud', and, since this protrait was penned late in 1553, the author could also assume that such pride had rendered him disloyal to the Tudors.

Pride, hypocrisy and an insatiable greed: every writer has cited these to explain how Northumberland brought about his own end. In fact, since his alleged traits can be explained circumstantially, it is more likely that accident felled him. Realism and consistency marked his words and actions even at the moment of his death. The circumstances of his so-called 'conversion' exemplify this. Northumberland was not essentially a spiritually minded person, so that it is futile to expect to find in him the qualities of the sincerely religious. The key to his character lies in the discovery that as a servant of the Tudors what mattered to him most was obedience and not faith, official obedience to the sovereign's will in matters of religion. Looked at in this way his 'religious' stance under Henry VIII, Edward VI and Mary makes sense: consistent to the end he accepted Mary's religion, if not her faith. In August 1553 he might have uttered the words he wrote to Cecil in 1552: 'I . . . stand to one kind of religion in the same which I do now profess'. Some, he knew thought him a dissembler, but feigning faith, as he implied to Cecil, was never his purpose.[27] He might have said that for him faith was irrelevant. Thus, his famous speech on the scaffold, like his attendance at mass the day before, signified his compliance, not his conversion. He thought that his compliance would persuade Mary to save at least his life. It did not, of course, though it probably guaranteed that the *manner* of his execution (beheading, not hanging) would not be dishonourable. Surely Mary knew that this was of powerful psychological importance to a gentleman soldier. Compliance should also have guaranteed to his heirs the inheritance of his titles and lands. In any case, on the scaffold Northumberland was careful to profess adherence to a Catholicism not shared by papists.[28]

Allegations of avarice are irrelevant here. Was there anyone at court in Edward's last hour who had not benefited materially by the Reformation? If Northumberland is to be judged on this count, a whole generation of courtiers and Crown servants must be condemned. Given the conditions of a royal minority, only the rate at which he acquired property was unusual by Tudor standards, and even that was not unique. The duke of Somerset appears to have been more avaricious, more ostentatious, more wealthy at the height of his power, more shamelessly proud. By 1551 Northumberland's power required a pre-eminence (a dukedom) and an income appropriate to his rank. Essentially without salary, he rewarded himself in the acceptable manner of the age.[29] To the charge that the Edwardian nobility held power only to enrich themselves (a complaint aired in the House of Commons), he replied privately to Cecil that he would never 'willingly do anything either by procuring to myself any benefit with hurting the common wealth or ,consenting to any such act'. Of course, he was hardly unbiased in this matter, but there is in his confidential letters to Cecil the hint that by the end of 1552 he could not always control the process by which his colleagues voted themselves the property which was legally the King's. On 9 December 1552 he openly admonished the members of the Council to be ready to spend not only 'our goods, but our lands and our lives for our master and our country and to despise this flattering of ourselves with heaping riches upon riches, honours upon honours, building upon building', and by 'ourselves' he did not by this time mean to include himself. It was only in men's 'evil imaginations', he said, that he had neglected the government of the King's realms.[30]

But what of his actions *vis-à-vis* his opponents? In every case it is possible to interpret his stance in more cogent terms than those usually advanced. As already stated, the *coup* of October 1549 did not immediately reward him with the power which is supposed to have been the object of the conspiracy. In fact, among his co-conspirators his enemies outnumbered him and they positioned themselves so well after the *coup* that he was forced to step quickly to avoid death at their hands.

Wriothesley was the real danger, not only to Northumberland, but to people such as Thomas Cranmer who feared the consequences of a conservative triumph. 'Hot' and 'very busy' was the way one eyewitness described Wriothesley's drive to power in October 1549.[31] It was Wriothesley's obsessive desire to send Somerset to the block that magnified the danger of the Catholic alliance, for, in riding Somerset down, Wriothesley's momentum (reported as 'earnestness') might have been sufficient to carry him on to leadership of a Council dominated by conservatives such as the earl of Arundel. Even before Somerset's arrest, the tide among the London conspirators was running swiftly in favour of the conservative cause. Expecting a Catholic reaction, reformers such as Hooper began to fear for their lives. Perhaps even Northumberland was frightened; he let it be known that he would not oppose a return to 'the ancient way of worship'. This pose cost him nothing politically, for, like Wriothesley, he was interested only in Somerset's removal. (Like Northumberland, Wriothesley was not religiously motivated.)

In trying to taint his opponent with Somerset's misdeeds, however, Wriothesley committed a fatal blunder: he forced Cranmer and Northumberland together, a notable achievement as the two had always been cool towards each other. Cranmer's objective was to save the Reformation; he needed Northumberland's political support in Council to block the expected conservative attempt to dismantle his liturgical reforms. Northumberland found that he had everything to gain politically by backing Cranmer and the reformers; he needed them and their leverage with the King – Cranmer appears to have been the one man the boy really trusted – to defeat Wriothesley. It was thus purely coincidental that a critical moment in the history of the reformed Church coincided with the decisive moment in Northumberland's personal career. The results were momentous: because Northumberland perceived Wriothesley's threat to be politically 'Catholic', he adopted an officially radical Protestantism, thereby isolating the conservatives, some of whom still dreamed of a Marian regency backed by the Habsburgs. The events of November–December 1549 thus both explain and connect two otherwise baffling developments after that time: Northumberland's early promotion of doctrines more Protestant than the King's and his determined efforts to outlaw Mary, the only person whose faith mattered more to him politically than the King's.

When Northumberland discovered that the conservatives had linked his own fate to Somerset's, he worked mightily to secure the latter's release, and, having done so, could not deny him a place on the Council. His only mistake in reinstating Somerset was to overlook the depth of his great rival's jealousy. Envy as well as renewed ambition drove Somerset closer to treason during the course of 1551; he later confessed to have 'contemplated' Northumberland's apprehension. By October 1551 his not-so-secret intentions posed an intolerable danger to Northumberland personally, as well as to the progress of the Council's programme of reform. It was especially important to him that England's hard-won financial stability be preserved. Reluctantly, therefore, he chose to destroy Somerset in the only politically safe way: trial by a hand-picked jury whose members were bound to return a verdict of guilt. Since Northumberland had struck first, it became necessary to present to the jurors what Somerset probably would have attempted before the end of 1551: Northumberland's seizure or illegal arrest. That is why Northumberland felt that he had to fabricate the case against Somerset, and it weighed very heavily on his conscience thereafter.[32] Nevertheless, his calculated action probably saved England the spectacle of a bloody counter-*coup* and the administrative chaos of a revived protectorate.

Contrary to what has been thought, the scheme to alter the succession originated in Northumberland's camp and not in King Edward's brain,[33] but, although Northumberland rightly accepted responsibility for it (his capacity for truthfulness has been underestimated), he was also right in saying that 'some others' shared his responsibility. Whoever first thought of the scheme, it was Sir John Gates who convinced Edward VI of the utility of the plan.[34] The 'Devise' was not altered without the King's knowledge, however, and the production of the final draft in Edward's hand is consistent with what we know about the origins of the boy's other 'state papers': very probably the King copied out the 'Devise' from his secretaries' notes or perhaps even from dictation. In any case, barring Mary from the succession was a cause in which the young King believed. The chronology of the whole episode leaves one with the impression that the original object of the 'Devise' was not to make Northumberland the manipulator of a puppet queen, but simply to ensure the rule of any one of a number of Protestants, all of whom were to be male. Indeed, it was not originally apparent (by the terms of the first draft) that either Northumberland or his family would benefit by the 'Devise', for at the time of his son's marriage Lady Jane Grey had not been named an heir to the throne. Only when it was realised that Edward VI really was dying and had not willed the throne to anyone alive did Gates persuade the boy to revise the draft in favour of Jane.

Since a Parliament could not be called in time to modify Henry VIII's Act of Succession (Edward VI was now comatose and so could not have signed a parliamentary statute anyway), a familiar type of authority was made ready: letters under the Great Seal signed by the Council and a group of important officials. One often forgets that, while this piece of paper was of questionable legality, the idea it embodied was acceptable politically to almost all of the signatories, since the alternative of Mary's rule carried too many liabilities. So far from being a desperate gamble, the 'Devise' to alter the succession is consistent with the decisive political realism of a man who, understanding the treasonable risks, made everyone else in high office co-partners in a crime less *un*acceptable than the accession of a papist. The 'Devise' recalls other solutions to intractable problems of state, when acts judged to be politically necessary by the Tudors were cloaked in dubious legalities. Northumberland was rightly found to be a traitor, but only after the political fact, for on the day of Edward VI's death no one could have predicted Princess Mary's triumph. Her resistance was probable, but not her success. Northumberland's mistake was not in misjudging Mary – she had shown him her characteristic defiance before – but in misjudging the extent of her support. When his colleagues saw this they abandoned him.

In sum, Northumberland's behaviour after December 1549

exhibits not the treachery of an inherently evil man, but the realistic calculations of a sixteenth-century soldier who had risen to the pinnacle of political leadership at a court already noted for its factious politics and rough justice. Because he inherited Somerset's wasteful disorder and misrule, he was determined to put right the administration of royal affairs. The administrative history of his regime bears out his decision to rationalise the Privy Council's conduct of state business. As Protector, Somerset had failed sufficiently to employ the Council in the formulation and execution of government policy. As President of the Council, Northumberland exploited fully the board's administrative competence. In this respect, Northumberland should be viewed as the architect of some of Elizabeth I's methods of government: he taught Sir William Cecil, the future Lord Burghley, how a prince should properly employ his councillors. The place and importance of the Council in the Elizabethan 'system' of government was thus prefigured under Northumberland and, as Dr Weikel shows in the next chapter, not even the indecision of Mary or the calamities of her reign disrupted its operation.

It is true that Northumberland ambitiously sought to dominate Edward VI's courtiers and councillors. His acquisition of the offices of Great Master and President, and not his supposedly Machiavellian character, explains how he accomplished this. Religion also served the maintenance of his power. Fearing a 'Catholic' counter-*coup*, he adopted Protestantism in order to test the conservatives' political loyalties. The introduction of the reformed faith into England thus came as a by-product of the intrigues of October 1549 to February 1550. Northumberland's true objective was not to promote the Reformation *per se*, but to provide for the government's stability, and this could be achieved only by neutralising political strife at court and reordering the King's finances. It is in this context that one must read the politics of the period after 1550. Thus, at the time of Somerset's trial (December 1551), Northumberland's purpose was to preserve the conditions of political stability necessary for the execution of the government's vitally important financial policy. Only Edward VI robbed him of ultimate success in this regard. The duke's treasonable attempt to correct the consequences of Edward's premature death should not blind us, however, to the nature and significance of his administrative achievement. Indeed, given the circumstances which he inherited in 1549, the duke of Northumberland appears to have been one of the most remarkably able governors of any European state during the sixteenth century.

# 3. The Marian Council Revisited

## ANN WEIKEL

THE so-called 'sterility' and failure of Mary I has been a fundamental part of the whole theory of the mid-Tudor crisis. Historians have tended to accept the portrayal of a weak Queen combined with an ineffective Privy Council which could not adequately advise her to pursue a wiser course, or, conversely, implement more effectively her so often condemned policies. This essay will examine whether these tradtional views apply to the Council's actions during Mary's reign, especially during her first and most critical year as Queen.

Mary has been most roundly and perhaps justifiably criticised for her decision to marry Philip II of Spain and for her religious policy. The marriage decision caused a serious rebellion in 1554 and indirectly led to the loss of Calais in 1558. Her religious policy failed to reconvert England to Catholicism. To what degree does the Council share responsibility for Mary's policies? Once determined, did the Council faithfully execute them? Did the opposing views of the two rivals, Lord Chancellor Stephen Gardiner and Lord William Paget, split the Council along easily identifiable lines creating consistent factions? If faction existed, did it impair the Council's daily operations or cripple that body in a crisis?

Our understanding of the Marian Council is based largely on the work of A. F. Pollard and the more recent elaboration of his fundamental interpretation by E. H. Harbison, G. R. Elton and D. M. Loades. Pollard, whose work predates the availability of some essential sources, condemned both Mary and her Council. She was weak. She chose her advisers with an eye to security and Catholicism. This produced a Council that was too large, faction-ridden and inefficient to provide sage advice or good governance. Government all but collapsed; England had fallen on evil days. Although the introduction of the original correspondence of the foreign ambassadors in Harbison's *Rival Ambassadors at the Court of Queen Mary* added considerably to our knowledge of the reign, it did nothing to alter Pollard's view of Marian government. In fact, Harbison's concentration on the diplomatic contest between the Spanish Renard and the French Noailles tended to emphasise the ineffectiveness of both the Queen and her Council. Geoffrey Elton, who originally joined the mid-Tudor detractors in his *Tudor Revolution in Government*, has begun to modify his view, owing to the work of his students on the Council under Edward and Mary. Although he no longer sees government in partial collapse and acknowledges some administrative vitality and continuity, his most recent text, *Reform and Reformation*, still retains some of the old assumptions about Mary's reign and ignores some of its positive aspects. The Marian historian David Loades has also adopted the traditional view. He elaborated it specifically in his discussion of Wyatt's rebellion in *Two Tudor Conspiracies*, where he portrays a factious Council that crippled government at the very moment that Wyatt threatened Mary's throne.[1] Interestingly, none of these conclusions have emerged from a detailed examination of the Council itself. When that is done a more accurate picture of Marian government emerges.

The traditional interpretations share a reliance on the reports of the Spanish ambassador, Renard, and the French ambassador, Noailles. This has created a distorted interpretation of the reign. Neither Renard nor Noailles was an infallible observer of English politics. Both were biased. While Noailles relied on informers, Renard was often at court and close to Mary. His judgements are more important and must be scrutinised carefully. Renard's criticism of the Council, its members and their actions, has created the unfavourable picture of an unmanageable, quarrelsome body, paralysed in crisis. Although skilled in court intrigue, Renard was a pessimist who had a propensity to panic during an emergency, reporting opposition and honest disagreement over policy as deliberate obstruction or treachery. Just as the Councillors were resolving their differences or handling a crisis, Renard's disparaging comments reached the height of their intensity. A more critical reading of Renard's reports combined with a thorough examination of conciliar activity suggests that his assessment was often inaccurate and undermines the standard interpretation of factionalism and ineffectiveness.

The traditional view of conciliar faction in Mary's reign derives from two sources. One is Pollard's portrayal of Gardiner as the religious zealot and Paget as the *politique*. The other is Harbison's description of two fairly well defined factions, in which Gardiner led Mary's Household servants,

> most of them devoted Catholics and few of them possessed of any political experience. Gardiner's zealous interest in restoring the old religion, his narrow legalism, and his honest patriotism were characteristic of the group, as was also his lack of finesse and flexibility in political matters. The other faction, led by William, Lord Paget, a shrewd and supple *homme nouveau* who managed to get on well with four successive sovereigns, consisted of the nobles and civil servants who felt that they had a natural right to govern the country . . . Gardiner's party looked to Rome, Paget's to Brussels.[2]

These factions consistently played a detrimental role in three critical episodes: the marriage decision, Wyatt's rebellion and the Catholic restoration. With regard to the marriage, Harbison skilfully describes the manoeuvring of the wily Renard, his ally Paget, and Gardiner, who rallied the novice Catholic Councillors in opposition. The end result was governmental confusion and the heightened unpopularity of the subsequent marriage to Philip. The marriage decision led to Wyatt's rebellion in January 1554. At that time conciliar faction is said to have paralysed the effort to safeguard the Queen and her kingdom. Both Harbison and Loades present a reprehensible picture of backbiting, untrustworthy Councillors who created chaos. In the spring Gardiner and Paget's rivalry got out of control over the best method of restoring Catholicism, and their quarrel on that issue spilled over from the Council chamber to the deliberations of the House of Lords during the second Marian parliament. It is generally agreed that at this point the conciliar system of government had broken down. If this interpretation is correct, then the Council indeed must share responsibility for many of the problems of Mary's reign.

Yet, if one uses additional source material, some of which was not available to Pollard, and employs it along with a critical assessment of Renard's reports, a different view of the Council emerges, as the subsequent discussion will demonstrate. And, further, if Dr Peter Donaldson is correct in attributing to Gardiner the Machiavellian treatise he has translated, he has contributed a great deal to a re-evaluation of conciliar politics. The treatise indicates that Gardiner and Paget were not as far apart politically as previously assumed, and the picture of rigid conciliar factionalism can be altered. While Gardiner opposed a foreign marriage, he later advocated Philip's rule of England, and the treatise was written to instruct him to that end. Gardiner's patriotism and zealous Catholicism can be seen in a new light. He sincerely wished to return England to Rome as fully and rapidly as possible, but he did not ignore the political advantage of an alliance of the poor with Catholicism. The battle between Gardiner and Paget in 1554, then, was not a simple contest between religious zeal and propertied practicality. Since Gardiner would have countenanced the execution of Elizabeth for political reasons, he can hardly be portrayed as narrowly legalistic. In trying to apply Machiavelli to English politics he may have lacked 'finesse', but he certainly had 'flexibility'. The treatise reveals Gardiner as more compatible with the 'shrewd and supple' Paget, and, indeed, before Gardiner died, in 1555, the two rivals were reconciled.[3]

But, even if Gardiner did not write the treatise, he and Paget shared a devotion to the Tudor dynasty which, because of the preoccupation with their political rivalry, has been overlooked. Gardiner, who had opposed the reforms of Thomas Cromwell, represented the old order. Although he had accepted Henry's religious reforms, he was a conservative, and had been imprisoned as part of the opposition in the reign of Edward. These and other attributes made him a logical choice for the Woolsack in 1553. Paget, perhaps the most talented Marian Councillor and the man most closely identified with Cromwell's reforms, had struggled to maintain his ideals under the adverse conditions of Edward's reign. That very involvement barred him from Mary's initial trust and from the place of leadership he thought he deserved. While he was also a religious conservative, he was not concerned with the fine points of theology. He sought the preservation of secularised Church lands and thus, in his judgement, the maintenance of order in English society.[4] Paget and Gardiner's theological differences were not monumental, but their means of implementing religious change were. As Cromwell's protégé, Paget deplored Gardiner's administrative methods, but both shared a concern for good government. Above all, both men were loyal and unselfish servants of the Crown: a crucial similarity which is obscured by those who have emphasised factionalism.

That emphasis derives from a conflict theory of history that does not necessarily apply to Mary's reign. The term 'faction' implies conflict and the existence of groups or parties with consistent allegiance to a person, programme or principle. That situation existed for a time in Edward's reign, and again in Elizabeth's Council, but it has led to a misunderstanding of conciliar politics under Mary. An examination of the problems in Mary's first year will show that faction, despite Renard's constant reference to it, actually played a minor role. Although some Councillors opposed Mary's significant decisions, their differing positions led to debate rather than paralysis, and they worked as diligently as possible to execute the Crown's will. Co-operation, then, was more characteristic than conflict. Further, the traditional view of the detrimental effect of the Council's size and the choice of Councillors needs revision. To demonstrate these points, I shall first examine three episodes isolated by Pollard and Harbison, and then analyse the criticisms of Mary's Council.

The clear division of opinion over Mary's marital choice has been cited as the first evidence of faction and the disruption of conciliar business. Two candidates were seriously considered, Philip II of Spain and the English Edward Courtenay, son of the executed marquis of Exeter: a handsome young man of the blood royal who had spent his youth in the Tower. Sides were rapidly drawn, but, once Mary had chosen Philip, the Council achieved a favourable treaty and there is no question that the Councillors co-operated in rallying the nation to a grudging acceptance of the marriage. Because Mary uncharacteristically did not directly consult the Council about the marriage until 27 October 1553, she inadvertently encouraged rivalry and misunderstanding. Different positions coalesced without royal leadership or guidance, but the Council did not divide into cohesive factions. Some members remained silent and some reserved judgement.

The political intrigues involved in promoting the candidates have too often diverted historians from the less glamorous but concurrent accomplishments of Mary's Councillors. The organisation of the new government, the coronation and the first parliament occupied the Council until autumn. In August and September, along with their regular duties, the Councillors handled Edward's funeral and some anti-Catholic demonstrations, and dealt with the disposition of Northumberland and Lady Jane Grey. At the same time they planned the coronation and drafted measures for the parliament. In October they managed that parliament. Haunted by the question of secularised Church lands, they began the work of dismantling the Reformation and confronted such problems as the title of Supreme Head, Henry's last will and the legitimate succession.[5]

Parallel with the Council's activities, but beyond its official purview, the marriage question simmered. Mary's selection of a partner was so important at home and abroad that speculation was rife in court and Council. But, since the Council was not consulted about the choice of Philip until 27 October, the marriage issue may be better understood in the context of court politics rather than of the Council's advisory capabilities. Sharing the view that women were unfit to rule alone, both Gardiner and Paget had quickly adopted as candidates men who would be indebted to them. This, as much as their different perceptions of England's interests, was at the heart of their competition. By 5 August

Renard knew that Paget favoured Philip, and after the coronation on 1 October he enlisted Paget's considerable political talent in the marital campaign. Gardiner, who feared a foreign marriage, supported Courtenay, the only viable English candidate. By 31 August he had mentioned Courtenay's name to the Queen, and throughout this period he rallied the novice Catholic councillors around the young man he had befriended in the Tower. In various audiences with the Queen in August and September, Renard gradually introduced Philip's name and secured a favourable response, although Mary feared conciliar opposition to a foreign marriage. As speculation increased, Paget obliquely mentioned the marriage, and Gardiner's supporters – Rochester, Englefield, Waldegrave and Southwell – spoke to her about Courtenay.[6]

Although the backstairs politicking had been intense, it was not until the Queen's announcement on 27 October that the Council became directly involved. The ten days following her consultation with the Council saw considerable political manoeuvring. Having been given little genuine leadership from above, the reaction was mixed. Only three of Paget's followers, Petre, Arundel and Bishop Heath, were clearly enthusiastic. Gardiner realised almost immediately that his support of Courtenay had shaken Mary's trust in him, and, because further opposition would have lost him the leadership of the Council, he accepted Philip. Rochester followed his lead. Renard's optimistic reports about increasing conciliar support continued until the parliamentary delegation of 16 November which protested the foreign marriage. That delegation included both Paget and Gardiner allies – Norfolk, Arundel, Shrewbury, Derby, Pembroke, Tunstall, Gardiner, Thirlby, Bedford and Paget.[7] Although the Queen blamed Gardiner and publicly humiliated him, it was probably his supporters, Waldegrave and Hastings, who were either directly responsible or let matters get out of hand.

There is no evidence that Gardiner was involved in organising the parliamentary delegation, and after the 16 November debacle he had to work diligently to regain the Queen's confidence. At the same time his perception of English attitudes and fear of foreign domination had not changed. He therefore used his previous opposition to produce the best

possible marriage treaty. In this instance the rivalry between
Paget and Gardiner had creative results, because the final
treaty was astonishingly favourable to England. Paget, Gardiner, Mary and Renard all took part in drafting the treaty.
But more important, when the treaty was presented to the
full Council on 7 December, Paget and Gardiner co-operated
to answer all objections to it.[8] Although there is no record
of the discussions, the treaty provisions show the beneficial
results of conciliar opposition to Philip. England would not
be Habsburg property. Philip's powers were strictly limited,
and he was not to involve England in war. Further, their
issue would inherit a generous portion of Habsburg territory.[9]
These terms were so favourable to England that it is difficult
to sustain the argument that they were achieved by an inefficient, faction-ridden Council. Rather, the treaty provisions
indicate the effectiveness of the Council in determining policy
when consulted. And, if Professor Donaldson is correct in
his estimation of Gardiner's Machiavellianism, we can assume
that Gardiner played a major role, particularly since both
he and Paget sought a consort to steady the royal hand.

Renard's reports of faction reached a peak in December,
but they lack credibility. Worried that another incident would
ruin his mission, he ferreted out every shred of opposition,
real or imaginary, and labelled it faction, thus giving a
false picture of conciliar activity. Although Renard either
knew nothing about or did not report Norfolk's criticism
of the marriage treaty, he did write about some strange
factions. On 3 December he reported, 'That body Sire is
so torn by faction that Paget tells me the Chancellor is
taking no pains in state matters. The earl of Arundel is
dissembling out of fear that if the heretics and French succeed
in setting Elizabeth on the throne he may suffer in his person
or estate . . . .'[10] But five days later Renard reported that
Gardiner was showing goodwill toward the match. Then
on 11 December he wrote that the earl of Derby was involved
in a plot to foil the marriage, and the next day that Derby,
Hastings, Waldegrave and 'several others' intended to aban-
don the Queen's service. They may have been excluded
from the inner circle, as Rochester had been, and were sulking.
They probably still had genuine reservations about a foreign

king, but there was no plot among them. Renard also reported a scheme to bring Cardinal Pole to England to prevent the marriage. This and other bits of information do not add up to coherent factions, but rather to confusion, a lack of cohesion and little organised opinion after Gardiner had accepted Philip. If Renard's factions did exist, they lacked durability, because they disappeared quickly after a few words from the Queen.[11] This is hardly the adherence to principle which characterised the factions of Elizabeth's Council.

The worst that can be said about the Council's performance in the first six months was that the Councillors indulged in clamorous differences of opinion. The Queen was well advised and served by the Council. The transition to the new ruler had been completed peacefully, moderation in religion still prevailed, and the advice to marry was correct in Mary's case. She still sought and needed someone she could trust completely, but Philip was the wrong choice. That decision was reached without the Council's participation. Once consulted, the Council did execute the royal will diligently. It negotiated a favourable marriage treaty and gave valuable service by inducing most of the political nation to accept the marriage. Furthermore, the Parliament during this period achieved its aims. Under conciliar control, it legitimised Mary, attainted the Dudleys and Lady Jane, confirmed the cancellation of Edward VI's subsidy granting tonnage and poundage for life, and repealed the 1552 Act of Uniformity. In view of the succession crisis and the knotty question of the Catholic restoration, these were substantial accomplishments. Still, the Queen had overridden conciliar opinion in her choice of Philip. Although the Councillors supported the marriage, trouble was brewing which they did not succeed in stopping.

Wyatt's rebellion was a serious challenge to Mary's rule because of its scope and proximity to the centre of government. By concentrating on rebel activity and accepting Renard's reports at face value, David Loades has elaborated upon the prevailing view of an incompetent Council so beset by faction that it was crippled during Mary's greatest crisis.[12] An outline of conciliar action and a critical reading of the reports sent by Renard and his aides suggests, on the contrary,

*Councill deals well with Wyatt.*

that once the Council had grasped the situation it handled
it with considerable energy and finesse.

The original conspiracy, which involved the Carews in
the West, Suffolk in the Midlands and Wyatt in Kent, would
have been devastating if the Council's early detection had
not precipitated rebel action before the planned spring rising.
The Council was spurred to action by the disturbing news
of a plot to marry Elizabeth and Courtenay. On 2 January
1554, ever wary of suspicious activity, the Council summoned
Sir Peter Carew to appear. His failure to do so alerted
it, and Sir John Arundel's detailed description of Western
agitation on 13 January led to decisive action. The Council
dispatched loyal agents to question the Carews, and on 22
January it ordered all justices of the peace to announce
the marriage, to explain the Queen's motives and to suppress
disorders, seditious rumours or attempts at rebellion. During
the same period, the final version of the marriage treaty
was negotiated, and after the signing the Council quickly
made its provisions public. On 21 January, Gardiner interro-
gated his protégé Courtenay, who gave Gardiner sufficient
information to handle the rebels without revealing Courtenay's complicity.[13] Given the information in its possession,
the Council gave no evidence of being paralysed by faction.
Rather, it appropriately concentrated on the West and on
Elizabeth.

On 23 January a letter from the sheriff of Kent outlining
Wyatt's activities galvanised the Council into new action.
While the Council temporised with Wyatt, decided to assemble troops by calling on reliable lords to raise their men,
and ordered the arrest and interrogation of persons spreading
the rumour that Edward VI was alive, Winchester organised
the London guilds, and Gage victualled the Tower. On the
26th the earl of Huntingdon set off to apprehend the duke
of Suffolk, and Northampton was arrested as a precaution.
The following day the Council informed Renard of the various
rebel activities and what it was doing to combat them. The
duke of Norfolk had been sent to Kent, men had been dispatched to arrest Carew, other men set to watch Noailles,
and 'all possible precautions' were being taken for the protection of London. The dispatches from Renard and his colleages

(who had joined him to help with the marriage treaty) indicated that the Council was taking timely action until their 29 January letter. Although it emphasised the danger and conciliar disorganisation, this report contains information that the Council was industriously maintaining its course. Military preparations were continuing, the marriage terms were being published by local officials and the clergy, Elizabeth had been summoned to court, and the French ambassador's mail had been intercepted.[14]

Just hours after the first of the ambassadors' critical letters had been written, the Queen's troops under Norfolk suffered a serious setback when his captains defected to Wyatt. It is this defeat, which opened the way to London, that has given credibility to the ambassadors' reports. Perhaps Norfolk, a respected but elderly soldier, should not have been given command, but the defeat was not the result of conciliar faction and incompetence. The Council still controlled the situation, because by 30 January the West was quiet, and, according to the ambassadors, Pembroke and Clinton were to lead 6000 troops to Kent.[15]

The Council's method of handling Wyatt after Norfolk's defeat demonstrated skill, perseverance and deliberation. The Council wisely rejected Imperial aid on land, and sometime between the 29th and the 31st decided on a final conciliary effort. Hastings and Cornwallis were sent to tell Wyatt that his actions were treasonable, but that the Queen would hear his petition if he believed that the marriage 'implied a divorce between her and her first spouse', the Crown of England.[16] The Council wanted to avoid bloodshed by inducing Wyatt to lay down his arms; if his reply were hostile, they would have gained a propaganda advantage and time to deploy the assembled troops to protect London. When their overture was rejected, the Council prevailed upon the Queen to make her famous speech from the Guildhall on 1 February. In true Tudor fashion, Mary rallied the London citizenry to her cause. Wyatt's entry into London on 7 February was met by Pembroke's troops. It quickly turned into a rout: Wyatt had been defeated by the Council's clever manipulation and its military preparations.

Where then do we get the picture of a faction-ridden,

incompetent or paralysed Council? This is based on the political actions of Gardiner and Paget, and on the ambassadors' dispatches from 29 January to 8 February.[17] Neither Gardiner nor Paget were above playing politics during the crisis – Gardiner by protecting Courtenay, and Paget by trying to demonstrate his indispensability. Paget implied that Wyatt had allies at court and that only he, Paget, was raising troops. Their manoeuvring perplexed Mary and bewildered Renard, but neither action paralysed the Council. Renard's confusion and lack of solid information made him suspicious, and that accounts, in part, for the nature of the ambassadorial reports.

Aside from one allusion to dissension (probably over Courtenay) Renard was more than satisfied with the Council's actions until 29 January and the reports gave every evidence of efficient activity. Then the tone of the letters changed dramatically. Suddenly nothing was right. This dispatch and the next (31 January) were intended to serve two purposes: to convince the Emperor that the situation was so grave that he should send aid, and that the Imperial ambassadors should be recalled. What has been taken as governmental disorganisation can be interpreted as ambassadorial nerves. The letters are contradictory because they portray a crippled Council at the same time as they detail actions representing a reasonable attempt to put down the rebellion.

The key to the changed tone of the 29 January dispatch is the querulous statement that the Council had not kept the ambassadors informed and, still worse, from their point of view, it had not indicated that they would receive protection. With an understanding of the letter's purpose and a knowledge of conciliar action, the description of the Council seems to be the produce of the overactive imagination of nervous foreigners inclined towards prejudice against the unpredictable English. They charged the Councillors with a lack of unison which abetted the rebels, with neglect of public affairs and the Queen's safety, and with failure to carry out their decisions. They reported a curious situation: the Queen was puzzled by the split in her Council and for four days the Coucil had failed to provide any additions to her personal guard. She asked Paget in Renard's presence

why the Council did not communicate with the envoys as
she desired. 'This failure was of such description that he
would not and could not say it though his life depended
on it . . . .' The ambassadors interpreted this to mean there
were 'suspicious persons ill disposed' toward the Emperor
and with 'evil intention'. Paget also said he had been trying
to raise troops for a fortnight, but that he was one voice
in the Council and could not do everything himself. Although
the ambassadors portrayed the Council as divided, incompetent and incapable of executing its decisions, this dispatch
later included information that the Council was taking timely
action. Norfolk's defeat was what gave credibility to this
description. Before the dispatch was sent off, news came
that the French ambassador's mail had been intercepted,
and the rest of the letter became optimistic.[18]

In the 31 January dispatch the ambassadors continued
to be critical and suspicious. That is not surprising, since
they had just learned from Gardiner that the Council had
rejected Imperial aid on land. This dispatch is clearly written
to illustrate the reasons for the ambassadors' sense of danger.
They wrote that they had asked Gardiner for protection
and it was offered. The dispatch goes on to say later in
the evening Renard was called to the Queen, whom he
portrayed as distressed by the absence of a guard for her
person. In essence, the letter asked the Emperor to believe
that Gardiner offered protection to the ambassadors while
the Council denied protection to the Queen.

Abandoned by his ambassadorial colleagues, who fled London on the night of 31 January, Renard's report of 5 February
was more agitated and fanciful: the Queen and Council
were sorely perplexed by Wyatt's 3000 troops, Courtenay
was part of the rebellion, Elizabeth was raising troops, Councillors were in the plot and the Council was quarrelling
over whether the rebellion was caused by Gardiner's haste
in religion or Paget and Arundel's success in negotiating
the Spanish marriage. Even if Renard was right about the
quarrelling, the Council still functioned, as the rest of the
dispatch shows with its report of the mission to Wyatt and
the Guildhall speech. By that time, Wyatt was camped outside
London and Renard was transferring his own fear to the

Council. His 8 February dispatch indicates that he was oblivious to the Council's clever handling of Wyatt and was unaware of other positive developments, such as the mood of London. Instead he reported a 2 a.m. visit to the Queen. The Council had urged her to flee London and she bravely sent for Renard. According to his boastful account, he persuaded the Queen over the advice of a craven Council that fleeing would be a blunder. Either Renard singlehandedly held the Queen and Council together or the report is dubious, because the Council had gathered troops which were ready and waiting before Wyatt entered London.

The danger over, Renard did not report an incompetent, split Council as long as it moved energetically and rapidly to punish the rebels. Again, as in the marriage question, Renard's reports reached a crescendo of criticism at the very moment when the Council was resolving the crisis.

The concurrent problems exacerbated conciliar relations in the spring of 1554: the disposition of Elizabeth and the remaining prisoners, and the question of religion. Renard's accounts of faction in this situation are confusing, because, although he reported the issues facing the Council, he did not always distinguish them. He was primarily concerned with insuring Philip's safe arrival in England. Because of his concern, Renard again read faction and treachery into honest disagreements over policy.

The disagreement over the treatment of Elizabeth does not demonstrate faction, but, rather, demonstrates that Mary and Gardiner were at odds with most of the Council. Gardiner lost men who had been his allies up to that point. Many were obviously torn between their religious predilections and the legitimate Tudor heir. When the Councillors delayed conveying Elizabeth to the Tower, Mary reprimanded them by saying they would never have dared to do such a thing in her father's lifetime. Another incident in this connection related by Renard shows his confusion about the nature of faction. On Sunday 18 March the 'heretics' of the Council met and decided to ask the Queen to be merciful and not shed noble blood (Elizabeth and Northampton). They further advised the Queen to pardon most of the remaining prisoners. Inducing Paget to take their side by playing on his animosity to Gardiner, they prevailed upon her to pardon six men. Mary began to suspect a plot and confronted Paget, who defended himself by accusing Gardiner of neglecting the Council. According to Renard, the split had widened because, as Paget said, the Chancellor despised his colleagues. This led him to act without their consent, take private measures in matters of religion, proceed faster than was wise, and plant suspicions about Paget and Arundel's loyalty. All this apparently refers to the aftermath of rebellion.[19]

Only when the question of restoring Catholicism arose during the second parliament did the rivalry between Gardiner and Paget threaten to disrupt the conciliar system of governance.[20] Renard naturally reported faction, because the Catholic restoration brought out fundamental differences of opinion in the Council. However, this was not a simple conflict between Catholic and Protestant. Paget was concerned primarily with good governance and order, not theology. He saw religion as the cement of society; he did not object to a Catholic restoration, but found a more cautious approach preferable to Gardiner's 'blood and fire' course. Personal rivalry and political ambition also played a role. Paget was trying, as before, to demonstrate his indispensability to the Queen, and that he could be a great nuisance if his advice were not taken. The underlying issue, then, was the method of returning to Catholicism; the major question was the security of secularised lands; and the catalyst was Gardiner's heresy bill. Since the bill did not refer to property, it must be concluded that Paget felt that haste would stir unrest and that the success of the heresy bill would ultimately endanger secularised property.

In February Gardiner began to agitate for a parliament at Oxford and to propose harsh religious legislation. Gardiner lost his bid for an Oxford parliament and Paget was defeated on the question of the proposed bills in the Council's legislative committee. At this point, according to Renard's account of faction, Gardiner had arranged to bring his proposed agenda for Parliament before the Council, but, in order to avoid consenting to the article on religion, Paget and Arundel had gone home without leave. It would appear that Paget had been overruled in the committee, but that

Gardiner, faced with the whole Council, was having trouble getting his programme approved. The situation was serious, but not as dire as Renard implied when he wrote, 'the confusion is such that no one knows who is good or bad, loyal or treacherous, constant or inconstant'. Only Renard was that confused. At this point Paget and Petre proposed reducing the size of the Council. They did not suggest dismissing Councillors, but suggested employing them elsewhere. A smaller Council would not remove Paget's opposition, but might reduce Gardiner's power and influence. It would limit the attendance of the novice Catholic Councillors, who rarely sat at the board, but who as Members of Parliament would presumably be present at the Council meetings and favour Gardiner's religious programme.[20] Temporarily outwitted, Gardiner agreed to the reform, and Renard enthusiastically reported an effective, reduced Council.

Although he had mentioned warning signs of difficulty in Parliament, Renard was shocked when trouble broke out between Gardiner and Paget in the House of Lords. To Renard the situation in the Council appeared chaotic.[21] Gardiner apparently perceived that he had been outmanoeuvred in the Council, and decided to move his religious bills in Parliament. Meanwhile Paget had assumed that he had succeeded in blocking Gardiner, and, taken by surprise, was stung into opposition. Paget faced the choice of checking Gardiner in the Lords, or saying nothing and losing his power base in the Council. The former risked incurring the Queen's wrath, the latter political failure in the Council. Paget chose to obstruct the legislative programme in order to convince the Queen that neither she nor the Chancellor could govern without him and his allies in Parliament and Council.

The transference of conciliar business to Parliament by Gardiner and Paget has led to the conclusion that the system of Tudor governance had collapsed under the burden of faction. Obviously, the rivalry between Gardiner and Paget had got out of control, but the evidence shows that, while the system functioned badly, government did not collapse. What is not clear from Renard's reports and, as in the case of Wyatt's rebellion, cannot be verified is whether the reduced Council actually failed, or whether faction seriously impeded the larger Council. Some Councillors did become involved in this dispute, but the drama of the political contest should not obscure the quiet management of Parliament by other Councillors. It attained its major purpose (ratification of the marriage treaty) and also limited Philip to the crown matrimonial through the co-operation of Gardiner and Paget.

If nothing else, the battle between Gardiner and Paget in Parliament settled the question of conciliar leadership. After the second parliament Paget lost his place in the Queen's favour, and Renard abandoned him. Throughout the spring of 1554 Renard continued to relay unfavourable accounts of Paget's behaviour.[22] In spite of the Emperor's instructions, Renard made no attempt to heal the breach; in fact, he spurned several of Paget's attempts to explain his behaviour. Since Renard continued to report faction in the Council, his motives are again suspect. This time, in addition to nervousness about Philip's impending arrival, Renard may have been trying to prove his own indispensability to the Emperor, because he himself was under investigation for possibly having accepted bribes in August 1553. Rumoured plots involving Paget, Arundel, Howard, Pembroke, Derby, Sussex, Elizabeth and sundry heretics have no real factual basis. A reading of the *Acts of the Privy Council* and other sources for this period indicates that most of these Councillors were carrying out their duties.

These three episodes serve as a paradigm for the rest of the reign. They demonstrate that the council did not dissolve into warring camps as has been traditionally thought, but rather, despite a lack of royal leadership, managed to respond to the administrative demands made upon it in times of crisis. Furthermore, Harbison's 'fairly well defined' factions do not survive the test of consistency on the issues discussed here or at other times when two distinct sides can be identified. Tudor Councillors were individualistic and cautious. Most did not commit themselves openly enough to have their names reported by the ambassadors, and some deliberately dissembled. During the first year, Gardiner had one consistent ally (Richard Southwell) and Paget had two (Petre and Arundel).

How then did the other members of the alleged factions

behave? On the marriage question, only Bishop Heath, usually considered a neutral, can be added to Paget's side. Gardiner had the additional support of Rochester, Waldegrave, Englefield, Gage, Bourne, Hastings and Hare (Household); Derby, Pembroke, Clinton, and Winchester (Edwardian nobility and civil servants) joined them. When the question of Elizabeth's future arose, the situation was reversed: now Gardiner stood almost alone. Rochester, Gage and Hastings, with two others of the Household not previously mentioned (Jerningham and Cornwallis), supported Paget. The position of Waldegrave, Englefield and Hare is not known. Paget also gained the support of the earls of Pembroke and Sussex, Lord William Howard and the civil servant Sir John Mason. The religious settlement found Rochester, Waldegrave, Gage and Bourne reunited with Gardiner. Englefield and Jerningham joined them. Paget retained the support of the nobles (Pembroke, Sussex and Howard) and two of the Household (Hastings and Cornwallis). Lord Rich emerged from obscurity to support them in the Lords.[23]

Another indication of Gardiner's support was the protest against Paget's plan to reduce the Council before the second parliament. Southwell, Rochester, Waldegrave, Englefield and Bourne objected, and they were joined by Lord Treasurer Winchester, Thomas Cheyne and Edward Peckham (nobility and civil servants). In the aftermath of the second parliament, Renard linked the nobility (Arundel, Pembroke, Sussex, Derby, Shrewsbury, and Howard) with the civil servant Mason in suspicious activities, but his evidence is questionable and this alliance seems doubtful.[24]

The divisions cited above do not demonstrate consistent adherence to a person or programme and do not justify the term 'faction'. Further, 'faction' has often been employed indiscriminately as a generic term to describe all differences of opinion and quarrels within Mary's Council. The divisions, friction, and quarrels that existed were not all equally serious or significant in the internal politics of the Council. Three examples suffice to reveal the cross-currents of co-operation, competition and contention which could affect political alignments. Arundel, Paget's consistent ally, and Gage, who usually supported Gardiner, engaged in a dispute over a piece of land in Sussex. Winchester and Baker, both sometime Gardiner supporters, and both skilled in finance, clashed over Exchequer operations but still served together on a financial committee and were responsible for considerable reform in that area. Derby, a Gardiner man at one point, and Shrewsbury, whose previous alignment is unknown, were quarrelling over a post on the Scots border at a time when Renard listed both as Paget supporters.[25] An analysis of committees of the Council, not to mention the work done by Councillors on commissions, is further evidence of co-operation at times when Renard noted faction.

Students of the Marian Council would be wiser to follow the more reliable analysis of Paget, an experienced Tudor Councillor who applied the principles of governance he had learned from Thomas Cromwell. After more than a year of working with Mary and her Council, Paget discussed England's governmental problems with the Emperor Charles V in a manner reminiscent of his letters to Somerset.[26] Although he sought to explain his disruptive behaviour in the second parliament, he analysed the Council candidly and with considerable perception. Faction was not one of the problems he cited. Since he defended dissent at Council meetings and was not reticent in describing the Councillors' strengths and weaknesses on a professional basis, the omission of the word 'faction' leads to the conclusion that it did not impede the Council's operation. Further, since Paget's reforms did not involve faction, we should take his word that it was not an explanation of what was wrong.

Paget said openly that the multitude of Councillors and their disparate interests and degrees of experience and ability were the causes of difficulty. He was also concerned about the Queen's ability to play her role in the Tudor system of governance. Paget protrayed a gentle, inexperienced and therefore ineffective sovereign whose chief minister (Gardiner) promoted misunderstanding and a lack of co-operation in government. Gardiner also neglected certain important matters, and his 'self-sufficiency and asperity' were incompatible with the spirit of frank and loving co-operation necessary for the successful conduct of conciliar government.

In his proposed reforms Paget implicitly outlined the basic

principles of good conciliar governance. Paget wanted Mary to take the initiative toward the Council or act on its advice as the circumstances required. He desired more royal control and recommended that Philip II, as the Queen's husband, should assume the sovereign role and allow himself to be assisted by the most qualified in a reduced Council. That body would have a monopoly on advice, and be efficient in administering the realm.

Pollard and his followers have not adequately considered, as Paget did, the circumstances of Mary's choice of advisers. No other Tudor faced, unprepared, the crisis of a disputed succession. Once Northumberland's attempt to place Lady Jane Grey on the throne had failed, Mary confronted a difficult political and administrative problem as she formed her government. Few men combined both governmental experience and trustworthiness with proven loyalty to her person and her religion. Without men of these qualities, Mary compromised intelligently by choosing a balanced Council of three basic but not mutually exclusive groups: Catholic loyalists, personal adherents, and experienced Henrician and Edwardian Councillors. The loyalists, men such as Rochester, Englefield, Waldegrave, Bedingfield and Jerningham, were those who had previously demonstrated their Catholic orthodoxy, or had aided Mary in those desperate days of July, 1553. None of them, however, had held high office. To fill her Council with these men would have crippled government. The Edwardians – Paget, Secretary Petre, Lord Treasurer Winchester, the powerful earls of Arundel and Pembroke – were men who were familiar with current problems, but all were implicated in Northumberland's plot and untrustworthy. To balance the loyalists and the Edwardians, Mary selected a few men – bishops Gardiner and Tunstall, the duke of Norfolk, Richard Southwell, John Baker – who, while they had participated in Henry VIII's destruction of the world Mary cherished, were known conservatives and had demonstrated hostility to Edward's regime. It is difficult to see how Mary, harrassed and threatened by physical and political dangers, could have done otherwise. To argue with Pollard that there was 'no wisdom' in the Council is to deny the experience of those with previous service, the administrative continuity provided by Thomas Cromwell's protégés, and the abilities of the newcomers. The only fault to be found in the composition of the Council is the absence of the talented William Cecil. Mary needed such a man, a Councillor who either agreed with her on the vital issues or was capable of persuading her to change course. Neither Gardiner nor Paget was able to perform the valuable service that Elizabeth received from Cecil.

Mary has also been criticised for the number of men she appointed. Pollard's 'multitude' has a ring of truth when compared to Paget's remark that the Council was like a 'republic'. Certainly forty-three men were too many, but very quickly the significant Councillors emerged, and for others the office became 'honorary'. The number of men who consistently attended meetings compares favourably with records of the Privy Councils under Henry VIII and Elizabeth I. This inner circle was informal, but its members directed the Council. In February 1554 the Council established committees (dominated by the inner circle) for more effective administration of the realm. There is ample evidence that the surplus Councillors served in their counties certainly with added prestige. These Councillors were a valuable and effective link between central and local government. Furthermore, Paget began agitating for a reduction of the Council, and when Philip left England in 1555 a Select Council was established.[28]

The final criticism of Mary's Council has been that her choice of members – and their sheer number – inevitably led to factionalism which crippled operations. But, as we have seen, this is simply not the case. Although there were difficulties over the marriage decision, a serious rebellion, and a tumultuous parliament, the issues were resolved. The marriage took place peacefully in July 1554, and in November Mary's most tractable parliament joyfully received Cardinal Pole, who reconciled England to Rome. The Council had served the Queen well. It was Mary who was ineffective. She did not include the Councillors early enough in the marriage decision and ultimately made the wrong choice. While her Councillors were indisputably loyal during Wyatt's rebellion and worked energetically, she did not direct them.

In backing Gardiner's 'blood and fire' approach to the religious settlement, she initially ignored the interests of a vital segment of loyal Councillors until Paget's actions convinced her that the protection of property was fundamental to the success of the Catholic restoration. If two other, later policy decisions which have also been criticised are taken into consideration, the same pattern applies. The policy of religious persecution did not have wholehearted support, yet the Council executed it. The question of the war with France in 1557 was hotly debated. Mary followed Philip's will and Paget's advice into military disaster over the vociferous objections of many Councillors. Again the Councillors strained to rally a reluctant nation to an unpopular cause. Indeed, there was a disagreement in the Council and the rivalry between Gardiner and Paget was spirited in the first year, but their competition had some positive results; the Council had functioned effectively and it continued to do so throughout the reign.

The Marian Council was much stronger and more cohesive than traditional interpretations would lead us to believe. Not only was the Council more competent than traditionally thought, but, in addition, it was capable of important administrative initiative in domestic policy, as suggested later in this volume by Tittler (chapter 4) and Slack (chapter 5). The Cromwellian system of government, designed with a strong adult ruler in mind, more than survived two weak Tudor rulers. Its strength throughout the Tudor period can now be affirmed, and it now seems more appropriate to characterise the theme of its operation as one of co-operation rather than of conflict.

*The war*

*I e. urban & social policy*

# 4. The Emergence of Urban Policy,* 1536–58

## ROBERT TITTLER

THE general attitude of the Tudors toward the towns and boroughs of the realm is by now broadly familiar to those well acquainted with the era. Tradition has long identified that dynasty with the interests of towns and townsmen, and, even if the old chestnut about Henry VII's alliance with the towns against the nobility can no longer be defended with much effect, Professor Elton has reminded us of the concern which, in his view, Thomas Cromwell felt for those interests in the 1530s.[1] What has perhaps not been accomplished in a satisfactory manner is some more precise statement of the forms which this concern took; how, when, and why it emerged as it did; and by what means it was implemented.

Such a statement is particularly appropriate to the theme of this volume, for it sheds much light upon the tenor and strength of mid-Tudor government in the face of almost constant domestic crisis. My point, in brief, is that the attention of the Crown, Council and Parliament to urban problems in the 1530s marks at best but a formative stage in the development of what could be called a national urban policy.

---

* It might be helpful to note at the outset that I take 'urban policy' to mean that corpus of principles which the central government sought to implement toward the political structure, legal jurisdiction, or economic well-being of the towns, boroughs and cities of the realm.

In my view the relatively mature form of that corpus of principles arises only in the years from 1540 to 1558, when, despite what one has been led to expect on the part of mid-Tudor government, conscious support for urban communities at Westminster became more precise in detail, more comprehensive in scope and more regular in execution than ever before.

I

Direct attempts to support the interests of towns and boroughs were, of course, not new in the middle of the sixteenth century, or even with the Tudors. They were spurred on particularly by the general decline in many urban communities in the later Middle Ages, and probably increased in frequency with the stabilisation of central government after about 1485.[2] An examination of the statute book and reference to town charters and other such sources yields at least three lines of development toward this end which were reasonably well established prior to the sixteenth century and which were perpetuated at least through the middle decades of the century.

First, exemptions from payment of subsidies, tenths, or fifteenths for impoverished towns, or rebates from such payments, are well precedented in the early years of the Tudor dynasty, and extend to even before Bosworth Field. It was quite common, for example, to remit as much as £12,000 from every grant of tenths and fifteenths, to be divided among the poor towns of each shire, while such towns as Great Yarmouth, Cambridge, Lincoln and even New Shoreham were sometimes completely exempted from such payments.[3] For the most part, Henry VIII seemed content to follow the example established by his father in this matter, although there were omissions from what by then had become the usual list of exemptions in a number of subsidy bills.[4]

This device did not end with Henry. In a move with strikingly modern overtones, and one which *could* have marked a watershed for the development of future fiscal policy, Edward's government attempted to remit the payment of all fee farms of English towns and boroughs for a three-year period. The statute of 2 and 3 Edward VI, c. 5, was probably inspired by an anonymous brief on dearth in the realm which was presented shortly before.[5] By its terms, the money which would have gone into the Exchequer was instead to have been placed aside to employ the poor in public works under the direction of the overseers of the poor. Unfortunately, however, the scheme ran foul of a situation with an equally modern ring to it when the Crown began to miss the lost revenue. In the following year the act was amended, and the remission was limited to a single year, which by then had already come to an end.[6]

A second time-honoured form of government support for towns and boroughs is represented by the principle of defending the monopolistic privileges enjoyed by particular trades, industries or towns themselves. So common was this practice in the economic system of pre-industrial England that one need not dwell upon it further, except to note that such expressions of government support had in the past nearly always been issued on an *ad hoc* basis, and in quite specific terms.

Thirdly, in what began in the fifteenth century as an effort to restore land to tillage in an age of depopulation and enclosure, and which gave rise to an effort to restore the dilapidated housing of many decaying towns by the mid-sixteenth century, several statutes passed in the reign of Henry VII or afterwards authorised punitive measures against town property owners who permitted their buildings to fall into decay.[7] At first these measures dealt with individuals, not towns, and emphasised the return of land to tillage rather than the poor state of housing. In the 1530s, however, two successive acts made general reference to the rebuilding or repair of dwellings and other buildings in Norwich and King's Lynn: 26 Henry VIII, cc. 8 and 9. Here we find the principle of corporate responsibility for improvement, and the government's ardent desire to replenish housing in many towns of the realm. The owners of decayed buildings were obliged to rebuild within a specified period or, ultimately, to surrender their property to the borough corporation. But the responsibility for rebuilding devolved along with the edifices themselves, and the corporations took on the statutory obligation to rebuild within a specified time.

A few months later, in a third statute of this nature,

27 Henry VIII, c. 1 (again probably the result of local initiative), several other decaying towns were listed. By 1540, with two more acts to the same effect, 32 Henry VIII, cc. 18 and 19, nearly sixty towns were listed in what was by then obviously more than an *ad hoc* expedient. In effect, what had begun in the council chambers of Norwich and King's Lynn in 1535 had in a five year period become a general statement of support by the institutions of central government for the re-edification of decayed towns under the aegis of local corporate authority. Still more towns came under this statutory regulation by acts of 1542 and 1544: 32 Henry VIII, c. 36, and 35 Henry VIII, c. 4.

This theme, with specific reference to housing, is not only evident in the legislation of the late 1530s and 1540s, where it coexists with a continuing interest in the restoration of pasture lands to tillage, but is also reflected in the communication between the Privy Council and individual communities. An oft-cited illustration of this is the Council order of 28 June 1549, in answer to the complaint of the town fathers of Godmanchester.[8] Anyone owning more than one house was commanded to rent out the additional housing; anyone having converted a dwelling to some other use was ordered to reconvert it; all open fields formerly belonging to guilds were to be divided to the use of cottagers. An equally vivid case of such policy enforcement derives from the difficulties of poor tenants in the borough of Boston at roughly the same time. The officers of the corporation had complained of the activities of a man named John Browne, who apparently made his livelihood by buying up derelict buildings, most of them houses, stripping off the building material, and selling whatever he could to a multitude of ready purchasers. This sort of activity was common enough after the dissolution of the monasteries, but the borough officials were much grieved at the pillage of buildings which were not only, it appears, in the very centre of town, but also still occupied by local artisans. When they proved unable to stop Browne themselves, they appealed to the Crown through William Cecil, whose seat at Stamford made him their closest friend at court.[9] The appeal brought the wrath of the Council down upon Browne in short order.

II

Instances such as these were not uncommon in the mid-century years, and they lead one to suggest that government support, characteristically prompted by local initiative and by concern for the re-edification of urban dwellings, established a favourable and perhaps even necessary climate for what Professor Hoskins has termed 'the Great Rebuilding'.[10]

Taken together, these older policy directions dealt largely with a concern for the physical or financial state of towns: concerns which arose long before the middle decades of the century, and which were pressed with renewed vigour in the late 1530s and 1540s. To contemporaries, however, the authority of local government, and its role in social and economic issues, seemed of equal or greater importance. Professor Elton has recently reminded us that, under Cromwell's guiding hand, and with the aid of well reasoned advice from his 'brains trust', this awareness grew rapidly in the 1530s.[11] Like their patron, several of the humanists and social critics whom Cromwell brought to court had enjoyed extensive experience in the more richly developed urban society of the Continent. This could be said of Richard Morison, Steven Vaughan, Richard Taverner and others, but one need look no further than to Thomas Starkey for a perceptive analysis of English towns drawn from this perspective.

Starkey had gained extensive experience of the most highly developed of all urban cultures, that of Italy, where he had been a member of Reginald Pole's circle at Padua. His *Dialogue Between Reginald Pole and Thomas Lupset*, probably written in 1532–3, shows his dismay that the towns of his own land fell far short of the civility, beauty and orderliness which he remembered – or imagined having experienced – in Padua and elsewhere. In the *Dialogue*, Pole is made to decry the lawlessness and incivility of English towns. Foreshadowing the precocious Rousseau of a later era, he offers that, 'if this be civil life and order, to live in cities and towns with so much vice and misorder, meseem man should not be born thereto, but rather to life in the wild forest'.[12] Lupset agrees that urban life was not as it should have been, but insists that, 'though it may be so that man abuseth the society and company of man in cities and towns, giving himself to all vice, yet we may not therefore cast down cities and towns and drive man to the woods again'. The fault lay not in the towns, but in their governors.[13] As Lupset affirmed later on in the *Dialogue*, 'Every gentleman flieth into the country; few . . . inhabit cities or towns; few have any regard for them; by the reason whereof in them you shall find no policy, no civil order, almost, nor rule.'[14] In the end, two solutions are put into the mouth of Pole: taxes should be raised to rebuild the towns, so that gentlemen might be encouraged to return, and officials should be appointed in the decayed towns to take charge of educating the youth in useful crafts and thereby relieving poverty.[15] Later on Starkey comes back to the latter theme, this time through the figure of Lupset, who proposes the appointment of 'overseers of the city', with charge over 'health, wealth, and ornaments of the cities and towns'.[16]

One finds in Starkey's *Dialogue* genuine and acute analysis of urban problems and a viable guide to possible legislative remedy. Assuming that he meant the landed gentry, Lupset's comments about gentlemen fleeing the towns may lack some historical accuracy when applied to England, but quite perceptively recognise the declining influence of the traditional feudal magnates upon society in general and upon urban life and institutions in particular. Morison, in his *Remedy for Sedition*, and others of Cromwell's advisers recognised the same. If, as Anthony Fletcher recently put it, 'the relationship of land-lord to tenant was the prime cohesive of Tudor society',[17] then the growth of towns and the erosion of feudal ties – at least in a figurative sense Lupset's 'fleeing gentlemen' – posed a grave threat for the traditional social equilibrium, and gave rise to that sort of languishing urban community which so struck the person of Pole in the *Dialogue*. (It is also possible, on the other hand, that 'fleeing gentlemen' referred to the flight of the substantial townsmen who, as Charles Phythian-Adams shows, were overburdened by the costs of their role in the towns.[18] Such flight would, of course, work to decrease the tax base, and encourage the deleterious effects of absentee landlordism on the urban fabric.) Erosion of urban leadership had been a problem from well before Cromwell's time, and helped exacerbate the problem of social control to very serious proportions indeed. Had the government needed proof of that social disintegration, the role of townsmen in the Pilgrimage of Grace in 1536, or in the risings of 1549, offered stark confirmation.

In this situation, the mid-century governments, guided by the social theorists of the age, made the most significant strides of the century toward what amounted to a national urban policy. Here three new themes of action stand out with particular clarity: town authorities were given new economic and social regulatory powers; they were given newly defined jurisdiction over military organisation – at least in the larger towns; and, more than ever before, they were given enhanced status before the law.

The needs of merchants and craftsmen to regulate the conditions of their trade and manufacture, both to assure standards of quality and to limit competition, is nearly as old, and hardly less fundamental, than the institution of the town itself. The recognition of this principle by central government, at least to a perfunctory extent, extends back nearly as far. Yet the government action toward this end had usually been expressed in particularist terms, toward the regulation of specific trades or industries, or toward individual towns.

In the Reformation parliament alone, for example, we have statutes for the protection of rope-makers in Burporte, Dorset; worsted weavers in Great Yarmouth; the economic regulatory powers of the borough of Southampton; and clothiers in the five chief towns in Worcestershire. This particularist form of government support continued unabated throughout the century.[19]

Yet the importance which Cromwell's decade placed on the economic plight of towns took on additional significance in the years after his fall. From about 1540, faced with the rapid acceleration in the rate of economic change, the government at Westminster experienced a suddenly more pressing need to arrive at broad solutions to problems of complex nature and national impact. These forces of change swept up merchants, craftsmen, labourers and consumers and had a variety of effects: the greater mobility of population, the search for new trade routes as old ones proved uncertain, the diversification of manufactures, the increased incidence of industry outside the bounds of corporate jurisdiction, the production of cheaper and shoddier goods, the decline of such traditional forms of labour organisation as the guild and the practice of apprenticeship, and, of course, the laconic facts of inflation and poverty.[20]

The themes of government response to these problems, as suggested by F. J. Fisher nearly four decades ago, were restriction and control: themes well documented in the statute book during the 1540s and 1550s.[21] On balance, though he emphasised foreign trade rather than domestic economic policy, Fisher's assessment of government attitudes has fared reasonably well. Although it is not my intention to treat either this economic change or the government's reaction to it as ends in themselves, their implications for the theme of urban policy are centrally important. The reinforced need for social control after 1536, and the upsurge of what one might legitimately call early 'economic nationalism' in the years immediately following, called forth an examination of the local authority upon which naturally rested the responsibility for enforcement. It is thus entirely logical that the government at Westminster should have made a concerted effort at this time to identify and fortify such local authority. This was particularly important in the towns, moreover, where jurisdiction was frequently more contentious than in the traditional setting of the countryside, where the expression of social or economic discontent could be most menacing, and where the label of 'urban crisis' has appropriately been applied to the era.[22]

The policy of economic and social control of which Fisher wrote is most familiarly exemplified by the Statute of Artificers of 1563, 5 Elizabeth, c. 4, the longest and most sweeping regulatory act of the century. It would be misleading, however, to focus on that landmark in isolation, for it came as the last and most comprehensive of a long series of acts which embodied its basic principles. Of greater importance for the theme of urban policy is the fact that nearly all the regulatory legislation of the mid-century decades has a distinct bearing upon the role of towns and town authority, and upon the economy of towns rather than the countryside.

It is also interesting to note that the development of government support for such local authority, even if, in part, as
a side effect of a more forceful national economic policy,
does not begin in earnest until *after* the fall of Thomas Cromwell: some of the very principles embodied in these acts,
including the ban on retail trade of a number of items outside
corporate jurisdiction, had in fact been considered and
rejected in the 1530s.[23]

The economic flux felt in the mid-century decades made
inroads upon traditional economic patterns in a variety of
urban types. In the smaller towns, where the economy rested
largely on the commerce and revenue of the market-place,
it was common in this period to experience what amounted
to a seigneurial reaction. Thus, as Alan Everitt has shown,
as soon as business picked up in the market place with
the expansion of population and internal trade, the feudal
landlords reasserted claims to legal and fiscal jurisdiction
which had tended to go out of use, and thus they threatened
the relative degree of economic self-determination which had
often accrued in the interim.[24] At times, as in the Essex
market town of Thaxted, such seigneurial challenges, carried
out in protracted litigation, eventually overcame even the
most determined resistance of the townsmen.[25]

Larger towns were often more secure of status, and were
usually sustained by one or more local industries, of which
woollen cloth was the most common. Here the economic
flux of the 1540s and 1550s had proportionately more complex
consequences. Typically, those towns would have evolved
formal institutions to regulate the standards of production,
the numbers of producers and the conditions of employment.
The guild, which controlled both the economic lives of
craftsmen or merchants and the quality of production, functioned alongside the authorities of the town itself to assure
the ideal of the just price, the just wage and a sound product.
The system worked well in conditions of relatively static
economic conditions. But, faced with the sharpened competition for overseas trade, the expanding and more mobile labour
force at home, and the burgeoning rate of inflation, it became
difficult to reconcile the traditional patterns of regulation
with the new demands for freedom of economic action. Such

demands came from craftsmen and investors who found it unprofitable or inconvenient to function within the bounds of corporate jurisdiction, from labourers who were unwilling to observe conditions of apprenticeship, and from the forces of the market itself, where the pressures of competition sternly challenged traditional corporate jurisdiction.

Bolstered by the writings of such critics as Sir Thomas Smith, William Latimer, William Forest, and Thomas Becon, who may be seen as ideological successors to Starkey, the government appears rapidly to have become convinced that the resolution of these pressures lay in a new assertiveness in support of traditional mechanisms for control. In political terms this meant either the strengthening of burghal jurisdiction already in force or, in many cases, the recognition of such authority where it had grown by custom alone. In economic terms, this meant attempting to reassert, or to assert anew, corporate control of the market-place and the workshop.

One aim of this emerging policy was to provide a check against the apparently declining standards of production which were widely held responsible for the diminishing saleability of English wares abroad. This could be done in statute by limiting the proliferation of industries in the countryside, where traditional mechanisms of regulation had no effect; by specifying details of a manufacturing process; or by reinforcing regulatory mechanisms where they did exist. Such policies were strenuously urged by a number of contemporary writers, of which the anonymous author of the *Discourse on the Common Weal* is perhaps the most familiar. He tells us that

> another thing I reckon would help much to relieve our towns decayed, if they could take order that all wares made there should have a special mark, and that mark to be set to none but to such as be truly wrought. And also that every artificer dwelling out of all towns, such as cannot for the commodities of their occupation be brought to some town to inhabit . . . such should be limited to be under the correction of one good town or other; and they to sell no wares but such as are first approved and sealed by the town that they are limited unto.[26]

The second thrust of these measures was to bolster the economic condition of the town itself, largely through the increased
employment of its workers, and through the increased revenue
accruing to the town from commerce and industry. Here
again the *Discourse* presents an accurate description of unem-
ployment in the towns.[27]

The response to this widespread sentiment may be seen
first in the host of individual statutes of this period which
call for proper manufacture of particular wares. However
diverse their objectives, these bills nearly all had the additional
effect of placing regulatory jurisdiction in the hands of the
local authorities: the mayors, the guild wardens, and their
deputies. By the middle of the century, legislation toward
this end turned from the particular town or industry to
the general principle of legal authority: a principle which
was expressed and endorsed by the Crown, Council, and
Parliament. I should like to emphasise that this development
from the particular to the general, and from the *ad hoc*
to the systematic, does not appear to have taken place under
Cromwell's direction, nor did it begin as late as the Statute
of Artificers. The most visible milestones of this development
came in the form of three legislative acts passed in the reign
of Mary.

The first of these came in 1554. Recognising that much
prosperity had been lost to towns through competition in
retail sales by denizens of the countryside, Mary's third parliament strove, in the Retail Trade Act (1 & 2 Philip and
Mary, c. 7) to prevent country dwellers from retailing woollen
or linen cloth, haberdashery, groceries, or mercery wares
except at regular fairs, or within corporate limits, upon pain
of fine or forfeit. The act applied not only to those retailers
who had moved from town to country in order to avoid
corporate control, but also to the growing number who pursued their activity as a supplement to agricultural occupations.

In the same vein, the Weavers' Act of 1555 (2 & 3 Philip
and Mary, c. 11) not only applied to clothmaking in all
parts of the realm, but also attempted to limit the extent
of such manufacture outside the bounds of corporate towns
and boroughs. Weavers and clothiers operating outside such
bounds were limited to two looms and one loom respectively,

and no new clothiers were to be permitted to take up their work after the passage of the act.

The point was driven home even more forcefully in the next parliament in perhaps the most comprehensive clothmaking legislation of the century: 4 & 5 Philip and Mary, c. 5, the Woóllen Cloth Act. Here we find specific attention to the 'decayed, destroyed and depopulated' aspect of 'diverse ancient Cities Boroughs and Towns Corporate' resulting from the removal of cloth manufacture from the towns to the countryside so as to avoid regulatory jurisdiction. The remedy specified that none should begin to make cloth outside such jurisdictions, under pain of a £5 fine per cloth: a rather stiff deterrent. Despite the fact that under clause 25 many areas seem to have been exempt from this provision, the policy of defending town authorities in their jurisdiction over England's chief industry had, for the second time in a short span, been stated firmly and clearly, as it had not been prior to this era.

A further very serious economic concern of this period was of course the question of poverty and its alleviation. Thanks to the diligent work of Dr Paul Slack reflected in chapter 5 of this volume, I shall not need to dwell upon this theme at length, but it would be remiss not to summarise, however briefly, the implications for urban policy of the almost universal preoccupation with this contemporary nemesis. Simply put, the responsibility for the prevention and relief of poverty, once considered the legitimate function of the Church, devolved after the 1530s upon the shoulders both of private individuals and of civil authority, especially at the town *cum* parish level. This greater responsibility gave rise first to an impressive degree of initiative from many of the chief boroughs of the realm – of which number London, Norwich, Ipswich and Bristol were particularly outstanding – and secondly to the provisions of statutory policy as promulgated in legislative acts passed between 1536 and 1555[28] and summarised in the more familar Elizabethan Poor Laws of 1597 and 1601.[29] In both cases, the result was the establishment in the towns of a quasi-uniform system for the relief of poverty, and augmentation, necessary to the operation of such a system, of the authority of the municipal corporations.

Along with the severe economic problems of this time, virtually all governments of the period 1536–58 faced at least the threat of internal unrest and the need for military preparedness. Henry faced serious rebellion in 1536 and war in the early 1540s; Edward's governments faced severe uprisings at home in 1549; and Mary, like her father, faced military crises of both sorts. At this very time, however, the traditional military organisation of the realm was undergoing a rapid and profound transformation wrought by the prevalent social change of the era. The breakdown of traditional social ties, the unreliability of feudal levies, and the increasingly obvious necessity to encourage the further development of a viable, post-feudal system of raising men and supplies, made mid-Tudor government extremely vulnerable to military demands.[30] In this shift from reliance on the feudal levy to a militia system, contention inevitably arose regarding jurisdiction over mustering in towns and boroughs. The issue was of the utmost practical importance, especially when a rebel force could commandeer regional military resources as readily as the Devon rebels had done in 1549.[31] By the 1520s the principle had seemed well established that the larger urban centres could carry out their own musters independent of shire authorities, while lesser communities continued to be mustered under the latter.[32] In the ensuing decades, however, and as a function of a general encroachment by shire magnates upon burghal liberties, this local control of the musters came under repeated challenge.

What evidence we have for the attitudes of Henry's government toward this question remains inconclusive, as examples both in support[33] and in contravention[34] of burghal authority may be cited. Despite the military expertise of both Somerset and Northumberland, little progress on this issue seems to have been forthcoming under Edward, beyond the usual calls for the fortification of specific military towns. For this and other reasons, the situation had become so serious that in the opinion of the most recent analyst only the fortuitous presence of foreign mercenaries in England permitted Somerset's government to escape even as lightly as it did from the risings of 1549.[35] Mary's government, however, seems to have resolved this dilemma by coming down firmly on the side of at least the larger towns against the claims of the lords lieutenant and other military officials of the shire. This is evident in several *ad hoc* decisions of her Privy Council,[36] specific mention in several corporate charters of the right to muster (the first such provisions which I have found in charters of borough incorporation since at least 1509[37]) and, finally, in the comprehensive statute known as the Militia Act: 4 & 5 Philip and Mary, c. 3.

A milestone in the organisation of the English military in many respects, the Militia Act made it plain for the first time that all towns and boroughs corporate which had either the status of a county or the enjoyment, by right of charter, of their own justices of the peace, should be accountable to no power but the Crown for purposes of mustering their own inhabitants. In addition, inhabitants of such towns were protected against being called to muster by authorities outside the town. Although this recognition of corporate authority was not always respected by the Crown in later decades, the Militia Act marks a high point of support for the privileges of corporate towns and boroughs on the part of central government.[38]

Underlying the issues of both economic and military jurisdiction is the even more fundamental issue of the legal status of the urban community. Although it subsumes questions relating to economic and military organisation, it is also an issue in itself and it too became a new and central concern of the Crown in the middle decades of the century. The reasons for this new awareness are complex, but they have much to do with the changing political position of the borough within the feudal context of the shire, and with the internal difficulties which beset towns and boroughs at this time.[39] In many cases structures of town government were insufficient to ensure the exercise of authority as demanded by the conditions of the time. Some towns were compelled to defend assumed, but unsanctioned, liberties against the threatened resurgence of seigneurial claims. In other cases towns needed all the economic resources at their command in the intensifying competition for regional trade. Whichever of these or other motives applied, the perceived need of towns and boroughs for a greater or more formal recognition of rights and liberties is most graphically evident in the revival of petitions for royal charters of incorporation and, as I have described elsewhere (an article in *History*, 1977), by the granting of many more such charters themselves in this period.

Legally, the charter of incorporation provided the ultimate recourse in the increasingly common battle to establish borough authority. Politically, it was the most direct and comprehensive means by which the Crown could define the nature and function of the urban community. The sudden revival and concentrated incidence of these charters after about 1540 indicates without further question that the governments of the mid-century decades were more aware of the problems and needs of urban communities, and of the value of their well-being for the realm, than ever before.

An examination of the documents themselves reveals a great deal about the nature of this awareness, and of the stages by which it developed within the remarkably short span of two decades. In terms of form and content it appears quite significant that, while those charters issued under Henry VIII were rarely more than *ad hoc* expedients employed to remedy specific difficulties and, as such, were highly sketchy in content, some of those charters issued under Edward and nearly all of those issued under Mary were fairly full in content and quite similar in form and even wording. This tendency toward standardisation of provisions in this important class of documents may be gauged, albeit somewhat crudely, by isolating and examining several key categories of privilege which might have been included in a 'full' charter of incorporation: one, in other words, which might well have been employed, as indeed many of them were, as a comprehensive instrument of government. If one then compares each charter with regard to these central categories, some idea may be gleaned of the fullness or sketchiness of the grant.

Such an analysis, based on a list of forty-three boroughs receiving incorporation or, in a few cases, confirmation of earlier incorporation (see appendix to this chapter) supports the conclusion that even in the years between 1540 and 1558 the Crown moved rapidly toward endorsing urban rule by what Messrs Clark and Slack have appropriately termed 'small knots of reliable men'.[40] With rapidly increasing frequency, incorporative charters actually named specific individuals to mayoral and conciliar office, endorsed the principle of selection through the process of co-option by incumbent officials, and, conversely, shut the door to popular or direct elections of town officials. Those magnates who had traditionally ruled over town affairs – at least in a metaphoric sense, Starkey's 'fleeing gentlemen' – were being replaced not by the landowning aristocracy, but from the ranks of the merchant patriciate. While this was not intrinsically new in the sixteenth century, it was now being more or less officially encouraged at Westminster.

Coupled with the Crown's evident desire for social control through the rule of urban oligarchy, I find genuine concern for the ability of corporate towns to hold their own, legally and juridically, against the interference of feudal landlords or shire officials from without the town walls, and against the threat of civil dissent from within. Burghal autonomy, as provided for in the charters, was characteristically embodied in such institutions as a regular court of record with the mayor sitting, retention by the borough of fines and fees issuing from it, a gaol, return of all writs to the Crown and Exchequer, a coroner, and even, as we have noted, the right to muster apart from the shire. Again, incidentally, the Marian charters stand out above those of her predecessors in their clarity and fullness.

As with the statutory evidence, one also finds here much emphasis on economic regulatory powers and well-being in the corporate towns of the realm. Here the incorporating charters generally ensure the right to markets and fairs, and the revenues issuing from them; assizes of bread, wine and ale, as well as powers to inspect other manufactures; exemptions throughout the realm, for their inhabitants, from various tolls and fines; and certain judicial functions, such as the court of piepowder, held in conjunction with fairs or markets.

A further indication of the success of these mid-century charters as instruments of government comes with the analysis of their endurance provided by the parliamentary survey of English and Welsh chartered boroughs commissioned preparatory to the Municipal Corporations Act of 1835. In this effort thirty-five of the forty-three boroughs incorporated between 1540 and 1558 were surveyed and, despite the long saga of town–Crown relations under the Stuarts in particular, fourteen of them – three Henrician foundations, two Edwardian, and nine Marian – still considered their mid-Tudor charter as their basic instrument of government.[41]

Finally, it is worth emphasising that the reign of Mary stands out with particular clarity as the high point of this spate of incorporation. Neither the governments of her predecessors or those of her successors came near to matching the rate of over four incorporations a year achieved in her reign,[42] while the Marian charters themselves were also, as I have noted, more formalised and comprehensive than their predecessors.

The suggestion that Mary's government in particular relied upon a strong link with the towns is reflected by two additional and especially suggestive bits of evidence. The first is the statute of 1554 against seditious words and rumours, 1 & 2 Philip and Mary, c. 3, in which, for the first time in the long history of legislation to curb sedition, the officers of all corporate towns were singled out for specific responsibility to repress such offenders, and were given the *ad hoc* powers of justices of the peace for that purpose alone. The second is the laconic attempt of Mary's Privy Council to determine on several occasions the selection of a mayor.[43]

III

What may one conclude from this evidence? By 1536, in the aftermath of the initial break from Rome and the quite unsettling experience of the Pilgrimage of Grace, several of Cromwell's advisers recognised the relationship between economic uncertainty and the breakdown of traditional concepts of social order on the one hand and the threat of social unrest on the other. At roughly the same time, many English towns themselves began to experience the multitude of changes in their traditional patterns of life which characterised the middle years of the century. They reacted to the consequent array of new problems by a variety of local initiatives, but also by seeking from Westminster greater recognition of the formal authority which they considered essential in carrying out such initiatives. Reviving as it did intense concern about the role and viability of towns, a concern drawn both from theory and practice, it is entirely logical that we should find the first signs of a concerted approach to urban problems by central government at this time.

At first, government action was irregular and was limited in scope. In the mid-1530s, Parliament, acting on local initiative but obviously with government approval, showed a more systematic concern for the physical state of towns, and for the increasingly important problem of housing and physical decay in general. As economic and social difficulties mounted in the years which followed, so did government try to keep up with urban problems; it began to work at the regulation of labour, commerce and manufacture, the relief of poverty, the state of military organisation, and the very basis of local government itself. Here one finds certain clear patterns of development and intent. In the first sense, government policy emerged at Westminster along lines established by local initiative, and proceeded from cases of intervention in specific, *ad hoc* matters to the promulgation of general principles which were widely, sometimes universally, applied. In terms of interest, the government seemed concerned to fill with sanctioned authority the void in many facets of local authority left by the break with Rome and by the disintegration of feudal ties. In this quest to assure trustworthy authority in the towns, the leading merchants themselves were identified as the most likely replacements for traditional clerical or seigneurial authority, and the merchant oligarchies became, at least for a time, the focal point of government support for town interests.

The cumulative weight of legislation, acts of the Privy Council, charters of incorporation, and other expressions of government will point to the establishment at Westminster between 1540 and 1558 of a post-feudal and uniform concept of town government. In this era we find a firm foundation established for the legal and administrative demarcation of the town from the countryside, and of municipal government from the manorial court. On that foundation the government at Westminster could hope to arrest the decay of English towns and to erect comprehensive strategies for the orderly government, the economic viability and the general prosperity of the realm. Although in the long run the role which was envisioned for towns and town authorities in the mid sixteenth century gave way before the demands both of a burgeoning capitalist economy and a resurgent, largely post-feudal landed class, we may find much of the basis for the relative stability of the Elizabethan regime in the emergence of a national urban policy in the two decades preceding 1558.

*Appendix: borough incorporations, 1540–58*

| Borough | Date | Patent roll (C66) |
| --- | --- | --- |
| Abingdon, Berks | 24 Nov 1556 | 911/m.30 |
| Aldeburgh, Suffolk | 15 Dec 1547 | 814/m.12 |
| Axbridge, Som | 1 Feb 1557 | 908/m.35 |
| Aylesbury, Bucks | 14 Jan 1554 | 865/m. 10 |
| Banbury, Oxon | 26 Jan 1554 | 873/m.3 |
| Barnstaple, Devon | 29 May 1557 | 912/m.5 |
| Beccles, Suffolk | 10 Mar 1543 | 721/m.10 |
| Boston, Lincs | 14 May 1545 | 771/m.32 |
| Brecon, Brecons | 20 Mar 1556 | 899/m.36 |
| Buckingham, Bucks | 17 Jan 1554 | 866/m.27 |
| Carmarthen, Carms | 17 May 1546 | 793/m.50 |
| Chippenham, Wilts | 2 May 1554 | 866/m.33 |
| Colnbrook, Bucks | 4 Aug 1543 | 737/m.2 |
| Droitwich, Worcs | 19 Apr 1554 | 878/m.36 |
| Exeter, Devon | 22 Dec 1550 | 827/m.33 |
| Faversham, Kent | 20 Jan 1546 | 783/m.34 |
| Great Dunmow, Essex | 16 Feb 1556 | 903/m.3 |
| Hertford, Herts | 17 Feb 1554 | 872/m.1 |
| Higham Ferrars, Northants | 14 Mar 1556 | 904/m.27 |
| High Wycombe, Bucks | 27 Aug 1558 | 933/m.10 |
| Ilchester, Som | 11 Dec 1556 | 916/m.24 |
| Launceston, Cornwall | 15 Feb 1556 | 903/m.13 |
| Leominster, Herefords | 28 Mar 1554 | 878/m.26 |
| Lichfield, Staffs | 2 July 1548 | 811/m.29 |
| Louth, Lincs | 21 Sept 1551 | 838/m.7 |
| Maidstone, Kent | 4 July 1549 | 815/m.9 |
| Maldon, Essex | 18 June 1554 | 868/m.13 |
| Maldon, Essex | 25 Feb 1555 | 885/m.32 |
| Monmouth, Mon | 23 June 1549 | 815/m.14 |
| Newark-upon-Trent, Notts | 21 Dec 1549 | 825/m.25 |
| Reading, Berks | 18 April 1542 | 711/m.1 |
| Saffron Walden, Essex | 18 Feb 1549 | 816/m.3 |
| St Albans, Herts | 12 May 1553 | 853/m.1 |
| Seaford, Sussex | 4 Aug 1544 | 737/m.5 |
| Sheffield, Yorks | 8 June 1554 | 869/m.34 |
| Stafford, Staffs | 1 Dec 1550 | 834/m.34 |
| Stratford-upon-Avon, Warwicks | 28 June 1553 | 863/m.2 |
| Sudbury, Suffolk | 30 May 1554 | 868/m.20 |
| Thaxted, Essex | 21 Mar 1556 | 902/m.6 |
| Torrington, Devon | 24 Sep 1554 | 890/m.6 |
| Warwick, Warwicks | 10 May 1545 | 772/m.23 |
| Warwick, Warwicks | 12 Nov 1554 | 882/m.6 |
| Wisbech, Cambs | 1 June 1549 | 818/m.45 |
| Worcester, Worcs | 12 Apr 1555 | 884/m.33 |

# 5. Social Policy and the Constraints of Government, 1547–58

## PAUL SLACK

I

THE social policy of mid-Tudor governments embraced a host of subjects and uncovered, and tried to remedy, a multitude of sins. Those many questions of 'reform and renewal' which had been aired in the 1530s were still of moment after 1547, and Edward VI's reign in particular was as much an era of social and economic projects as the years of Cromwell's ministry.[1] Yet the official reaction to social problems under Edward and Mary has attracted less attention than contemporary literary comment on them, despite its importance in bridging the gap between the much-trumpeted innovations of Wolsey and Cromwell on the one hand and those of William Cecil on the other.

Not all the pertinent issues can be considered here. Themes with major social implications, such as economic and educational policy, must be left on one side. I shall concentrate largely on the subject of social welfare, particularly the welfare of the poor. In many respects, however, it was typical. In this area as in others, established policies had to be reconsidered and in some cases reshaped. The pressure of new circumstances and the weight of traditional social ideals combined as productively here as elsewhere, moulding and modifying legislation and executive action. Achievements were admittedly more banal and more confused than aspirations. There was no coherent well-defined programme, no readily agreed response to major challenges. But there was more continuity in policy, and more effort applied to its execution, between 1547 and 1558 than is sometimes supposed. There was also one exceptional achievement, the foundation of the London hospitals, which is too often taken for granted. And, if progress was generally slow and halting, more than one part of the machinery of the mid-Tudor polity may be illuminated by a consideration of why that was so.

Much of the difficulty lay in the fact that social problems, though evident, were not simple. Short-hand reference to a 'mid-Tudor crisis' should not be allowed to conceal the perplexing variety of its manifestations. It was, of course, an age of inflation, accelerated by deliberate debasement of the coinage between 1542 and 1551. But this trend was obscured by an alternation of two different sets of economic circumstances. Most conspicuous were the short-term crises caused by harvest failure – in 1545, between 1549 and 1551, and, finally and most spectacularly, in 1555 and 1556. No less worrying, however, were the intervening years, when, notwithstanding good harvests, the price of products other than grain remained high. Attention therefore switched backwards and forwards between corn supplies, which occupied the Council in 1550 and 1555–7, and such matters as the scarcity of cattle and dairy produce, the burdens of purveyance and the activities of middlemen, which were discussed in the parliaments of 1548–9 and of 1554 and 1555.[2]

Another underlying trend, evident since at least the 1520s, was population growth. Its effects were visible in crowds of vagrants on the roads and in increasing pressure on land, particularly commons and wastes. Yet the bugbear of 'depopulation' remained as powerful as ever. It was not simply that the government's military needs made it acutely conscious of a lack of stout husbandmen able to fight its battles for it, and that engrossing and conversion to pasture were still live issues. There was also the real decay of many provincial towns, typified by, but not confined to, the dilapidated property of dissolved religious foundations.[3] Some urban populations were stagnating; and, where they were not, a dwindling

proportion of prosperous citizens could feel overwhelmed by
distress among the lower orders, especially in the depression
which followed the collapse of English cloth sales in Antwerp
in 1551. Enclosure itself was a problem for townsmen as
well as villagers, as the frequent conflicts over town closes
and fields in the first half of the sixteenth century demonstrate.[4] That the decay of towns was central to many of
the social concerns of the period can be seen even from
so agrarian a document as John Hales's bill on tillage.[5]

Finally, these problems were aggravated and overshadow-
ed, not clarified, by demographic crises and epidemic
disease. There were serious outbreaks of plague in London
in 1543 and 1548 and in many parts of the provinces in
1544–6 and 1549–51. There were the 'new' diseases of the
Tudor period: syphilis, whose virulence and power to shock
had not yet begun to decline in 1550, and the sweating
sickness, which returned in epidemic form in 1551 and,
although not serious in terms of mortality, hit the upper
classes as well as the poor. Worst of all was the demographic
disaster of 1556–8, when epidemics of typhus and other
'famine' diseases were followed by an outbreak of influenza
which caused the greatest mortality crisis of the sixteenth
century.[6] We should not conclude that the poor were poised
on the brink of a Malthusian situation in this period. Whatever else the revolts of 1549 may have been, they were
not risings of a starving peasantry, and even in the crisis
of 1556–8 it was a virus infection, not one or more deficiency
diseases, which did most of the damage. But rampant disease
was easily interpreted as a symptom of general social decay
and a demonstration of the direct threat it posed to the
social and political élite.

The concepts of disease and decay were thus more than
metaphors when used, as they often were, to describe the
social problems of the 1540s and 1550s. Yet they did little
to indicate precise modes of action, to distinguish between
moral exhortation, economic management and investment
in social welfare as remedies. On the contrary, they reinforced
traditional assumptions that the organism of the body politic
could be threatened by disharmony in any part of it, and,
conversely, that single ills were, in the words of an Edwardian

proclamation, the product of 'sundry disorders in the whole commonwealth', all of them needing reform.[7] It was this commonplace structure of attitudes, rather than any more precise programme, which bound together those writers who speculated about the deficiencies of society and government, doctors as well as clergymen and lawyers among them. Thus John Caius, the most eminent physician of the day, attributed the sweating sickness of 1551 to the excessively luxurious tastes of the rich and the deplorably alehouse-oriented habits of the poor; and the Council thought it a divine punishment for 'that insatiable serpent of covetousness wherewith most men are so infected that it seemeth each one would devour another, without charity or any godly respect to the poor, to their neighbour or to their common wealth'.[8]

It followed from these fundamental preconceptions that strategies for social reform ranged far and wide, from regulation of prices, marketing and manufacturing industries, protection of towns and tillage and control of dress and diet, to the closer regulation and relief of the poor. It followed also that any single measure was aimed at more than one target. The act of 1552 for the licensing of alehouses, for example, clearly related to popular manners, public order and prices in the drink trade; for all these reasons it proved enormously popular with justices of the peace, despite some doubts about its efficacy.[9] Similarly, another measure of 1552, the Usury Act, was designed to kill two birds with one stone. It was part of the reaction against uncontrolled monetary speculation which followed the coinage and exchange crisis of 1551: the bill's progress in Parliament paralleled that of a measure regulating exchange dealings, and the two issues were bracketed together in Edward's 'Discourse on the Reform of Abuses'.[10] But without the general moral opposition to usury as a symbol of covetousness, that 'vice most odious and detestable' as the statute described it, it would be difficult to account for its rapid passage, or for the failure to repeal it despite its manifest and quickly recognised imperfections. The ban on usury plainly hampered some charitable purposes, such as the use of loan stocks and orphan money, and it was inconsistent with other projects, including a pawnshop licensed in London which copied foreign methods of furnishing credit to the poor.[11] No matter how broadly based the consensus of assumptions behind social policies, the Usury Act shows how difficult it was to apply it to particular circumstances without unforeseen and unwelcome consequences.

If innovation was to be drawn out of this Gordian knot of complex problems and blurred assumptions, it required decisive political will. Here the omens were slightly more propitious in 1547, with the accession of a new king, whose uncle was determined to be protector in more than name, and with the promise of thoroughgoing religious reform. This is not to say that Somerset was any more altruistic than his predecessors or successors: every new regime needs to find novelties to prove its identity and enhance its authority and prestige. Neither should it be argued, as was once fashionable, that Protestantism provides a sufficient explanation for new trends in poor relief. Many ostensible innovations had their parallels before the Reformation or in Catholic as well as Protestant countries.[12] Yet the circumstances of 1547 undoubtedly made a difference. No less than events a century later, in the 1640s, they raised expectations of radical change. It was only too easy to suppose that religious purification would lead to social reform, the next triumphant item on the agenda. 'Now that the true worshipping of God' was set forth, the King and his Councillors would surely pluck 'up by the roots all the causes . . . of . . . decay and desolation'.[13]

As in the 1640s, such intoxicating aspirations soon cooled. They were tempered almost immediately by the obvious problem of resources. Projects had been encouraged by the apparent availability of Church lands for their support (another parallel with the mid-seventeenth century); but the government's military commitments negated most of the good intentions proclaimed in the Chantry Act. It often needed prolonged pressure by local interests to preserve hospital foundations, for example, and efforts to procure further chantry lands for charitable purposes were rarely rewarded.[14] More intrusive methods of raising finance were inevitably unpopular, even when they had the ostensible commonwealth appeal of the relief on sheep and cloth of 1549. When that tax collapsed, so too after a short interval did the *quid pro quo*, the release of towns from their fee-farm payments so that funds could be diverted to poor relief and 'other deeds of charity and commonwealth'.[15] Successive bills in the Commons between 1549 and 1553, apparently designed to encourage endowments for schools, repair of roads and poor relief, tell us something about disappointed expectations.[16]

Equally discouraging was the regularity with which the government's attention was diverted away from social policy, or directed only towards the harsher aspects of it, by more pressing concerns. Somerset's Scottish war is merely the first example. Popular rebellion in 1549 and 1554, religious reaction and war again under Mary, all focused conciliar energies on the more concrete issues of domestic security and government finance: lords lieutenant, riot, the militia, legal procedures and revenue courts. Ket's rising and the accession of a Catholic queen were enough in themselves to discredit any notion of religious radicalism and social reconstruction marching hand in hand.

Yet even so, despite temporary fractures and increasing caution, there was considerable continuity in social policy, and this for two reasons. On the one hand there was the tradition of commitment to social reform which we associate with civic and Erasmian humanism, which the commonwealth theorists inherited, and which appealed to all statesmen from Wolsey onwards as a useful weapon in their battles for domestic power and a reputation for 'civility' abroad. On the other hand there was the realisation, above all on the part of local authorities, that the actuality of disorder and decay demanded remedies. The two impulses often met: in Parliament, in the Council and, as we shall see, in the deliberations of the rulers of London. Throughout the period, therefore, the question was not whether to act at all, but how to define acceptable strategies and how to guarantee their execution.

II

The problems of definition can best be seen in one of the end products of policy-making, parliamentary statutes. That there were sometimes interrelated clusters of social legislation seems clear. Although the output of statutes (as distinct from the number of bills) on social and economic matters declined after 1553, each regime of the period presided over one productive session. There were the sessions of 1548–9 and 1552, which considered more than a dozen social and economic measures, some of which have been mentioned; and there was the highly disturbed assembly of October to December 1555, which passed not only industrial legislation and a poor law reminiscent of 1552, but also acts on tillage, dairy cattle and purveyance which remind one of bills discussed in 1548–9.

It is easier to examine the statutes and titles of bills in the *Journals* than to establish their origin, however.[17] We know that John Hales was deeply involved with several proposals in 1548–9, but we cannot be sure that all of them had conciliar support, and one of those which almost certainly did (the 'milch-kine' bill) nevertheless failed.[18] The direct evidence of government interest in the social legislation of 1552, to be found in Edward VI's own papers,[19] is counterbalanced by the fact that many of the proposals in the background documents did not reach the statute book, and by the evidence of independent parliamentary initiative. When we come to 1555, our knowledge extends little further than the form of the acts themselves. The poor law looks as if it may have been an 'official' measure, but it seems unlikely that the agrarian bills, which had to be taken in hand by William Cecil, were.[20] While the latter were perhaps accepted by the government in the hope of appeasing opposition to its religious proposals in the session, they indicate continuity of interest in commonwealth issues in the Commons rather than in the Council in Mary's reign.

This mixed genesis of legislation is no more than one might expect, given the nature of Parliament and the convention that it should have a regular and formative voice on matters of common weal. The habit of making acts valid only until the end of the next parliament, which was usual in the case of poor-relief legislation, made return to the subject and further revision likely. There was often more than one bill on a particular subject in a session, as with vagrancy in 1547 and tillage on several occasions. Some issues, such as sumptuary regulation before 1555 or forestalling and regrating after 1548, proved so complex or contentious that legislation came only at the end of protracted debate.[21] In the process vested interests and government caution could inhibit all but the most superficial solutions to outstanding problems.

The agrarian statutes of the period are familiar examples. The problem had always been acknowledged to be wider than enclosure itself: it was the decay of 'houses of husbandry' and of tillage, caused by engrossing as well as conversion. But the conventional solution, the restoration of tillage as it had been at a specific point in the past, was scarcely effective, though resorted to again and again from the statutes of 1515–16 onwards. It may have been the aim of an unsuccessful bill on tillage and houses of husbandry drawn up by a committee of peers at the beginning of Edward's first parliament.[22] The alternative was to try to deal with causes rather than symptoms, but efforts to set real limits to engrossing met with insuperable opposition, as Wolsey had found in 1515 and Cromwell in 1534. Even Cromwell's attempt to deter conversion by restricting the size of flocks of sheep was modified in Parliament in 1534. Their successors made no further progress. Hales's bill against engrossing of 1548–9 and apparently similar proposals made in 1552 and 1554–5 failed, as did a bill in 1552 further to reduce the size of flocks.[23]

The story after 1547 was not wholly one of failure in the face of vested interests. With the advantage of hindsight we can see the new problems of demographic growth and inflation beginning to make their mark on agrarian legislation. Pressure on commons and wastes was admitted and to a degree accommodated in an act of 1550, although this looks very much like an official stop-gap measure, rushed through at the end of a session which had considered at least four other agrarian bills after the collapse of Somerset's enclosure commissions. The high cost of meat and dairy produce was attacked in an act of 1555 to encourage the breeding of cattle, a measure reminiscent of Hales's abortive bill on the same subject in 1549.[24] As far as the major issues

were concerned, however, the failure of 1549 had been decisive. The centrepieces of later agrarian legislation, the tillage
acts of 1552 and 1555, were conventional, seeking in vain
to restore arable farming as it had once been; and the Elizabethan statute of 1563, despite Cecil's renewed interest in
the problem of engrossing, proved hardly different.[25]

Something of the same reluctance to depart from established
models characterised mid-Tudor legislation on poor relief.
But there were differences which made the final outcome
more positive. The problem – at its simplest, crowds of
vagrants and beggars – was easier to identify than agrarian
grievances and was demonstrably growing worse; and the
solutions promised an increase in social control, not the disasters of 1549. As a result, the strategy anticipated in Thomas
Cromwell's famous draft bill of 1535 and in the final short-
lived act of 1536 was adopted with fresh vigour after 1547.[26]
Although the pattern of advance and retreat to be seen
in the 1530s was also repeated, Edwardian parliaments acknowledged again the superficiality of simply whipping
vagrants and licensing beggars, procedures enshrined in the
poor law of 1531 and due for renewal in the first parliament
of the reign. Instead, as effective solutions to both problems,
they returned to the three new areas of action identified
in 1536: the provision of work for vagrants and the idle
poor, regular collections for the relief of the impotent, and
in consequence a complete prohibition of begging and indiscriminate almsgiving.

The first venture along this road, the Vagrancy Act of
1547, was vastly ambitious but a total failure. As C. S. L.
Davies has shown, its central provision, that vagrants
could be bound as slaves for two years, proved hopelessly
impractical.[27] Yet it should not be dismissed merely as an
instance of the dangers involved in allowing social theorists
to have their heads. The act was not a paper plan imposed
by government fiat: it developed out of several bills presented
to Parliament, and in its final form it was a comprehensive
poor law. Like the statute of 1536, it banned begging and
prescribed weekly collections for the impotent poor. The
slavery provisions were themselves a brutally simple means
of employing paupers, designed to overcome the difficulty

of persuading masters to take them on. There was even a reference to public works, a direct echo of 1535. However, volunteer slave-owners, whether public or private, did not materialise, and these clauses damned the whole statute. When it was repealed in 1550 and the elementary provisions of 1531 restored, little was salvaged beyond a section allowing the compulsory employment of poor children. The major question of work for the adult poor was not grappled with again until the 1570s.[28]

The other tactics of 1536 and 1547 were readopted in 1552, however, and this time successfully. The statute of that year not only imposed weekly collections and condemned begging in words very close to those of the 1536 Act; it also backed up its prescriptions by encouraging the regular measurement of responsibilities and resources in every parish. There should be local registers of the needy poor of the kind which some towns were already compiling. There should also be records of the amounts which parishioners agreed to give toward their support, thus committing themselves in advance to weekly payments. This was an important step towards a permanent poor rate, and the original intention of some interests in Parliament may well have been to go the whole way: the first bill on the subject (in 1552), introduced into the Lords and committed to a group including Hooper and Coverdale, was entitled 'for Taxes and Assessment for the relief of poor and impotent persons'. It clearly had a mixed reception, and it was replaced with a new bill simply for 'provision and relief of the poor', which was rushed through all its parliamentary stages at the end of the session. Although it is impossible to be sure of the details in the absence of the original bills, it appears that the government intervened to save as much as possible in a measure, possibly not official in origin, whose taxation provisions had proved controversial.[29]

As it was, the legislation of 1552 was a major advance, effectively laying the foundations of the Elizabethan Poor Law, but it was the last of the period. If anything, the danger in Mary's reign was rather of reaction. The act was not renewed in the parliament of 1554–5, perhaps because the government was contemplating some revision. In the event a new act, passed in the following session at the end of 1555, repeated the provisions of 1552 almost word for word. It may have had government support, since it went through the Commons smoothly enough and was apparently not amended in the Lords, despite being committed there. Yet it was not uncontroversial, for three peers, including Rich, voted against it.[30] Whether they thought it too radical or too conservative it is impossible to say. What is certain is that the new act made only three modifications to its predecessor, and only one might imply a change of attitude.

Two of the new clauses simply reflected local experience: the first ordering collections in London to be paid to Christ's Hospital, and the second providing that rich parishes in cities should pay their surplus to other city parishes. But the third amendment was a step away from earlier attacks on casual almsgiving: where the poor were too numerous to be relieved, they might be licensed to beg. It would be rash to attribute too much significance to this qualification. Like the other additions to 1552, it may simply have been a recognition of reality in large towns. The fact that it was repeated in the Elizabethan statute of 1563 suggests as much.[31] Yet it is impossible to ignore its consistency with other evidence, considered below in the context of London, that in Mary's reign there was a greater tolerance of indiscriminate charity. By directing attention to the donor as well as the recipient, the Catholic doctrine of good works may well have made casual alms more acceptable and any further move towards compulsory rates unthinkable. Certainly the negative point stands. It was left to the parliament of 1563 to advance beyond 1552 and introduce, albeit as a last resort, compulsory assessment by quarter sessions.

Even in the field of poor relief, therefore, the legislative machine proved itself cumbersome and unwieldy, unable to build lasting structures quickly on the common ground which undoubtedly existed between the government and the local interests represented in Parliament. Action was more immediate and more effective when either central or local authorities acted independently, and it reveals their ambitions more clearly than does the tortuous history of parliamentary bills.

III

It was a commonplace among contemporaries that statutes were so much waste paper unless there were adequate means for their enforcement. Proclamations did something to help, and circular letters insisting on the enforcement of specified acts were even more useful. In Mary's reign, for example, they testify to the government's central concern with public order, with the apprehension of suspect strangers, punishment of vagrants, and control of alehouses and unlawful games – all of which contradict any view that Marian policy was tender-hearted toward the poor as a whole.[32] The most effective vehicles for the government's more important aims, however, were special commissions.[33] Whether issued to all justices or to select groups of notables, they permitted an immediate and flexible response to local circumstances which was impossible in legislation, however ambitious its drafting. It is not without significance that the precedents for their use were set not by Cromwell but by Wolsey.

The most famous examples, Somerset's enclosure commissions, admittedly were scarcely as encouraging as their model, Wolsey's inquiry of 1517. Although they showed a salutary readiness to distinguish beneficial from harmful enclosures, they were destroyed by the revolts of 1549 and not revived for more than a decade. Yet it is a remarkable testimony to their indispensability that there was provision for commissions in the tillage statutes of 1552 and 1555. The Marian act even permitted them to 'take order and direction for the reformation' of offences, a power which may have helped to undermine Somerset's second commission.[34] Much more successful, and no less important, however, were the commissions for surveys of grain and provision of markets in years of dearth, where the example set by Wolsey in 1527 was followed both by Northumberland and by Mary.[35]

In November 1549 the Council sent out circular letters to all justices complaining that the 'insatiable greediness' of middlemen had inflated corn prices, and ordering them to institute local searches of barns for grain and see it brought regularly to market. Ten months later, immediately after a second bad harvest, surveys of corn were again commanded, and 'special men in every shire' appointed to supervise them when the justices were thought to have been negligent. The results are to be seen in local searches in towns such as York and Shrewsbury.[36] Although the records of conciliar action are irritatingly incomplete, it is clear that further searches were instituted in 1556–7 at the height of the next harvest crisis. A complete census of grain survives for one of the hundreds of Norfolk, for example, listing every family in each parish, the number of mouths to be fed, the stocks of corn in each household and how much could be spared for local markets.[37] Here was the firmest indication in practice, far clearer than statutes on regrating, that the government was willing to intervene forcefully on behalf of poorer consumers when necessity dictated.

It was more difficult to establish an acceptable policy than this brief summary may suggest. In 1550, for example, there were two conflicting proclamations on the subject, apparently reflecting differences of opinion between Northumberland and the rest of the Council, including Somerset. The second proclamation, probably at Northumberland's instigation, toned down the penalties threatened in the first, and introduced a Cromwellian note: it appealed to parliamentary authority by trying to fix maximum prices for a range of victuals under a statute of 1534. The price controls proved unworkable, given differences in local circumstances, and had to be dropped before the end of the year. There were also objections, repeated more forcefully by suspiciously interested parties later in the century, that the cure was worse than the disease: that intervention in the market created scares, encouraged hoarding and prevented the necessary movement of grain to large centres of population.[38] Nevertheless, searches for grain remained a central plank in Tudor social policy and they culminated in the book of dearth orders of 1586, whose influence, not least on popular mentality, persisted into the eighteenth century.[39] The government's motives were not unmixed. It was taking precautions to preserve public order, and also protecting its own interests as a consumer. But there were sufficient local benefits for it to earn some part of the paternalist reputation it so coveted.

Local authorities, and especially urban corporations, were even better equipped than the central government to act quickly in a crisis and to invent new methods of coping with it. That towns were responsible for initiating many of the novelties in the poor laws of 1552 and after is well known. They were also fully aware of deficiencies in parliamentary and conciliar recommendations and sought to remedy them. It was clear, for example, that they needed corn stocks as well as market regulations in order to protect themselves against dearth, and these were provided, in some of the largest towns well before 1547. The inadequacy of parochial control of poor relief in urban societies was also apparent and some corporations were imposing greater centralisation. They had tried to reduce begging, a keynote sounded first in several towns between 1517 and 1520, and were beginning to organise collections for the impotent and to turn them into compulsory assessments. The earliest to be more than a temporary expedient was probably that established in Norwich in May 1549, on the very eve of Ket's rebellion. Above all, there was a move towards more discrimination in social welfare. It often began with small changes, like that in Exeter in 1548 when the wholesale distribution of doles of bread was stopped because of the danger of 'great infection . . . by reason of the great press of people'. But it developed into the prescription of different solutions for different categories of pauper and the careful measurement of social problems in censuses and surveys of the poor, such as those taken in Coventry in 1547 and Worcester in 1556.[40]

What is difficult to investigate in the English provinces is not the character of welfare measures but the steps which produced them, the processes of evolution which we have tried to trace in the case of legislation. The incentive to prevent starvation, eliminate begging and employ the poor was obvious in 'decaying' mid-Tudor towns: the first motive of urban magistrates must simply have been to clean up the streets. They were sometimes encouraged by, though not dependent on, central initiative – as in York, where the Council of the North regularly supported action against vagrants and abuses of the market. In York too we can see the important stimulus often provided by emergency cir-

cumstances. The coincidence of bad harvests, high prices
and outbreaks of plague and the sweating sickness between
1549 and 1551 elicited a comprehensive reaction: censuses
of corn, surveys of the poor, searches for vagrants, close
control of alehouses, quarantine measures, and a compulsory
assessment for the poor, first raised in 1550.[41]

This was exactly the combination of crisis and elaborate
response reproduced in other cities in Western Europe in
the early sixteenth century.[42] But even in this case we cannot
easily follow, as we can in the case of Lyons or Venice,
the stages by which some options were taken up and others
discarded or modified. For that we must turn to London
and the greatest experiment in social welfare in Tudor England.

IV

The five London hospitals, St Bartholomew's, St Thomas's,
Bethlem, Christ's and Bridewell, can be compared only with
poor-relief institutions in major cities on the Continent. In
conception and in reality they were unique in England. The
impulse behind them might be similar to that which inspired
innovation in other English towns, but it was voiced in
more articulate and sophisticated form. The first orders for
St Bartholomew's, published in 1552, claimed that in the
past five years it had cured 800 poor 'of the pox, fistules,
filthy blanes and sores . . . which else might have . . . stunk
in the eyes and noses of the city'; and its beadles were
enjoined to throw vagrants in gaol and bring in any sick
loitering in the streets 'to the noyance and infection of the
passers-by'. Christ's Hospital housed children whose 'corrupt
nature' arose from the 'dunghills' from which they were
taken. But these crude incentives were papered over with
the vocabulary of Christian humanism more commonly
employed at court and on the Continent than in the provinces.
As 'faithful ministers of God', the governors of St Bartholomew's claimed to be furthering 'this most necessary succour
of their poor brethren in Christ'.[43]

Although some of them gave their name to lesser institutions
in provincial towns, the hospitals were also unlike many

others in England in scale. They attracted enormous endowments, absorbing nearly one half of all charitable benefactions by Londoners in the 1550s. By the end of the century they were supporting (or in the case of Bridewell punishing) more than 4000 people in the course of a year.[44] Moreover, their organisation initially placed them outside the main stream of development of English poor relief. They were controlled not by justices of the peace but by a body of governors. They did not, at least at first, copy the parochial structure of English social welfare, but centralised relief for the whole capital. Most important of all, they were not designed to be dependent on a parochial poor-rate: the famous half-fifteenth raised for St Bartholomew's in 1547[45] was a once-for-all levy to found the hospital, and it was hoped, vainly as it turned out, that charitable collections and endowments would take care of the future.

The parallels with London do not lie in England but elsewhere in Europe, where organised charity and remodelled hospitals, some of them for children, accompanied the municipal centralisation of poor relief: in Geneva, for example, where the Hôpital-General had been founded in 1535, or in Lyons with the activities of the Aumône-Générale, also in the 1530s.[46] Like many European towns between 1520 and 1550, London was a stage for the productive interplay of humanist ideals and mounting social problems.

Although there is much that is still obscure in the genesis of the London scheme, we can identify the men most active in its conception and execution, those aldermen and councillors who regularly served on the committees considering the poor over the decade from 1547 to 1557.[47] As yet we know little about their attitudes or connections, but they appear to have formed a broad-based coalition. They included established aldermen such as Richard Gresham and George Barne, and thrusting younger men still rising in the civic hierarchy, such as Thomas Lodge. The Protestant patrician Rowland Hill was deeply involved, but so also was the famous Catholic philanthropist Thomas White. The importance of medical interests is suggested by the activity of two surgeons, John Ayliffe and Thomas Vicary, surgeon to both Edward and Mary.

The chief figures holding this coalition together, and driving the hospitals forward, were two other city men with close government connections. One was Richard Grafton, first treasurer of Christ's Hospital and government printer; he at least must have been familiar with humanist ideas and he had travelled on the Continent. More prominent still was Martin Bowes, goldsmith and under-treasurer at the Tower Mint until 1550. He sat on virtually every relevant committee, 'devised' successive orders regulating the hospitals, and was finally enthroned as their 'comptroller-general' when the scheme reached completion in 1557. He was also one of the City's Members of Parliament in 1552 and 1555, although we have no means of knowing whether he influenced the poor-relief acts. That he had some knowledge of Continental welfare schemes is suggested by one of his early unsuccessful proposals, for a 'brotherhood of the poor', a fraternity of charitably minded merchants like those to be found in Venice and elsewhere. If any single man can take the credit for the London hospitals, it is this little-known figure whose other claim to fame is his central role in the Edwardian debasement of the coinage.[48]

The London experiment did not spring fresh and whole from Bowes's or anyone else's mind, however. Its final shape was the result of gradual elaboration, and there were modifications in the light of experience which ultimately distanced it from its Continental equivalents. The dissolution of the monasteries provided the crucial opportunity to use institutions to fulfil established policies. Petitions to the King beginning in 1539 were rewarded in 1544 with the promise of St Bartholomew's, Bethlem and Greyfriars (the site of the future Christ's Hospital). The first major committee on the project met in 1545, and St Bartholomew's opened its doors to the sick poor two years later, Bethlem continuing as a hospital for the insane.[49] For the moment that was all, and St Bartholomew's was for long known simply as 'the house of the poor'. But the removal of diseased beggars from the streets merely revealed the size of the problem and uncovered other categories of pauper to be isolated and thus contained.

A project for revising the hospitals was therefore sent to the Protector for his consideration in March 1549. Action was postponed by Somerset's fall and in 1550 the corporation was more concerned with combating dearth than with long-term problems. The extension of the city's jurisdiction to include Southwark drove home the need for more adequate provision, however. Discussions with the Council were resumed in 1551 and new plans quickly made. The additional grant of St Thomas's met the need for room for the incurably impotent and old; and Christ's Hospital was opened for foundling children in 1552.[50] Finally, Edward's sudden gift of Bridewell palace, apparently at the instigation of Bishop Ridley, allowed Bowes and his colleagues to tackle what they now saw as the essence of the problem: the wilfully idle poor and those who were willing to work but could find none. It was to be both a lock-up for rogues and a workhouse, and it represented the ideals of close social control and profitable employment which had replaced the earlier, more loosely defined ambition to find a lodging place for beggars.[51] Successive surveys and committees, and not least the availability of several institutions, had prompted the identification and treatment of different layers of poverty.

The first threat to this carefully ordered scheme came with the death of Edward VI. Mary hesitated to confirm the grant of Bridewell until February 1556; the administration of Christ's and St Thomas's was not fully perfected until 1555, although they were grossly overcrowded by 1556; and it was not until September 1557 that the hospitals were united and the system finally completed.[52] The delay was partly a result of the uncertain status of monastic property at the beginning of the reign. In particular, former Greyfriars led by William Peto set out to destroy Christ's Hospital, which had taken their place.[53] Another setback was the fall from political favour of men such as Grafton and Barne, who had been too obviously associated with attempts to exclude Mary. Wyatt's rebellion amply confirmed the government's suspicion of any manifestation of the city's autonomy. But there was also a significant change of emphasis in the new regime's approach to charity which dictated a cooler response.

It should be stressed that there was no complete reaction. Cardinal Pole, for example, fully shared the city fathers' enthusiasm for hospitals for the sick and foundling poor. In fact he complained about London's failure to match the achievements of Italian cities with which he was familiar. Some of the Spanish clergy in London admired and defended Christ's, and Bishop Bonner was no less concerned than Ridley had been to encourage legacies to the hospitals.[54] Even the central objective to which the corporation had turned by 1553, the disciplining of vagrants and the idle poor, was entirely consistent with the Marian government's campaign against these potentially seditious elements.

Yet the government's attitude was wholly ambivalent. It had precisely the same reservations as those expressed by the Catholic Sorbonne in a notorious judgement on the Ypres poor scheme in 1531.[55] In the first place, there are signs that it deplored in principle the attack on indiscriminate charity which was fundamental to the whole effort. Mary's chief personal work of charity was characteristic: the refoundation of Henry VII's Savoy Hospital, which gave food, alms and a night's lodging to any poor who came to its doors. It was a far cry from Bridewell, which had been endowed with the Savoy's lands by Edward VI. Secondly, Catholic attachment to the established privileges and jurisdiction of the Church meant resistance in practice to any encroachments from secular authorities, including the governors of the hospitals. While Gardiner interfered to restore or introduce daily mass in the new institutions, Bonner fiercely contested Bridewell's open punishment of 'moral' offences normally tried by ecclesiastical courts. He did not get very far. The city successfully appealed to its 'liberties' against him. But, when a preacher at St Paul's Cross in 1558 could openly attack the harshness of Bridewell, the aldermen understandably felt isolated in their battle.[56] They can have felt secure only with the accession of Elizabeth.  ·

These were not the only problems afflicting the hospitals, however, and they were not in the long term the most serious. If they could be abused in Mary's reign for doing too much, they had earlier and more accurately been criticised for accomplishing too little.[57] They had not removed the spectre of poverty from the streets, and they had neither the financial resources nor the physical capacity to do so. Charitable endowments, generous as they were, proved inadequate, and unpopular levies on the city companies and new revenues from cloth sales at Blackwell Hall were not sufficient to make up the deficit.[58] More fundamentally, the confinement of the sick, old, orphans and rogues still left a vast segment of poverty uncatered for. Bridewell could not, and had never attempted to absorb more than a tiny fraction of the unemployed; and there remained the problems of casual labour and low wages to force men temporarily onto the streets. These were the respectable 'decayed householders' identified and counted when different kinds of poverty were first clearly distinguished in 1552.[59] The comprehensive ambitions behind the scheme had to be modified almost as soon as it was begun.

The logic of the situation led inevitably towards a parish rate and the regular provision of outdoor relief. As early as 1547 Bowes had planned a scheme to encourage parish collections for the poor, which developed into voluntary agreed contributions of the kind envisaged in the act of 1552. In that year the collections, amounting by then to £160 a month, were centralised in the hands of the treasurers of Christ's Hospital, and part of them redistributed in the form of outdoor relief.[60] By the 1560s parishes were retaining some of the money for their own poor and thus by-passing the hospitals, and regular aldermanic exhortations to them to increase contributions had become the next best thing to compulsion. Circumstances, and not least the inexorable growth of the city, had made parish collections and parish payments an essential element in metropolitan poor relief.

Thus, the character of welfare provision in London gradually approached that in other English towns. The ambition to use monastic property and charitable donations to solve the problem of poverty painlessly had failed. The problem remained wholly exceptional in London, and it grew worse. But the challenge was not met with comparable originality again until the introduction of the Corporation for the Poor in that other decade of social experiment, the 1640s.[61]

V

The early history of the London hospitals exemplifies many of the themes considered in this essay. It illustrates the mixed motives which underlay attempts at social engineering: fear of disorder, disease and decay; and a quest for civil harmony, civic decency and the triumph of Christian charity, however defined. It shows too how radical ambitions lost impetus when confronted by sudden political change, first in 1549 and then, more seriously, in 1553, as enthusiasm for social projects temporarily dried up.[62] At the same time, intractable realities cut grandiose aspirations down to size.

Yet the example of London also displays the continuities which permitted major achievements in Tudor social policy. First in importance was continuity at the local level. Since the basic social problems did not go away, policies only fitfully blessed with government approval were necessarily maintained and developed in the localities. Social reform was a prime objective of many authorities in the years after 1540, and their attention was not confined to the sphere of poor relief, on which we have concentrated. Other concerns can be seen in the redirection of charitable endowments, in the foundation of grammar schools, and in the copying by several towns of London's Orphans' Court, which looked after the interests and property of the heirs of freemen.[63] If the circumstances of the 1540s made the regulation of the poor a focus of municipal activity, it proved in the following decades to be only one aspect of a much wider effort to create orderly local communities.

There was more fragile continuity – but continuity none the less – at the centre, where national policies were formed and local endeavours encouraged and orchestrated. We have seen the problems of definition and execution which bedevilled attempts to manufacture social strategies in the Council and in Parliament. But these difficulties were no greater in the reigns of Edward and Mary than before or after. They arose from the constraints involved in government by consent and co-operation between different forces: between social theorists and hard-headed politicians preoccupied with more immediate issues, between the Council and the interests represented in Parliament, between the central government and local authorities. Out of this maelstrom there emerged some genuine advances, as in the case of the poor laws. There was parallel progress in other fields, not considered here. Much of the economic legislation of the mid-Tudor decade (on apprenticeship, for example) modified the initiatives of the 1530s and prepared the ground for Elizabethan achievements. By the 1560s many aspects of Tudor policy had been refined by experience: ends had been more clearly articulated and means more realistically assessed.

Continuity had one further important consequence. As familiarity with commonwealth ideals increased, so the notion of public responsibility for social welfare came to be widely accepted. Continuous insistence from the centre, as much as continuous experiment in the localities, made social policies part of the intellectual and administrative baggage of every justice of the peace. In 1540 that process was only just beginning; by the 1560s it was at least half-completed.

It would not be inappropriate, therefore, to see the career of the London magistrate Sir Martin Bowes as symbolic. He was an early representative of that section of the Tudor ruling class which found in welfare reform an ideal means of satisfying its authoritarian impulses while salving its conscience. He is also a suitably Janus-like figure with which to conclude this account of mid-Tudor social policy. Having materially contributed to social problems through his management of the debasements of the 1540s, Bowes spent his later years presiding over the greatest charitable enterprise of the period. Like the 'good duke' himself, he illustrates the ambivalence of government and governors at a time when covetousness was never more attacked and the opportunities for it never more seductive. Whatever their failings, it was men such as he who took up the 'policies of paternalist publicity' of Wolsey and Cromwell[64] and tried to forge practicable tools out of them.

# 6. The Legacy of the Schism: Confusion, Continuity and Change in the Marian Clergy

REX H. POGSON

I

HINDSIGHT is one of the historian's main weapons; but, if its assumptions are accepted uncritically, it can easily turn against him. Nowhere is this more true than in the study of the Church under Mary Tudor. In a broad view of the Tudor period, Protestantism and national feeling emerge as dominant themes; and against such a background Mary's reign can be dismissed as a brief and isolated losing streak in English Protestantism's winning game. Against the later glare of the Armada bonfires, the fires at Smithfield that consumed the Marian martyrs seem pale, and their apparent futility can encourage a dismissive interpretation of all Mary's policies.

There are, however, a number of dangers in this picture. First, and most obviously, it should not be forgotten that the Englishmen of 1553 did not share our hindsight: Protestant leaders, gloomily contemplating the reversal of Edwardian reforms, prepared their flock for a long trial of faith under Antichrist; several hundred of Mary's most important opponents fled to indefinite exile; and, at least until the end of 1555, Mary's expectation of a son, three parts Spanish, seemed to threaten another generation of Catholic rule. If we take the Marian failure too much for granted, we lose the sense of tension, hope and fear which were such important influences in a troubled reign. A second danger in the use of hindsight is that we may neglect Mary's own intentions: she and her cousin Reginald Pole, who joined her as legate from Rome at the end of 1554, had extensive plans for Catholic revival which have received scant credit. Too strong an assumption of failure can prevent our examining the Marian policies in their own terms and context; our responsibility is not only to chronicle the ultimate winners, but also to discover the losers' aspirations. Thirdly, and perhaps most significantly, a concentration on the stake, on the doctrinal conflict, can obscure a theme which is crucial to our understanding of the reign: confusion. To some Englishmen the doctrinal differences may have been clear-cut; but John Foxe's *Acts and Monuments* (the famous 'Book of Martyrs') and Pole's legatine register show a large number of anxious people who are not readily categorised as 'Protestant' or 'Catholic'.[1] The prevailing impression at all levels of society is that uncertainty was the chief legacy of the schism.

These reservations about the use of hindsight lead into our themes for this chapter. Our concern is to show how the confusion of the schism obstructed and diverted the reforming plans of Mary and Pole, occupying most of their severely limited time; and how their failure can be explained not so much by long-term historical inevitability as by their specific misjudgements of the problems which they inherited. The task, then, is not to diminish the better-known themes of persecution, plotting and revolt, but to fill in another section of the same Marian story by illustrating the stresses of mid-Tudor ecclesiastical government.

The argument will be constructed round one main example: the attempt to restore the quality of the Catholic clergy. This was of the first importance to Mary and Pole; a Roman revival would depend on stirring clerical leadership, from Lambeth right down to the poorest parish. Yet to stimulate this leadership was a task of great legal and doctrinal complexity, for most of the clergy on whom Pole would at first depend had been schismatic conservatives under Henry VIII, and many had slipped into or condoned heresy under Edward VI.

Both Pole and his opponents ascribed many of the changes of the schism to inconsistent clerical guidance. Some had revelled in the opportunity: 'the greatest cause', said Woodman at his trial for heresy in 1556, 'that I was compelled to read the scriptures was because the preachers and teachers were so changeable'.[2] But Catholics asserted that most of the English flock had found this unpredictability an alarming rather than invigorating experience. Pole wrote of the schism as a second Tower of Babel, and Stephen Gardiner, Henrician and Marian bishop of Winchester, remarked caustically that in Edward's reign the people were lectured rather than comforted.[3] To rescue chaotic and schismatic minds from such confusion, Pole called on the sane 'exterior light' of agreed Roman traditions.[4] But he could not find 9000 untainted clergy to spread that light; the legacy of the schism required a cleansing of old clerical sins to allow continuity of Roman tradition, but also an infusion of new spirit to meet the unprecedented changes of the previous thirty years. The difficulty of the task is self-evident; so too is its importance as an illustration of our themes.

II

The striking changes wrought in English society by the schism form an essential background, and deserve a (necessarily brief) section to themselves. The statutes of the 1530s, fashioned by the talents of Thomas Cromwell and exploiting the anticlericalism and national feeling of the political nation, had announced and defined as Erastian royal supremacy. Among clerical and devout lay leaders, this had varied effects: it could confirm an existing mistrust of the traditional church, produce a clash of loyalties, or lead to an interim position of uncertainty. We can take two examples to hint at the political and spiritual questions which the royal supremacy asked of the leading clerics. First, Stephen Gardiner: his training and experience, shared with so many of Henry VIII's bishops, were legal and administrative; he rose in the 1520s through service to Wolsey and the King, and was a candidate for the highest advisory position. But the opportunites of the divorce gave an opening to the radical Cromwell. By

1532 the conservative Gardiner had to choose between Pope and King. Self-interest and loyalty to the Crown made the choice an Erastian one, and the book *De Vera Obedientia* of 1534 confirmed the decision. But Gardiner was still not fully trusted by Henry, and the events of the 1540s, culminating in the reformers' coup of 1547 and the dominance of Seymour, belatedly convinced Gardiner of something which More had seen immediately – that without unity with Rome Catholic orthodoxy was crumbling. Gardiner resisted what he saw as misuse of the supremacy through a little boy, spent some years in the Fleet and Tower, and emerged as Lord Chancellor in 1553 convinced not that the papacy was divinely ordained, but that Rome was certainly needed for a Catholic revival in England. He justified obedience to Rome because Marian statute demanded it, a far cry from an automatic acceptance of eternal truth through Christ's one vicar. The events of the schism had led this Henrician back to Rome, but they had left their Erastian mark on his thinking.

For our second example, Thomas Cranmer, the bitterness of such choices was even longer delayed: he reached Canterbury in 1532 as a supporter of the divorce; he was shaped by and in turn influenced the changes in Continental and indigenous Protestantism during the 1530s and 1540s; he ascribed a clerical as well as royal significance to Henry's supremacy; and he played the biggest part in the brilliant doctrinal and liturgical developments of Edward's reign which turned English Protestantism from a heresy into a national creed. Then, in the last three years of his life, the legacy of the schism caught up with him in the form of a clash of loyalties. He was torn between his Tudor loyalty and his faith, and recanted from Protestantism six times before going to the stake in 1556. His hesitation was not cowardice; it was a demonstration of the confusion and harrowing demands made on those caught up in the schism and its consequences.[5]

Mary and Pole did not intend to work with Cranmer; but they had to work closely with Gardiner. Their success in reinspiring the upper clergy would depend on their ability to allow for and counter this inheritance of confusion and bitter choice. Protestants were able to claim that the Marian bishops themselves had taught England to reject Rome in earlier reigns; time and great sensitivity were required of a legate who hoped to construct a strong Roman hierarchy in such a situation. Nor was this the only worrying inheritance. Erastianism had its physical effects too. The Henrician dissolution of the monastries, and the attack on the chantries in 1547, had been followed by a long series of Edwardian commissions which systematically plundered the churches, and towards the end of the reign even became apologetic. because most of the valuable land and ornaments seemed to have been taken already![6] The beauty of holiness, so vital to Roman ceremonial and belief, could not be restored overnight in 1553. Moreover, the early fears that the dissolution would damn all departed souls naturally abated with passing time; monasticism as an integral part of English society needed continuity, for twenty years without monks raised doubts about the value of their return. This was particularly true because of the sale of ex-monastic lands to the gentry; Mary's parliaments now felt a vested interest in Erastianism, and, if Rome had to return, the Pope must promise not to touch the new lands of the English political nation. This was one of the issues which delayed Pole for over a year in his journey from Rome to London, and which gave the legatine mission such an inauspicious start.[7] Could former Roman glories be revived after so drastic a change in ecclesiastical wealth?

Pole also faced the spiritual consequences of the schism. From small cells at Court and in the universities, and from localised pockets of surviving Lollardy, Protestantism emerged by 1553 as a strong faith in the south-east and a significant, if uneven, force elsewhere. The new faith's influence was not restricted to its devoted converts: even conservative bishops were drawn into doctrinal and liturgical innovation in the 1530s and 1540s; Londoners 'swarmed like bees' to hear the challenging sermons of Ridley and other great Edwardian orators;[8] avid reading of the English Bible and the Edwardian surge in secular educational foundations are two very different indications of a widespread interest in new ideas. A Catholic reforming clergy had to be ready for a fight, not an automatic reoccupation of lost ground. This is not to say that there were no militant conservatives: Foxe relates an incident of a bewildered parish whose church was disrupted every night by rival gangs pulling down and putting up an altar or communion table, according to their opposed faiths.[9] But this example itself shows the struggle which the Catholic authorities would encounter locally. It may be that there was a silent majority of confused conservatives in 1553, waiting for guidance; we see glimpses of them in the petitions, so anxious to please, in Pole's register. But to comfort and mobilise such a majority, if it existed, and to resist Protestant fervour and quieten schismatic doubts, would require great clerical patience and inspiration. And in the midst of the bigotry and confusion there remained the lasting problem of clerical ignorance and poverty at parish level, so depressingly highlighted by Edwardian inquiries in the south and west.[10] If the Marian clergy were to have the calibre to lead a revival, much work had to be done.

III

This was the inheritance of Mary and Pole. Before we look at the attempt to regenerate the clergy, we need an idea of the quality of their judgement of the problems of 1553. Both were obsessed by the sin of the schism, but also dangerously blind to some of its implications. Mary, embittered by her mother's divorce, had accepted the royal supremacy only for safety, and had been an embarrassing Catholic anomaly in her half-brother's reign. The welcome she received in 1553 convinced her not only of Tudor popularity but also of general acceptance of her views. In this latter assumption she was misled: she was hailed for Tudor blood not for Spanish or Roman policies.[11] But Mary, as Spanish observers quickly noted, was politically naïve.[12] She stated that there were qualities more important than human prudence, and issues more vital than political survival for its own sake.[13] She indiscriminately condemned all the developments of the schism, whether or not she had a chance of reversing them, and so encountered widespread opposition on her Council and in her parliaments. Nor did her initial religious steps appear creative or positive. Forced to retain the hated title of the supremacy until Pole's arrival, she used it to attack Edwardian bishops and deprive married clergy. Her legislative programme was dominated by repeals of schismatic laws and attempts to revive powers for the destruction of heretics. In her terms, she was cancelling the gross errors of a sinful schismatic faction, and releasing her people to return to the love of Rome; and from that standpoint her measures may seem positive. But they did not reveal any sympathy for the complex pressures which we have noted, nor an understanding of the depth of many changes. She was turning the clock back, not mending and adjusting the mechanism.

Pole had been even more isolated from the schism than his cousin Mary. Whereas she had withdrawn in spirit, he had been absent in physical exile since 1532. His reforming roots lay in the Christian humanism of the early decades of the century, in the group of cardinals who produced Paul III's plans for Catholic reform in the late 1530s, and in the bid of the moderate *spirituali* to direct the reforming programme of the Council of Trent.[14] He returned to England in 1554 convinced that the breach with Rome had been the work of a tiny faction, and that the Henrician bishops and nobles had succumbed through cowardice and 'too much love for the world'.[15] Pole expected obedience to Rome and a revival of Roman order to inspire Catholic belief once more. He spoke of the English problem not in Gardiner's terms, as a unique national development, but as a small part of the general issue of a divided Christendom.[16] In short, he was still using the language of Catholic reformers of the 1520s; and this fits in with his refusal of Jesuit assistance as unnecessary, and his disapproval of an evangelical campaign as too unsettling to the troubled flock.[17] He had many of the priceless gifts of the spiritual adviser – he listened well and sympathised closely with the individual sinner – but he lacked an informed overall judgement of the schism's impact. He had his chance to learn: as soon as he arrived in England, he met the stubborn English refusal to contemplate Roman obedience without assurances over monastic lands; and, when he discussed this issue with Mary's Council, he found that many of the bishops and councillors with whom he would have to work did not respond to the traditional ideal of a united Christendom.[18] It was a bitter lesson, often to be repeated; but a cleric of his background and beliefs could not bring himself to learn it. Among the confusions of the schism we must number the errors of Mary and Pole in underrating its results.

IV

The first priority for revival of the Catholic clergy was a respected and dependable episcopate. In view of Pole's openly expressed contempt for the Henricians, and of their belief that Pole had behaved as a traitor to Henry in the 1530s, it is hardly surprising that Gardiner was not overjoyed at the legate's arrival in 1554, nor that there were secret requests to Rome for his removal.[19] Indeed, it may be that the delays which Pole frequently noted in the arrival of information from the dioceses resulted from episcopal obstruction as well as administrative difficulties. But, in spite of these unpromising signs, Pole did make some progress in his relations with the schismatic bishops: Bonner worked hard in carrying out legatine instructions in the diocese of London; Tunstall of Durham showed some of the old friendship; Thirlby of Ely commented on Pole's helpfulness, and so on.[20] Above all, the bishops contributed to Pole's finest achievement, the London synod of 1555, which drew up twelve influential reforming decrees; and the legate depended on the bishops for intensive diocesan visitations in the following year to give him the local information necessary for the enforcement of the decrees.

All this, however, could be window-dressing unless followed up by a sustained revival of energy and direction in the bishops themselves. To acquire a reforming episcopate, Pole had to banish the effects of schismatic error in the existing bishops, and arrange the appointment of valuable new members to the episcopal bench. A suitable example of the difficulties of the former task can be found in the question of holy orders. The sacrament of orders, like those of baptism and confirmation, was taken to imprint an indelible 'character' on the recipient's soul. Only a duly consecrated bishop could officiate. Seventeen years of schismatic rites, and after 1550 three years of the Edwardian Ordinal, had wrought havoc with the concept of continuity of holy orders. A cleric who had received valid orders irregularly could receive dispensation from Pole to continue his ministry; but invalid orders required fresh candidature for ordination. The key question was whether or not the Henrician and Edwardian rites had retained the 'form and intention' of the Roman ceremony. To us it may appear trivial to concentrate on niceties while heresy flourished – fiddling with definitions while Rome burned – but we must remember how much rested on the legitimacy of the priest in a church where the sacrificial role at the altar was so crucial. Moreover, Pole wanted to emphasise – and did so in the sixth decree of his synod – the increased care which bishops should exercise in testing candidates for ordination; such a step would seem a mockery without careful elimination of past aberrations in the bishops themselves. This was a case where confusion was great and legal continuity essential.[21]

The popes did not assist in a speedy resolution of this difficulty. Julius III's original bulls of commission to Pole in August 1553 had omitted any mention of orders; when he rectified this in March 1554 he did so with such a lack of clarity that Paul IV felt compelled to offer two further interpretations.[22] Even these have proved sufficiently ambiguous to fuel a heated recent debate among Anglicans and Catholics over the relationship of English to Roman orders.[23] This debate, however, had concentrated more on the needs of modern ecumenism than on the realities of the Counter-Reformation. It is unthinkable that Paul IV, the inquisitorial Caraffa, could have contemplated acceptance of the Edwardian Ordinal, with its deliberate heretical omission of the priest's sacrificial role. The actions of Mary, Bonner and Pole are consistent with the view that the Henrician rite was considered valid but irregular, and the Edwardian ordinations invalid.[24]

Pole was left to absolve his bishops for schismatic sin, and dispense them for continued ministry. His reputation for careful assessment of individual needs is borne out in the varied wording of his dispensations: Tunstall's orders were pre-schismatic, and he only required absolution for the sin of the breach with Rome; for most of the others, there was dispensation to use orders which were 'less than correct', in the interests of continuity, and on the assurance of penitence; those who had broken the vows of the religious orders suffered rougher words for their lapse. The legate had to try to evoke a sense of shame and inspire a joy at reunion with Rome. In view of his strained relations with many of these men in the past, it was a delicate and lengthy task. Pole spent much valuable time on the past when he could have been considering the future. Mary's reign of five years always seems too short for her political hopes; Pole's mission, delayed sixteen months at the start of the reign and cut short in 1557 by the revocation of his powers, had an effective life of only half the reign. When we realise how much of that limited time was occupied by the past confusions of the schism, the brevity of his opportunity for reform can be fully appreciated.

Nonetheless, the legate did have the time at least to begin the shaping of the episcopate which would have supervised his long-term plans if he and the Queen had lived longer. Here we may hope to test the quality of his planning for the future.[25] Yet here too the schism cast its shadow: Francis Mallet, to take one instance, appointed to Salisbury at the very end of the reign, had been a chaplain to Cranmer and Cromwell in the 1530s before his chaplaincy to Mary in Edward's reign and his imprisonment for resisting change. Thus, even a cleric of integrity leaves a doctrinal trail difficult for the historian to follow; how much more difficult it was for Pole and Mary. No wonder they were obsessed by the schism, and lacked objectivity in assessing its results.

In view of this complex inheritance, the Marian criteria for appointments had to be strict. Pole and Mary concentrated on clerics with a theological and pastoral rather than legal and administrative background. The 'love of the world' which they detected in Henry's bishops was perhaps linked in the Queen's and legate's minds with a heavily political training; they looked to a new background for inspiration. Only three of the new Marian bishops were legists: there were four heads of colleges, a professor of theology, and a headmaster of Winchester. Three of the leading writers of propaganda and controversy were also chosen. In some cases the talent may have been spread a little thin, but the idea was a sound one.

In seeking a love for Rome among their bishops, Mary and Pole had to rely on personal knowledge and the trusted testimonials of others, rather than recent record. Gilbert Bourne had been an agent of Bonner in Edward's reign; James Brooks and Thomas Watson had been Gardiner's chaplains; William Glyn was a protégé of Thirlby; William Peto was an aged supporter of the Aragonese faction from the days of the divorce. Above all, Richard Pate and Thomas Goldwell had been in exile with Pole, and Ralph Baynes and John Christopherson had also gone abroad in Edward's reign. As much as possible, such signs of integrity were set against the confusion of schismatic careers, to seek continuity of commitment.

The appointment of Clynog to Bangor at the end of the reign may sum up the Marian hopes. He was young, only taking his degree in 1548, but he rose rapidly as chaplain to Mary, a member of Pole's household and a close friend of Goldwell. By 1558 he had already made his name in Rome. Young clerics nurtured by trusted leaders were Pole's long-term investment. This glimpse of Marian intentions is elusive because of the brevity and political misfortune of the reign; but it serves as a corrective to the assumption of inevitable all-pervading gloom.

However, there remains an awkward question. Elizabeth's inheritance, like Mary's, was confused, but in 1558 one of her striking advantages was the vacancy of ten sees. This lends credence to the retrospective view that 1558 saw the declining resignation of an incompetent era. In fact, illness and bad luck are more to blame than slackness. Three bishops died within a month of Mary's and Pole's own demise, and three bishops already nominated had not been consecrated in November 1558. Of the other three, Oxford was in the temporary care of John Holyman of Bristol, who had received detailed instructions from Pole on tending a vacant see;[26] John Hopton had died in August, when the Queen and legate were already ill; which leaves only Sodor and Man, admittedly vacant since 1556, but remaining so until 1570! The main reason for the delayed consecrations was Mary's troubled relationship with Rome: the elderly but energetic Paul IV hated Spanish power in Italy, mistrusted Pole's early record of sympathy for heretics in Italy, and so by 1556 was failing to support Marian plans in England. In 1557 he ignored royal quests for confirmation of episcopal appointments and revoked Pole's legatine powers.[27] It is ironic that the Spanish marriage and Pole's mission, both so close to Mary's heart, should draw her to a quarrel with her beloved Rome. In the circumstances, it is perhaps to Pole's credit that he did not altogether despair.

The opening months of Elizabeth's reign give us the only hint at the outcome of the Marian episcopal selection policy. The behaviour of the surviving bishops indicates that the events of the schism, and perhaps Pole's decrees too, had clarified the need for Roman loyalty. Only Anthony Kitchin of Llandaff accepted Elizabeth's supreme governorship in 1559. Pole did not try to inspire Counter-Reformation resistance: in 1558 he accepted Elizabeth as the future ruler, trusting God for the triumph of the true faith in the next reign.[28] Nicholas Heath of York, the senior surviving cleric, followed the same line of Tudor loyalty and a refusal to work under an Erastian supremacy. But the resolve of some of the bishops to combat heresy was apparent: Bonner and Tunstall went to prison; Watson was still in trouble in the 1570s; Scott, Pate, Goldwell, Christopherson and Clynog gathered at Louvain to act as the equivalent of the leading Marian exiles – to write, to lobby Rome for action, to keep in touch with Catholics in England. If hindsight tells us that these men were swimming against the tide, we should not forget the terror aroused in English Protestants for another century by the prospect of Catholic action at home and abroad. And we should note too that one-third of the surviving Marian episcopate, grouped at Louvain, clearly did not see the years under Mary as futile. We can see in Pole's assessment of his task and responsibilities an old-fashioned, misplaced confidence in a Roman obedience which could no longer be taken for granted; but we can also see the injustice of failing to give credit to these signs of renewed spirit which emerged from his years in England.

V

Hope for the regeneration of the English Church in 1553 rested not just on the quality of the bishops but also on the efforts of all the clergy. The parish priest was the local Catholic bulwark against the assaults of heretical preachers. More important to Pole (since he often thought in terms of the problems of the 1520s) was the role of a good resident clergy in resisting anticlericalism. Whereas Mary concentrated before Pole's arrival on depriving married clergy, Pole's record is of more positive thinking about the quality of the parish clergy: the third decree of the synod stressed the residence of the clergy, the fifth outlined the behaviour expected of them, and the ninth explored current abuses.[29] But once more we shall see his blueprint for reform blurred by complications left over from the schism.

We can illustrate the inherited difficulties which beset Pole, and his underrated talents for making the best of them, in the example of pluralism. This abuse – the holding of more than one living – had been condemned for centuries, without much effect; additional benefices had been used for so long as patronage and reward for prelates, and as a means of survival for poorer clerics, that a Church so dependent on political and landed assets could hardly change. Pluralism had been fiercely attacked in the anticlerical parliament of 1529, both for bestowing unmerited wealth on such as Wolsey, and for the absenteeism or inadequate residence it caused at parish level.[30] And the changes of the schism had worsened this already bad situation. For instance, impropriated benefices had been a longstanding issue, blamed for pluralism, absenteeism and the ignorance of poor assistant clergy. These impropriations were livings on monastic estates, where the monastry took rectorial income, paying only a part in stipend to a vicar. The dissolution presented an opportunity for releasing impropriated funds to the parish clergy, improving their income and so encouraging residence. But the climate of secular opinion in the 1530s was not conducive to such a move. Instead, the right to thousands of clerical incomes went with lead, plate and land, via the Crown, to leading gentry, and the money was locked away from Pole when he made his efforts to improve poor livings. Moreover, the schism had brought other ominous developments. Inflation (prices probably doubled in the 1540s) hit and bewildered the small cleric on a fixed income; pluralism could be the only hedge. And at the same time there was a shortage of priests. For example, the displacement of clergy in 1554 during Mary's purge on clerical marriage was a large upset.[31] Many of them seem to have found livings elsewhere, but in some areas the advancement of assistant clergy was rapid, and led to a vacuum lower down the scale. For this and other reasons Pole wrote in his reluctant dispensations for pluralism of the 'shortage of ministers', the 'acute shortage', and finally, as he received more information, the particular shortage of 'worthy' ministers. Like so many reformers before him, Pole had to accept the continuity of pluralism while preaching its dire consequences and the need for change.

In over 200 surviving dispensations, we can appreciate that Pole took all possible precautions against rubber-stamping. He made stricter demands of residence, and gave more rigorous instructions to his local officials in checking a petitioner's assertions, than we find in papal and legatine dispensations for English clerics just before the breach with Rome. He required testimonials of a priest's worthiness – taking one opportunity to conduct an inquiry personally, *viva voce* – and learned from experience to look carefully into the relative incomes of the two livings and the distance between them. On the rare occasions when local records cross-reference in detail with the legatine register, Pole seems to have conveyed at least some of his own urgency to the locality. We cannot tell how many petitions were refused, nor how much of a formality some episcopal officials considered the whole process; but we can tell that Pole took it seriously, and that his administrative staff wrote of individual cases on their merits. Not the least impressive feature of this and similar administrative exercises is the legate's evident determination to collect accurate local knowledge of deficiencies, abuses and needs. He wanted to cut through the ignorance of the effects of the schism: although we may doubt his overall administrative grasp, his intentions were admirable, and far from the usual picture of a depressed and incompetent regime.

It may be felt that Pole's staff was too occupied with this kind of administrative routine when more dramatic measures were needed to reconvert a nation; and, indeed, this is a fair criticism of Pole's view of his task. But in mitigation it should be recalled that Pole's first priority was the removal of obstacles to the reconciliation of England to Rome; so he was obliged to deal with a backlog of tricky legal and administrative questions from the schism. The scale of this obligation can be judged by a brief return to the subject of ordination. Not just the bishops but all the lesser clergy too needed clarification of their position over holy orders, and, although Pole's sixth decree in the synod of 1555 was concerned with the quality of future ordinands, it was not until the spring of 1557 that petitions about future ordinations at last outnumbered the continuing list of anxious queries about schismatic orders. Within a few months of that turning point, Paul IV was revoking Pole's powers. Obsession with apparently trivial cases from the past was thus forced on the legate for more of his time in England, and he showed much tact and patience.

Since he had come to give 'comfort' to the English people, Pole viewed this straightening of schismatic tangles as a vital stage of his mission. But only an increased number of suitable ordinands in the next generation could begin to defeat the inherited problems against which Pole dutifully struggled. Marian measures on the education of the clergy are thus crucial for the assessment of Pole's reforming quality. The eleventh London decree dealt with this theme, and it seems regrettable that Pole turned to this vital subject so late in the synod.[32] None the less, this was eventually the most influential decree of the twelve; though its active life was short in England, it was issued in time to affect the great educational decisions of Trent. Pole hoped to found seminaries in the English cathedrals, and eventually elsewhere, to remedy the alarming shortage of priests. The size of the diocese would determine the number of pupils, and boys of eleven would be prepared for the priesthood. It was hoped that others, not destined for clerical life, might also participate: Pole thus intended both a charitable education for the able poor, and a political success in educating the sons of the influential. The money for the project was to be taken from one-fortieth of all clerical incomes over £20. Here in theory is the blend of continuity and change which we have been seeking.

With so little available time, practice was certain to be less impressive than theory. But, even allowing for this, the record of the reign in education is disappointing.[33] Pole's fear of heresy and inquiry was greater than his desire to evangelise. He was suspicious of preachers and teachers because they had caused so much trouble in the past, and he and Mary spent more time worrying about the destruction of subversive literature than trying to spread works and sermons of which they approved. John Foxe suggests that Pole only turned to education 'having at all points established the Romish religion'; yet how did the legate imagine that such re-establishment could last without action as vigorous as the ideas of his eleventh decree?[34]

There were some hints at positive action. The convocation of Canterbury in 1558, still battling on despite the revocation of Pole's powers (and despite the common assumption that in its final year the Marian regime lost all will to live) set up a committee under Pole to formulate a uniform teaching method for all bishops to enforce. The cathedral school at York was fashioned to 'ward off . . . the ravening wolves' – perhaps a rather defensive image: and through episcopal initiative there seem to have been successes in the foundation of new schools at Wells and Lincoln.[35] But, against hopeful signs such as these, the legate's suspicion of Edwardian schools and his unwillingness to license preachers or appoint schoolmasters had a greater and deadening effect. There were complaints, as from Worcester, where the cathedral school lapsed in Mary's reign, or Coventry, where 'great damage' was done by the absence of a schoolmaster.[36] It is ironic that Pole's eleventh decree was instrumental in the European measures which led to such foundations as Douai, whence English priests came in the 1570s and 1580s to reconvert Elizabeth's England: ironic, because twenty years earlier Pole showed little enthusiasm for such an evangelical effort, and rejected the specialised help of the Jesuits. There is a gap here between the reforming words and the administrative grasp. The legate was sensitive to some of the minor schismatic confusion which had affected his clergy, but turned his back on the greatest challenge.[37]

Many of the most dangerous heretics had come from the universities; Pole and Mary would expect their ablest clerics to emerge from the same source. As Chancellor of both Oxford and Cambridge, the legate had an opportunity to cleanse and redirect at this important level. He is most notorious for arranging the burning of heretic remains: this is a good example of the way in which a snippet of information from Foxe can colour a whole mission with the smear of negative legalism.[38] In fact, Pole's energies at the universities went into visitations to enforce old statutes; again, we may feel this was designed for the restoration of order rather than for the reinspiration of zeal, but it was positive in intention and active in enforcement. Pole was consistent in his belief that sound ideas would only follow obedience and strict legality. All but three of the Cambridge colleges appointed new heads; doleful reports of apathetic ignorance after the visitation of St Benet's persuaded Pole to press for 'grave and wise masters'.[39] At Oxford there was the same pattern of general visitation followed by inquiries in the individual colleges, and in 1558 Pole was still pushing hard enough to supervise the precise statutory arrangements for the appointment of a new Warden at All Souls'.[40] Pole can be criticised for failing to reform the university curriculum (he had a few other things on his mind – European diplomacy, synods, papal quarrels) but he did restore the study of canon law.[41] Once again, Pole's strength lay in tidying up the irregularities of the past; once again, we may doubt the militancy which he was inspiring. But Ridley thought Pole had achieved the total Catholicisation of the universities; and, although he was doubtless exaggerating to impress on Protestants the wrath of God for their sins, it is clear that some of Pole's enemies were much more impressed by his efforts than hindsight would lead us to suppose.[42]

## VI

Within strict – and too narrow – limitations, then, Pole
was concerning himself with the next generation of priests.
But in what condition would these trained clerics find their
parishes? This was a crucial question for a legate who was
relying on good resistance and the beauty of holiness to
calm disturbed schismatic minds. His hopes were unrealistic
because of the appalling physical destruction which he inherited. Tunstall of Durham reckoned that by 1558 he had
still not restored the necessary ornaments to his cathedral;
this lack of ceremonial beauty was likely to be still more
true of less notable churches. Some detail can be drawn
from the archiepiscopal visitation of Canterbury in 1556 and
Harpsfield's archidiaconal inquiries in the same diocese in
the following year, and the first impression is the collapsed
state of the buildings. About two-thirds of the churches mentioned by Pole in 1556 suffered structural damage in fabric
as important as the roof or the chancel. A year later, almost
half the churches visited by Harpsfield had damaged chancels.
Any visitation will reveal some inadequacies, but not all
these problems can have been incidental or short-term; nor
are there signs of notable improvement with the passing
of time. In 1556 Acris, by no means a horrifying exception,
had a decayed chancel, no silver paten, no cloth for the
rood, no cover for the font, a badly-damaged altar, and
so on. In such churches did Pole hope to revive Catholic
loyalty.

The damage was more than merely material. Schismatic
contempt towards ornaments can be seen in the large number
of wrecked images discovered by Pole's visitors; and the
same pattern emerged in the visitation of Bath and Wells
as late as 1557. It was more difficult to remove this contempt
than to replace lost ornaments; not surprisingly, Harpsfield
in 1557 in Canterbury found backsliding and heresy most
prominently in the parishes which had been worst hit by
the destruction and confusion. Moreover, Edwardian plunder
had created local hostility to any visitors, so that even Marian
restorers met obstruction. Pole needed thirty years, not three,
to achieve a continuity of beauty of holiness; and in the

meantime he needed some vigorous campaign to convince the English flock that revived Roman services were worth striving for. Yet his exceptional inheritance did not inspire in him a desire for exceptional measures.[43]

He did, however, hope for a revival of dedicated monastic obedience and ceremony. Although the problem of the Church lands denied him a large-scale restoration, he and Mary were ready to demonstrate their piety where possible. This is a theme extensively covered elsewhere, but a few points add to our argument.[44]

The Venetian ambassador's report that by 1557 seven houses of strict observance had been restored reflected a considerable effort to deny the depressing effect of the loss of monastic estates.[45] A number of re-endowments are grouped together in Pole's register for the spring of 1557; clearly this is the result of detailed planning, and it is reasonable to suppose that, coming so close to the revocation of Pole's powers, these measures were only the first step in an intended programme. Pole owed much of his knowledge of the cloister to his role as cardinal protector to the congregation of Monte Cassino in Italy. He showed his experience in issuing legatine instructions to the Brigettine house at Syon, and he tried to bring two Cassinese reformers to England to help in re-establishing Westminster.[46] This last is a revealing point: his interest in this foreign assistance makes it unlikely that his rejection of Jesuit preaching was mere inertia; we are driven to the conclusion that he picked his Continental helpers carefully and placed the order and beauty of monasticism much higher on his list of priorities than a unit of shock-troops for Counter-Reformation preaching. He expected a quiet return to harmony, not a fight to the death; but the schism had made the first impractical and the second essential.

This is not to deny that the restoration of Westminster was a brave effort to continue a fine tradition. Feckenham, the abbot, a remarkable man, stayed with Scott of Chester and others to fight Elizabeth's supremacy verbally and impressively in the House of Lords in 1559. But Westminster in Mary's reign had less than half its pre-schismatic income; and decades of change had marked the monks as well as their possessions, for youth was lacking, and a contemporary likened the house to a college rather than an ascetic reformed cell.[47] Most poignant of all, four of Feckenham's community were with him only because their old house in Glastonbury had been converted in Edward's reign to a factory for Walloon weavers. This demonstrates the strange clashes of interests and the changes which Pole was not qualified nor prepared to appreciate. And, finally, the legate himself, even in an area of policy in which he showed great personal interest, lost opportunities by neglecting urgent calls for refoundation.[48] It was, then, not only a shortage of time which marred his efforts: his lack of drive was also responsible for missed chances.

VII

There are two broad conclusions to be emphasised. The first relates to our opening on the dangers of hindsight. We noted how easily Marian administration can be dismissed as isolated, arid and, in any case, doomed from the start. The material offered here suggests some reservations. Allowance has to be made for the immense complexity of inherited problems, which not only occupied Pole's limited time but also blocked plans for the future; in spite of these difficulties, Pole did have a coherent programme, based on the continuity of traditional order and stated in the synodal decrees; and his failures have to be placed against the extraordinarily short time in which he could work.

These thoughts are not intended to reverse the familiar impression that Mary's government was confronting enormous odds, but they may lead to a deeper and fairer judgement of the nature of the Marian failure. Above all, they demonstrate that the reign should not be seen as an isolated mistake: in the European context, Pole's work has to be linked with plans for Catholic reform from the 1520s to Trent, and it contrasts with some of the successful measures of the militant Counter-Reformation; in the English context, Pole faced a schismatic ferment which affected in a variety of ways all the rulers and ruled of mid-Tudor England, whatever their creed or standpoint. There were many mistakes in Mary's reign; but in their own context they were not merely arid, nor is it profitable to see them in isolation.

But the understanding which we may bring to the period cannot prevent our second main conclusion: that the view which Pole and Mary had of their task was fatally unbalanced. It is difficult to avoid the speculation that in a longer and luckier reign they would still have missed important opportunities to win back England to Rome. For Mary was embittered and legalistic about her father's sins, and Pole was too confident of the lasting conservatism and traditional obedience of the English people. His was the optimistic reforming language of united Christendom, applied to a divided and partly dismantled church. Pole's views on the quality of the clergy have provided our vehicle for this discussion, but the same strengths and the same blindness can be seen in his financial administration, his view of the persecution, and so on. Indeed, it is revealing that so much can be said of Pole's aims without mentioning the notorious burnings: the legate's weakness was not that he justified the destruction of obstinate heretics, as he did, but that he discounted their importance and was so surprised by their number. He showed sensitivity and the beginnings of success in understanding some clerical confusions; but the greatest changes of the previous reigns were underrated or ignored. He based his hopes on a continuity which was no longer possible.

# 7. Public Office and Private Profit: The Legal Establishment in the Reign of Mary Tudor

## LEWIS ABBOTT

> Let me be judged by the law,
> for I will seek no better defence,
> considering chiefly that it is my
> profession.
> Justice James Hales, 1553[1]

I

ON 11 June 1553, as the young King Edward VI lay dying at Greenwich,[2] Sir Edward Montague, Chief Justice of the Court of Common Pleas, received a summons to meet with the Council on the following day at one o'clock in the afternoon. In accordance with instructions, he presented himself on the 12th before the King and a select group of advisers accompanied by four of his colleagues, Sir John Baker, Chancellor of the Exchequer, Sir Thomas Bromley, a senior judge of the King's Bench, Edward Griffin and John Gosnold, respectively Attorney and Solicitor-General.[3] From this moment on, the legal establishment of England became implicated – albeit with the greatest reluctance – in the treasonable plot of the duke of Northumberland to divert the succession of the Crown from the King's sisters, Mary and Elizabeth, to his (Northumberland's) daughter-in-law, Lady Jane Grey. The story is a dramatic and tragic one which historians have told and retold over the last 400 years.[4] Yet it remains a compelling introduction to the involvement of the legal profession in the political conflicts of the mid sixteenth century. In effect, senior law officers of the realm were bullied under physical threats to draw up letters patent which embodied in expanded, formalised language the terms of Edward's so-called 'Devise'.[5]

Such a strategem was seen by the lawyers to make themselves and the Council parties to treason.[6] They did their best, however, to avoid being caught in the net. According to one account, they advanced an alternative whereby Princess Mary would be admitted to the succession provided that she agreed to make no religious alterations, nor meddle with titles to dissolved monastic estates, and that she allow the present ministers to remain in power.[7] Such a compromise was obviously unacceptable to Northumberland, whose plan depended on maintaining the reins of government through his son and daughter-in-law. Having agreed, however, to draw up the letters patent, the desperate legal advisers tried to protect themselves by extracting from the young King the promise of a general pardon absolving them from their crime. Given their predicament, one can readily accept Chief Justice Montague's claim that he and his colleagues went about their loathsome task 'with sorrowful hearts and weeping eyes'.[8] Yet even in the depths of despair a resourceful advocate never loses sight of his professional priorities: among the reasons listed in the letters patent for disinheriting Mary and Elizabeth was the fear that one or other sister might marry a foreigner: 'That then the same stranger, having the government and the imperial crown in his hands, would rather adhere and practise to have the customs of his . . . own native country . . . to be practised . . . within this our realm, than the laws, statutes and customs here of long time used.'[9]

Whether reflective of self-interest or familiar English prejudice against outsiders, the lawyers' prophecy was only partially accurate; but, as events were to prove, they saw to it that indeed 'the laws, statutes and customs here of long time used' would remain in place as securely as they themselves.

The constitutional nightmare conjured up by Northumberland must have conditioned the behaviour of the judges and senior lawyers alike to wariness for the rest of the century. Not until the elevation of Sir Edward Coke to the bench did the profession permit itself again to be entangled in a political crisis of such gravity. The five years of Mary's reign provide a consistent and illuminating pattern of professional conduct: ultra-conservatism in matters of law, property and social hierarchy; unswerving conformity to the re-established Roman connection, albeit in varying degrees of fervour; ostentatious loyalty to the regime combined with energetic cultivation of personal careers and patrimonies. For its part, the government had little choice but to rely on a handful of skilled and experienced men whose religion and politics might be suspect but whose expertise was indispensable. Between 1553 and 1558 the number of active, professional lawyers from whom the Queen could choose her law officers was, as always, limited by the long, exacting years of legal apprenticeship.[10] In practical terms one may exclude the puisne barons of the Exchequer and perhaps a third of the High Court judges and serjeants, who applied their talents almost exclusively to the intricacies of fiscal and land law. Given the nature and degree of involvement in public affairs, it can be estimated with reasonable precision that the actual number of common-law practitioners available for royal service never amounted to more than thirty of this highly structured, hierarchical profession.

The common lawyers also possessed – and still possess – a psychological weapon which is as formidable as that of the twentieth-century scientists: a virtual monopoly over what appears to laymen as the unfathomable mysteries of 'the law'. Their pronouncements were buttressed by centuries of accumulated procedure and precedent. No wonder, then, that the élite of the profession, the *sages de la ley* as Coke designated them, spoke with an air of supreme confidence which was the envy of their ecclesiastical rivals. This aura of authority influenced kings, confounded bishops and

over-awed laymen. 'We be informed by our judges', proclaimed Henry VIII, 'that we at no time stand so highly
in our estate royal as in the time of Parliament.'[11] It was the
extorted opinion of the law officers concerning the validity of
Edward VI's 'Devise' which ultimately persuaded
Archbishop Cranmer to sign the letters patent: 'methought
it became not me being unlearned in the law, to stand
against my prince'.[12] Stephen Gardiner was by no means
unlearned in the law, but he too, with less good grace,
accepted a claim that the King was bound by the statute of
praemunire. He swallowed this 'for a law of the realm because
the lawyers said so', but his 'reason digested it not'.[13]

The immediate repercussions of the conspiracy to deprive
Mary were, for the lawyers concerned, much the same as
for the majority of politicians and office-holders who sub-
scribed to Edward's will. After a few weeks of uncertainty
the ranks re-formed somewhat akin to the professional structure which had existed under the previous regime. The
changes engineered by Gardiner, now Lord Chancellor, while
calculating and shrewd, merely point up the restrictions imposed upon him, notwithstanding his apparent hostility towards the common-law jurisdiction.[14] As may be expected,
the hapless Montague was removed from his place despite
strenuous efforts at ingratiation with the new queen when
she reached London. Worse was yet to come: on 27 July
he and the Lord Chief Justice, Sir Roger Cholmeley, were
sent to the Tower.[15] (Perhaps it was at this point that Sir
Edward was inspired to inscribe his tomb with the epitaph
*pour unge pleasoir mille dolours.*) Yet it was Cholmeley who
had more cause to lament, since he and the Chief Baron
of the Exchequer, Henry Bradshawe, had avoided active
participation in the Lady Jane Grey plot; yet both were
deprived of their posts and Cholmeley ended up in prison.

Aside from subscribing to Edward VI's will, as did almost
all the officers of state, the motive for Cholmeley's dismissal,
as in fact Montague's, smacks of political opportunism.[16]
Both were old and expendable; their dismissal offered the new
regime a welcome means of creating vacancies on the
bench and hence bringing in some comparatively fresh
recruits. Despite his recent association with Montague, Sir

Thomas Bromley became Lord Chief Justice in place of Cholmeley – not, as Burnet assumed, because he 'was a papist
in his heart' (though he was hardly an ardent Protestant),
but because of a high reputation as an advocate and proven
ability on the bench.[17] It was also probably considered politic
to maintain confidence and stability on a bench soon to
participate in a goodly number of treason trials. Montague's
seat as Chief Justice of the Common Pleas was taken by
Sir Richard Morgan, a devoted Roman Catholic and steadfast
adherent of Mary's before her accession. Another to lose
office in the early months of the reign was John Gosnold,
the Solicitor General, whose place was filled by William
Cordell, destined for a long career in Tudor government.
Two months after the Queen's accession, Sir Robert Bowes,
the Master of the Rolls, retired *pure, sponte et absolute* and
the office was granted to Sir Nicholas Hare. Both Cordell
and Hare combined the necessary expertise and religious
conservatism to suit Gardiner's taste in legal appointments.[18]

One of the most celebrated casualties from amongst the
legal establishment was Sir James Hales, a highly respected
justice of the Common Pleas. Hales possessed strong Protestant
sympathies and a high sense of principle – a somewhat rare
combination within his profession. He was the only judge
who openly refused to sign Edward VI's letters patent.[19]
His conscience, unlike that of some of his colleagues, lacked
discretion, however, and he persisted in enforcing certain
politically, if not legally, outdated statutes against celebrating
the mass. Despite Hales's unwavering support of the legitimate
succession, the Chancellor was no man to stomach so impolite
a jurist, especially one who had participated in Gardiner's
trial and imprisonment in 1551. Hales's advanced age rendered him redundant and provided an unmistakable signal
– if one were needed – to other judges that their religious
and professional scruples should be kept within realistic limits.
He was not reappointed and was subsequently arrested. Later
released, he is reputed to have committed suicide at his
estate in Kent, an action which resulted in a protracted
and celebrated lawsuit.[20] His place on the bench was eventually taken by William Stanford, perhaps an even better
lawyer, if a poorer Protestant.

With the exception of Hales, even those who lost their places or were demoted continued to reap the rewards offered by a profession with a small membership but a wide array of duties in the public domain. Even Montague and Cholmeley were granted special privileges during their confinement, and upon release after six weeks they were found a variety of profitable commissions during the remainder of their lives.[21] Other practitioners whose involvement in Edwardian politics had been a bit too conspicuous tended to drift unobtrusively into less sensitive but recuperative areas of royal service. Two notable examples were James Dyer and the above-mentioned William Stanford, both of no fixed religious scruples, yet both linked with some of Northumberland's cruder assaults on the Church. The accession of Mary ended any further political aspirations they might harbour, yet their proven ability and experience in and out of Parliament compelled the government to retain their services. Dyer's patent as Queen's Serjeant was renewed and Stanford was raised to the same rank in October 1553.[22] In this capacity they attended the early parliaments of the reign. The Journals of both Houses indicate that the pair contributed in some measure to the remodelling of the Anglican Church, no doubt on the logical premise that they had gained considerable practice in such matters under Northumberland.[23] Dyer's labour and loyalty found their reward in his appointment as recorder of Cambridge and elevation to the bench in 1557. Stanford received his due even sooner, becoming a judge of the Court of Common Pleas in 1554 and receiving a knighthood shortly after.[24]

Certain other aspiring members of the profession whose religious credentials were open to question probably suffered no more than a temporary check on their careers. Men such as Ranulph Chomeley, Thomas Carus, John Walsh and Richard Harper might have received their call as serjeants sooner than 1558 had Edward VI lived.[25] In the 1555 call of serjeants the prominence of strong Marian supporters is unmistakable. Anthony Browne, William Bendlowes, Francis Morgan and William Rastell in particular evinced a clear distaste for the religious innovations effected by Edward VI's protectors. Some were to participate actively in the suppression of what came to be heresy in the years 1553 to 1558.

All save Bendlowes reached the bench by 1558.[26] On the other hand, a clear preference for Catholics on Mary's or Gardiner's part did little to obscure that familiar pragmatism which lawyers habitually brought with them to government office – namely, a talent for combining public service with private profit.

If the government had any doubts as to the basic allegiance of the lawyers when Mary gained the throne, these were largely dissipated over the next two years. Like the great majority of the propertied classes, they might question and even obstruct specific policies, but concerted opposition within or without constitutional bounds was severely censured. The implementation of parliamentary legislation as it devolved upon the institutions and officers of the law was energetically enforced in a display of loyalty which almost appears calculated to convince the sceptical that indeed the disgrace of 1553 was erased.

The aim of this essay is to reveal to the reader the scope of activities which engaged common lawyers of senior rank in what would now be categorised as the civil service. In mid-Tudor England this effectually meant direct involvement in the establishment and maintenance of public order. Aside from the traditional forum of the law courts, attention is directed to the notable role played by legal practitioners in Parliament, local commissions and various offices of state where their training best suited them. The absence of both the constitutional luxury of a 'loyal opposition' and a firm line between political and administrative spheres of government meant that these men had to display political dexterity of the highest order or be pushed aside by suspicious superiors or ambitious subordinates. Yet attainment of a senior crown appointment was an unparalleled opportunity for the advancing lawyer to enhance both his status and income. It is hoped that by tracing the careers of a select number of the legal profession in the mid-sixteenth century the reader will sense the exhilarating, if perilous, environment in which Tudor government and society operated. Equally important, it may provide some notion of the self-interest and acquisitiveness which activated such men in an age when the competing loyalties of God and Mammon were still on an equal footing.

II

It is sometimes alleged that historians are guilty of obsessive interest in the subject of organised opposition to mid-Tudor government.[27] On the other hand, there is little question that a considerable, although not necessarily an excessive, amount of time and resources was expended by Marian officials at the central and local levels of government investigating and suppressing disaffection of one sort or another. It may well be that an infusion of scholarly research could and should be directed towards the operation of law enforcement during this period, as has been done for the reign fo Henry VIII, rather than towards the resistance which helped promote it.[28]

Three closely related areas of opposition appeared in the eyes of the Marian authorities to threaten the established order: an obstinate refusal to accept the restoration of Roman Catholicism, direct attempts at overthrowing the government, and inflammatory language directed against one or both; in short, the offences of heresy, treason and seditious words. In combating 'the many-headed monster', the multi-faceted talents of the legal profession proved to be indispensable. Whether as judges, local magistrates, special commissioners, attendants at the House of Lords or Members of Parliament, the lawyers earned their place in government esteem – and at a profit.

The campaign against heresy reveals most vividly the remarkable way in which legal practitioners adapted themselves to changing conditions. The main areas of activity appear to have been London and East Anglia, with the county of Essex showing traditional rebelliousness.[29] For the magistrates, lawyers and laymen alike, the motive for proceeding against heretics was as much the control of subversive behaviour as the enforcement of religious orthodoxy.[30] The reimposition of Roman Catholicism in Essex provides illuminating evidence on the ambiguous role of the lawyers who were most active on the commissions concerned. Three members, William Bendlowes, Anthony Browne and Richard Weston, were Essex-born and well established in the profession. It would appear that their religious inclinations served only to invigorate their pursuit of troublemakers in general and heretics in particular. The most active of the three, according to martyrologist John Foxe, was Anthony Browne, 'a hot and hasty justice in persecuting God's people'. He brooked no interference, however, from clerical officials and seemed more concerned about clearing the prisons than indicting heretics.[31] A fourth lawyer of note was Serjeant Thomas Gawdy, a Norfolk man who was reputedly 'a favourer' of the Protestants and, according to Strype, 'the least fierce among them' as a persecutor of heretics.[32] All four sat on commissions of the peace and assize, and seem to have operated on the standard assumption that criminals came in all forms. Certainly the orders issuing from the government, especially during and after 1555, as compared with the previous two years, make it appear as if religious persecution was an expedient means of trying to quell popular discontent.[33]

The evidence from the second half of Mary's reign, however, indicates that public order was not to be maintained by burning scores of lower-class trouble-makers for heresy any more than by hanging a handful of upper-class troublemakers for treason. Nor did existing legislation against unlawful assemblies seem particularly effective.[34] The most frustrating challenge to vested authority lay in the popular pastime of rumour-mongering, verbal abuse and rowdy behaviour which contemporary chroniclers catalogued under the amorphous rubric of 'seditious words'. This is a subject which has received little attention from either legal or social historians, doubtless because of its ill-defined character and obscure past. Yet from all accounts the problem had reached worrying proportions right from the outset of Mary's accession.[35] One of the earliest proclamations of the reign was issued by the Council to suppress 'light, seditious, or naughty talk', particularly as it related to 'the great and most weighty affairs touching the Queen's highness, royal person and the state of the realm'.[36] Unlike the pamphlet warfare which raged between 1553 and 1558,[37] seditious words were largely the province of the common and uneducated segments of the population. The usual punishment for offenders was to be set in the pillory and to suffer assorted abuses to the ears, whether through nailing or removal. Yet, as Professor Elton points out, the law was unclear on the subject even after certain categories of rumour-mongering were made a capital offence, in 1542.[38]

From the foregoing sketch of public service and private profit in the mid-sixteenth century it would seem that the elite of the common lawyers succeeded, like the vicar of Bray, in adjusting with alacrity to changing political circumstances. That they did so without serious repercussions can be attributed in part to their indispensability, not merely in the courts of law, but, more significantly, in the legislative and executive branches of government as well. This fact is perhaps most graphically demonstrated in the Marian parliaments of 1554 and 1555.

It is sad but true that lawyers have traditionally been known to make fortunes out of other people's misfortunes. It happened when Henry VIII dissolved the monasteries and it occurred again when his daughter proceeded to reassert papal jurisdiction in England. But this is the background against which one can appreciate the rapid, almost casual manner in which the medieval heresy laws were reactivated by Parliament in December 1554, despite the apparent rejection of such a plan by the Lords six months earlier.[39] It is probably only a coincidence, but an interesting one, that among the lawyers sitting in the House of Commons at the time were William Bendlowes and Anthony Browne of Essex; Richard Weston, representing Lancaster borough; and both Sir Roger and Ranulph Cholmeley from London.[40] It is also worth noting that James Dyer, *servientem ad legem et solicitatorem domine regine*, was attending the House of Lords along with his partner William Stanford. William Cordell was also present, in his capacity of Solicitor General.[41]

Less speed and more contention marked the passage of 'The Great Bill' reconciling England with Rome than did putting heresy back on the statute books. In essence, much of the disagreement concerned priorities rather than policy, certainly with respect to the question of monastic lands and impropriated livings. Despite Cardinal Pole's obvious disgust with the cynical attitude of the laity towards its recently acquired estates, human nature and the tide of events throughout Western Europe ran strongly towards secularisation of ecclesiastical property.[42] The majority of the Commons seemed willing enough to swap Edwardian Protestantism for Marian Catholicism so long as it involved only their consciences and not their possessions. Here the opinions of those *de la loi d'Angleterre* who sat with them came to the surface. The lawyers, or at least those acting at the behest of the government, argued that adequate guarantees against resumption of Church property already existed in law, inasmuch as the Crown had since time immemorial held absolute control over temporalities. This opinion may have been good law, but it was bad history: the holders of monastic estates knew better and demanded that the agreed papal dispensation be inserted into the statute of repeal.[43] This position was supported by the judges, led by Lord Chief Justice Thomas Bromley, in conference with the Queen and Philip prior to the bill's enactment. Mary reportedly vented her displeasure by means of a 'grievious taunt' upon Bromley, whose unwilling participation in Northumberland's plot was evidently not forgotten: 'I would you could have as well considered the right of the crown in my brother's time.'[44]

The original bill had been initiated in the House of Lords under the tutelage of that crypto-Protestant Serjeant Dyer and his fellow land speculator William Cordell. After it reached the Commons on 27 December, Pole sought to have the dispensation enacted as a separate statute, so as not to make the bargain appear too blatant in the eyes of Roman Christendom.[45] The long and acrimonious debate which followed seems to have obscured the real significance of the issue; both sides acknowledged a *de facto* contract, and it was not the papal dispensation, but parliamentary statute and the courts of common law, which would guarantee proprietary rights. Here again the lawyers were seen to be at work, protecting the interests of the landed class and furthering their own livelihood as well. A series of clauses was tacked onto the bill, among them one which confirmed that 'the title of all lands, possessions and hereditaments in this your majesties' realm and dominions is grounded in the laws, statutes and customs of the same, and by your high jurisdiction, authority royal and crown imperial, and in your courts only to be impleaded, ordered, tried and judged and none otherwise'.[46]

Less than a year later the issue of lay impropriations was raised again. This time the problem centred around the question of the Crown's surrender of its first fruits and tenths. Even this generous, but futile, gesture could not escape being the source of squalid political wrangling. Not the least cause was the government's decision to bring the matter before Parliament, a decision apparently predicated on the opinion of 'experienced English jurists', who doubtless saw this as their best means of supervising the process. Dyer and Cordell were in fact once more on the scene, charged with transmission of the resultant legislation from the Lords to the Commons, where it passed only after heated argument.[47]

The grounding of these ecclesiastical revisions in parliamentary statute has, with some justification, been regarded as 'a negative form of constitutionalism' by which the rough foundations of a 'rule of law' were being established.[48] Of more immediate significance was the fact that at no time in the sixteenth century did the legal establishment exert its authority or exploit its specialised knowledge to greater effect than in the later Marian parliaments. The main reason was unquestionably the accumulation of unresolved constitutional issues which bore directly upon the fragile political structure of mid-Tudor England. None was more crucial for the Queen than the reorganisation of the English Church or clarification of her consort's status and, with it, reaffirmation of the Habsburg alliance. Each demanded extensive remedial legislation of a drastic nature which effectively placed government at the mercy of Parliament and those who drafted its statutes and guided its debates.

One of the most conspicuous services performed by the lawyers on behalf of the Crown concerned the law of treason, where the House of Commons more than the courts was their principal forum. In view of the Queen's marriage and the hostility it provoked, the Parliament which met in November 1554 was called upon to re-enact the more explicit legislation developed under Henry VIII.[49] On 6 December the Lords sent down to the Commons a bill designed to extend the protection of the treason laws to Philip. This was the second time that Parliament had undertaken such a scheme.[50] It received a first reading the next day and was committed to 'Mr Weston' – probably the aforementioned lawyer from Essex who was sitting for Lancaster borough in this parliament. The measure did not come up for a second reading until 17 December; it was then rejected out of hand, first on the justifiable premise that it was obscure and imprecise, and secondly on the questionable claim that it was unfair to one to whom the realm owed a debt of gratitude.[51] In its place was substituted a more comprehensive draft. This not only enlarged the scope of what constituted an offence, but also provided for the guardianship of any heirs and extended legal protection to Philip while resident in England, should Mary predecease him. Simon Renard, the Imperial ambassador, in an uncharacteristically explicit passage, identifies those behind this apparent effusion of affection for the Queen's foreign husband as John Pollard, Speaker of Mary's first parliament, and *ung nommez Bruin, de loi d'Angleterre.*[52] There is little doubt that this was none other than Anthony Browne of Essex, who was Member for Maldon.[53] Pollard was another member of the lawyers' elite whose allegiance to the Marian cause displayed that familiar blend of public devotion and personal aggrandisement. He had a long and distinguished career in legal, administrative and parliamentary offices, extending back to 1535.[54]

The revised treasons bill, which was drafted by a Commons committee, presumably under the guidance of Pollard and Browne, and read for the first time on 20 December, did not go directly to the Upper House. Over Christmas it took a circuitous and decidedly unusual route via the Queen and the Imperial ambassador. According to Renard's account, one is presented with the spectacle of a parliamentary committee laying before a foreign envoy the substance of an important piece of legislation.[55] Despite Renard's reservations about certain clauses and doubts over the Lords' willingness to approve it, the revised version was eventually passed and received royal assent during the third week of January 1556.[56] In retrospect, however, it is obvious that neither the lawyers nor the MPs generally were motivated by devotion to the Queen's consort so much as determined to see that his status was clearly defined and his authority precisely circumscribed. In the bargain they also codified both the sweeping scope and procedural uncertainties which marked the law of treason during the rest of the sixteenth century.[57]

A third area of parliamentary activity involving the legal establishment to a conspicuous degree concerned the problem of seditious words and rumour-mongering. Even before the 1554 parliament had begun considering the more volatile matters of heresy and treason, it addressed itself to the necessity of reinforcing the ramparts of rank and privilege against verbal attack. The first item of business after the session began, in mid November, was a bill for the punishment of seditious words and rumours. It was sponsored by Sir John Baker, Privy Councillor, Chancellor of the Exchequer, lawyer and former Speaker; a man popularly known as 'Butcher Baker' in recognition of his eager conversion to the Marian cause.[58] There was evidently considerable interest and debate on the subject; it was reintroduced in amended form on 22 November and given a second reading the next day. At that point, the Commons Journal states, there was 'argument upon' it. In the course of the ensuing week the bill was debated on three successive days before being approved and sent up to the Lords on the 29th.[59] After the first and second readings the measure was committed to William Stanford, the Queen's Serjeant, for 'the making of a proviso unto it'.[60] The bill as amended, was passed on 11 December and brought back to the Commons by Serjeant Dyer and Sir Richard Rede for acceptance. It was reread and approved over the next three days in tandem with the heresy bill.[61] The careful attention to detail which preceded passage of this act is of some significance, especially when compared with the lack of contention which attended revival of the heresy laws. Yet quite obviously parliamentarians from both chambers must have regarded the two pieces of legislation as complementary vehicles for the containment of popular unrest.

In essence the act 'against seditious words and rumours' revitalised the medieval offence of *scandalum magnatum*, which had originated by statute in 1275. It was now augmented, however, with clauses directed at anyone attacking by words those in positions of authority. The Marian act, together with another in 1559, empowered justices of the peace to punish the guilty on first offence by the loss of ears for abusive language and the loss of the right hand for seditious writings.[62] Although the act only makes specific mention of verbal affront to the monarchy, the terms of the statute were construed to include the spreading of false reports about noblemen, great officers of state and judges.[63] Eventually the criminal offence of *scandalum magnatum* would be adapted by the courts to fit the civil law of libel; at this stage, however, the lawyers and legislators regarded the remedy as political in scope.[64]

When it came to actual pleading in the courts, lawyers expended little time prosecuting accused traitors and dissidents, whose small numbers made such trials comparatively rare in relation to the massive volume of civil litigation.[65] Yet, as a means of furthering their professional careers, treason cases ranked second to none as visible proof of loyalty to the regime. Here the work was more ritualised and less productive – other than in its financial rewards.[66] It has long been accepted that treason trials in the sixteenth century were political in nature and abrogated the customary rules of evidence and procedure. Regardless of rank or religion, judges, serjeants and barristers alike vied with one another in abusing the accused, whose means of defence were severely curtailed.[67] In some instances the hearing was an empty formality. When Northumberland came to trial, the lawyers were there in full regalia, but judgement was pronounced by the duke of Norfolk, president of the court, without bothering to consult the judges.[68] Foreign observers marvelled at the hypocrisy of those who had been a party to Mary's dethronement and were now sitting in judgement upon their less adroit fellows.[69] Sometimes the victims went out with a whimper, as in the case of the marquis of Northampton; sometimes with angry defiance, as in the case of Sir Thomas Palmer.[70] Almost always their feeble attempts at defence were quickly demolished by 'learned counsel'.

The one and only exception, and something of an embarrassment to both the government and the profession, was the celebrated trial of Sir Nicholas Throckmorton in April

1554 for complicity in Wyatt's rebellion. With a panel of commissioners including four judges and a former chief justice, the prosecution was led by William Stanford and James Dyer, the Queen's Serjeants. Throckmorton not only presented a masterly defence but also had the temerity to cast at the men of law some pointed barbs which came uncomfortably near the mark: 'I know how by persuasions, enforcements, presumptions, applying, inferring, conjecturing, deducing of arguments, wresting and exceeding the law . . . that unlearned men may be enchanted to think and judge those that be things indifferent . . . to be great treasons; such power orators have, and such ignorance the unlearned have.'[71] Punishment for Throckmorton's ensuing acquittal fell principally on the jury – 'heretics to a man' in Renard's jaundiced opinion – but there was, it seems, a move to punish the judges. Curiously, in an age when the bench was manifestly vulnerable to royal displeasure, neither Queen nor Council could or would take disciplinary action. The judges did somewhat better when Sir James Crofts was arraigned at the Guildhall ten days later. They reaffirmed his implication in the conspiracy notwithstanding a plea that no overt act had been committed, although the prosecution had to empanel a second jury before a conviction could be obtained.[72]

The task of enforcing law at the local level, although the least distinguished in terms of success, probably comprised an essential ingredient in the legal profession's immunity to the harsher repercussions of political upheaval. The strains of enforcement invariably fell most heavily upon commissions of the peace, which naturally were staffed with a strong contingent of judges and senior advocates. Again, this is most noticeable within the Home Counties and East Anglia, where social dissatisfaction tended to emerge independent of religion and politics. In Essex seven practising lawyers appear on the 1554 commission as members of the *quorum*, including four familiar names, Cordell, Bendlowes, Browne and Weston.[73] The Norfolk commission included Edward Griffin, the tenacious Attorney General, as well as two local worthies, Serjeants Thomas Gawdy and Richard Catlin, another intriguing example of personal friendship tied into professional and political partnership. Suffolk contained many

of the same names but also had two royal favourites as
well: Clement Higham, Speaker of the November parliament
and Privy Councillor, and Sir Nicholas Hare, Master of
the Rolls. More surprising is the name of John Gosnold,
who lost his place as Solicitor General in 1553. In and
around London the dominant figure from the ranks of senior
practitioners was Serjeant Robert Brooke, 'zealous Catholic',
respected legal scholar, former Speaker and recorder of the
city. He sat on commissions of the peace for Middlesex,
Hertfordshire, Kent, Surrey and Sussex.[74]

It is evident from subsequent events, however, that attempts
to silence loose and inflammatory talk were hardly going
to succeed when efforts at suppressing printed propaganda
were patently unsuccessful.[75] Equally obvious is the fact that
as time went on the government came to regard heretical
and lawless behaviour as one and the same. Certainly after
1554 persecution of heretics superseded prosecution of seditious and rebellious persons. This may, as some maintain,
represent a cynical policy of expediency encouraged by secular
magistrates frustrated in their attempts at muffling popular
dissent.[76] It is surely significant that fully one-third of those
condemned to be burned at the stake were poor, unemployed
transients who seem to have fallen under the spell of millen-
arian fantasies, then so prevalent about the capital.[77]

If the heresy commission established in February 1557
is any guide, the legal community had few qualms about
the merging of its coercive jurisdiction with that of the
Church. Led by Edmund Bonner, the bishop of London,
it numbered among its members Sir Roger and Ranulph
Cholmeley, one a deposed Lord Chief Justice, the other a
reputed Protestant and newly appointed recorder of London.
Sir Nicholas Hare and Serjeant William Rastell, good lawyers
but better Catholics, were also included.[78] The commissioners
were empowered to inquire not only into 'divers heresies
and heretical opinions' but also into 'false rumours, tales
and seditious slanders'; to search out not only 'all such
persons as obstinately do refuse ... to hear mass', but also
'vagabonds, and masterless men, barrators, quarrellers, and
suspect persons' within a ten-mile radius of the city of
London.[79] This commission did not, as Froude suggests,[80]

mark an alarming accretion of power to the Crown, but, rather, something of a panic reaction to the threat of mob violence in the capital. Perhaps the frightening spectre of Münster in 1535 still haunted the English authorities.

It would appear that the conspicuous accommodation shown by Privy Councillors, if not the Crown, to religious change among government officials bred open contempt among the ordinary people, from whose ranks most of the so-called heretics were extracted. Certainly for the three native magistrates of Essex the confusing shifts in religious policy of the mid century caused minimal inconvenience but brought material rewards. Browne and Weston carried on a long and fruitful collaboration which extended at least from the reign of Edward VI until Browne's death in 1567. Weston had already enriched himself modestly as an agent of Thomas Audley's during the dissolution of the monasteries.[81] In 1551 Browne was one of a commission established to clear from the churches what plate and valuables still remained. While carrying out instructions, his regional committee managed to leave the bare necessities for conducting services. Yet he does not appear to have deviated markedly from the blanket indictment that the commissioners showed little concern for the religious implications of their actions. Two years later Weston and Browne were granted possession of a free chapel by the chantry commissioners. Browne also purchased the reversion of Brentwood manor in the same year.[82]

Having secured a sound base of financial operations within the inclement atmosphere of Edwardian Protestantism, it remained for the more adaptable of the lawyers to seek professional preferment under Mary. For Browne at least, there was a brief scare when his success as a collector of church valuables jeopardised his pro-Catholic credentials. He was detained in the Fleet during the last two weeks of July 1553. The following September the Council demanded that he deliver up plate removed from the parishes of Essex.[83] Thereafter, however, his zealous pursuit of heretics more than restored him to favour. Within a year the same Council was congratulating Browne and his colleagues 'for their travails in the well ordering of the shire, praying them to continue their diligence, and to cause all such that shall condemn the Queen's highness' order set forth in religion'.[84] In 1555 and 1558 Browne was again singled out for his 'accustomed care and diligence' in the execution of justice.[85] Both Browne and Weston received tangible proof of official favour: the latter became Queen's Solicitor in 1557, the former a serjeant in 1555 and Chief Justice of the Common Pleas in 1558.

Other productive partnerships developed in this period among lawyers who succeeded in bridging the transition from Edward VI and Mary. William Cordell was a transplanted East Anglian who fashioned himself a long and prosperous career in the second half of the sixteenth century. Having supplanted John Gosnold as Solicitor General in 1553, he went on to succeed Sir Nicholas Hare as Master of the Rolls upon the latter's death in 1557, was knighted and was appointed to the Council.[86] That same year Cordell and Browne, in conjunction with other favourites, were granted a number of properties in Essex held by Susan Clarence, the Queen's Mistress of the Robes, together with two manors forfeited by Sir John Gates upon his attainder for treason. Both men were also among a consortium which purchased the Essex manor of Almounton Spettell from Lord Wyndsore.[87] Investment among lawyers in real estate was evidently prevalent within other counties bordering London; in 1554, for example, we find Cordell and Serjeant James Dyer purchasing five manors in Kent. Cordell and Browne also went about gathering a number of minor but profitable sinecures during the same period, ranging from Clerk of the Swanimote Courts of Waltham Forest to the reversion of the office of Chirographer of the Common Pleas.[88]

One of the many lessons which Elizabeth apparently learned from her sister's reign was the futility of trying to determine legal appointments on the basis of religious affiliation. For the most part, the new Queen was prepared to accept the learned counsel of her predecessor; she had little choice. Only one judge was removed from the bench – namely, Sir Clement Higham, who had presided over the Court of Exchequer since March 1558. His status as a Privy Councillor as much as his Catholicism probably accounted for his departure. The fact that he possessed little court-room experience must also have been a factor. For the rest, Elizabeth's ministers performed an adroit piece of shuffling by which the more committed Marian judges were placed in less sensitive posts without the Crown losing the benefit of their experience. The familiar figure of Anthony Browne is typical: he had been appointed Chief Justice of the Court of Common Pleas in October 1558; now he was demoted to the rank of puisne judge to make way for Sir James Dyer.[89] Even as ardent a Catholic as William Rastell kept his position on the King's Bench. Admittedly the government had some room for manoeuvre inasmuch as several of those given preferment by Mary between 1555 and 1558 died just before or shortly after Elizabeth's accession. Robert Brooke, Nicholas Hare, William Dalison, John Pollard and William Stanford all fell into this category.

III

Whatever may be said about the general economic state of the realm in the last years of Mary's reign, it was a prosperous time for the legal establishment. Business in the common-law courts during the 1550s reached unprecedented levels of activity and many senior practitioners were productively employed in government. It was for the lawyers a seller's market: there was a shortage of experienced barristers to plead cases as well as a lack of serjeants to fill the bench.[90] Leaving aside those who had retired to obscurity or died, all the serjeants who had been called in 1552 and 1555 were either High Court judges, justices of assize or Crown servants of prominent rank by 1558. Prior to Mary's death there is no evidence to indicate that any lawyer had suffered a serious check in his career, aside from one or two victims of the 1553 shake-up.[91] Even Gilbert Gerrarde, who had incurred the Queen's displeasure, and Edmund Plowden, who had challenged her authority in the 1558 parliament, were summoned to take the coif that same year; so was Ranulph Cholmeley, whose labours on the London heresy commission must have stood him in good stead.[92]

It is all too easy to be cynical about the manner and means by which the legal establishment maintained its status close to the centre of political administration. That many of these

men were unscrupulous in their pursuit of royal favour is
undeniable, but others displayed high professional standards
in the performance of their duties. Those who possessed ruthlessness and agility, as well as real ability, more easily survived
the testing challenges of the mid-Tudor years to become
the trusted servants of the Elizabethan state. Readers of
*The Mirror for Magistrates*, published in 1559, might delude
themselves into believing that judges were bound to fall from
grace 'for misconstruing the laws and expounding them to
serve the prince's affections'; such was only rarely the case
in the sixteenth century, despite the legal profession's reputation, among the general populace, for greed and corruption.[93]

On both the administrative and the judicial side of the
legal vocation, mid-Tudor government displayed a self-inter-
ested form of enlightenment which recognised merit and rewarded service. Sir William Cordell, whose success as Solicitor
General led to his appointment as Master of the Rolls under
Mary, held on to the post after 1558 although he was removed
from the board of the Privy Council. Edward Griffin finally
lost his place as Attorney General, the office going instead
to Gilbert Gerrarde, the lawyer who had so effectively protected the interests of the then Princess Elizabeth in 1554
against threatened prosecution for treason in the wake of
Wyatt's rebellion. Richard Weston, who, like Browne and
Cordell, had laboured diligently and profitably in the Essex
vineyard for both Edward VI and Mary, received his reward
with a promotion to the bench, where political impartiality
was regarded as a virtue as well as a necessity.[94] These
and other adjustments in rank and personnel caused little
disruption within the profession; rather they heralded that
characteristic stability which marks those men of law in the
service of the Crown. By an obvious combination of luck
and design, a considerable number of Elizabeth's servants
shared with their mistress remarkable political and biological
longevity. Among the lawyers, Dyer, Cordell and Gerrarde
remained at their posts until the 1580s.[95]

A concluding reference to Anthony Browne may be fitting,
since he more than any other lawyer seemed to epitomise
that delicate balance between principle and profit. His eleva-

tion to the chief-justiceship of the Common Pleas was appropriate in that it was second in prestige to the office of Lord Chief Justice of the King's Bench, yet yielded a higher income. When Mary attempted to pre-empt his authority of appointing officials to the court, Browne, ardent Catholic, scourge of heretics and champion of the Queen's consort, did not hesitate to challenge his sovereign when his prerogatives and fees were threatened. Even after his demotion at the hands of Elizabeth, the issue of *brocage*, or dispensing of offices, escalated into a full-blown constitutional battle. It was Sir James Dyer, however, the new Chief Justice, who reaped the monetary benefits after the legal establishment had blocked the Crown's claim.[96]

Browne was by no means pinched for money. During the last ten years of his life he continued to accumulate property in his native Essex, purchasing, as in the past, dissolved monastic estates. He also seems to have retained a taste for controversy. This time it was the debate over the succession. With the assistance of his junior colleague, Edmund Plowden, he composed a treatise which advocated the claim of Mary Stuart and attempted to refute the arguments put forward by John Hales.[97] On less reliable authority, Browne is said to have been offered custody of the Great Seal in place of Nicholas Bacon but refused, because 'he was of a different religion from the state'.[98] In 1566, a year before his death, Browne was knighted by the Queen at the Parliament house, where he and so many of his fellow lawyers had begun their public careers.[99]

# 8. England and the French War, 1557–9

## C. S. L. DAVIES

MILITARY history is largely ignored except by enthusiasts. The strain which war placed on the workings of the state, and the burden placed on the subject for the maintenance of ships and artillery, of soldiers and sailors, by taxation or by more direct methods of expropriation are generally admitted. War was the stiffest test which any regime could face. Defeat or even the strain of victory could bring apparently impregnable political structures crashing down. But what armies or fleets actually did once they were assembled is passed over rapidly; 'drum and flag' history is of little interest to the general historian. The French war is always mentioned in accounts of Mary's reign. The loss of Calais hangs like a pall across the last year of the reign, second in notoriety only to the persecution of Protestants as the mark of a government which was incompetent and out of tune with the feelings of the nation. All the more reason, then, to set the events in context; to examine how far the Marian government deserves its reputation for dragging the country into a war in which it had no interest, how far the war itself was mishandled, and to what extent there was a deliberate subordination of English to Spanish interests.

The war of 1557–9 was the culmination of that long struggle for the control of Italy which had begun with Charles VIII's invasion in 1494; the culmination too, of a 150-year old feud between the kings of France and the dukes of Burgundy. The English, dependent as they were on the Antwerp market for the sale of their cloth, were the natural allies of the

Burgundian dukes and their successors the Habsburgs, now also kings of Spain. The importance of the English Channel as the link between Spain and the Netherlands was emphasised by the French conquest of Metz in 1552, which seemed to threaten the overland routes between Spanish territory in Italy and that in the Netherlands. England's strategic importance explains Charles V's anxiety to have Mary safely married to his son Philip. The English, on their side, were worried, and the marriage treaty included a clause that 'the Realm of England by occasion of this matrimony, shall not directly or indirectly be entangled with the war that is' between Charles V and the King of France. The marriage always carried with it a potential clash of interests; and, knowing this, the English were keen to negotiate peace between the Emperor and the King of France. Their attempts failed. Even so, without English involvement, a truce for five years was patched up at Vaucelles in February 1556. By that time Charles had abdicated in favour of Philip as King of Spain and ruler of the Netherlands.*

The truce was always uneasy. But it was the octogenarian Gianpetro Caraffa, now Pope Paul IV, who destroyed it. Paul fiercely resented Spanish rule in his native Naples and Spanish domination of Italy generally, which threatened the independence of the Papacy. Hysterically denouncing Charles V as a 'heretic, schismatic, and tyrant' whose whole aim had been 'to oppress the Holy See', and adding that Philip was little better, Paul managed to provoke an invasion of the Papal States by Philip's viceroy in Naples, the duke of Alva, in September 1556.[1] Henry II could not ignore the chance to re-establish French power in Italy. In November 1556 an army set out under the duke of Guise; in January

* The multiplicity of dominions over which Philip ruled makes for difficulties on nomenclature. Philip's army at St Quentin, for instance, included contingents from the Netherlands (themselves a collection of separate lordships), from the various Spanish kingdoms and from Italy, as well as German mercenaries. In referring to the Netherlands I have sometimes used the word 'Flemish' (for instance, to distinguish from troops from Spain or Italy), although, of course, Flanders was only one province. 'Netherlands' is too clumsy, and 'Dutch' is misleading to a modern reader. 'Spanish' is more difficult; I have sometimes used it to refer to Philip's continental dominions (as against England); sometimes to distinguish specifically 'Spanish' matters from those of the Netherlands. The context, I hope, should make the meaning plain.

1557 a surprise attack was mounted on Douai, on the Flemish frontier. By the end of the month Philip and Henry were formally at war.

Philip had no wish for war. He had very nearly exhausted his financial credit, he had qualms about fighting the Pope, and, in contrast to his father, he did not enjoy soldiering. Nevertheless, if war were forced on him, he would fight to the best of his (and his subjects') ability; and therefore he arrived in England in March 1557 to invoke English aid. There he found himself faced by a hostile Council, alleging England's inability to fight. Famine made it impossible to feed an army; trade with France was important, not least because of French supplies of grain; government finances and the threat of sedition ruled war out of court; finally, the marriage treaty did not allow it. (In fact the treaty was ambiguous: its wording could be held to apply only to the war raging in 1554 between Charles V and Henry II; and, in any case, the treaty of 1546, under which England was to come to the aid of the Netherlands if they were attacked, had been specifically reaffirmed in 1554.) The Queen referred back the Council's opinion. The Councillors, called in one by one to justify themselves, began to give ground. There was talk of financial aid to Philip, even of a small expeditionary force, though no formal English involvement for the moment; even that might be possible once the new harvest was in and the immediate threat of famine removed. In the event, Henry II's longstanding protection of English rebels cut the Gordian knot; on 28 April 1557, Thomas Stafford landed at Scarborough from a French warship, seized the castle, and proclaimed Mary's deposition. His little band was soon ejected and taken prisoner; but Henry had unwittingly provided a solidly English reason for a declaration of war.[2]

The threat of famine invoked by the Council was hideously real. The harvests of 1555 and 1556, taken together, had been the worst in living memory, with prices 50 and 100 per cent above the norm. The famine was general over Northwestern Europe; in the Netherlands only Amsterdam, with its lien on Baltic grain imports, was spared. France, too, suffered from widespread shortages, though the French ambassador, with his eye on political advantage, had arranged for shipments of French grain to London. In May 1557, however, the situation was suddenly transformed. The coming harvest was likely to produce a glut.[3] Grain was hurriedly brought out of store, the size of a penny loaf in London rose from 11 to 56 ounces, and merchants who had set off to import rye from Danzig found on their return that the bottom had dropped out of the market. The weather, as well as Henry II, had undermined the Council's position. War was solemnly declared on 7 June 1557.[4]

War was welcome to some, at least, of Mary's subjects. William Paget, the Lord Privy Seal, an enthusiastic supporter of the Habsburg alliance, had thought as long ago as November 1554 that the way for Philip to consolidate his position as King of England was to lead an English army in the field. Many of the aristocracy thought in terms of personal loyalties, rather than national interest, and to them it was natural and right that Philip should help his father, and that Mary and her subjects should help Philip. A personalised, rather patriarchal concept of loyalty, dependent on the tenure of land by inheritance and marriage, was, after all, the foundation of noble power. 'By the Mass', said the Scottish earl of Cassillis to the earl of Westmorland in 1557, 'I am no more French than you are a Spaniard.' 'Marry,' replied Westmorland, 'as long as God shall preserve my master and mistress together, I am and shall be a Spaniard to the uttermost of my power.'[5]

War itself would provide the opportunity for service, position, honour and profit; an opportunity eagerly plucked, to all appearances, by men such as the earls of Pembroke and Rutland and Viscount Montague, all of whom held important commands in the French war; by the earls of Shrewbury and Westmorland, with commands in the north; by the Lord Admiral, Lord William Howard, and his successor, Lord Clinton; and by Lord Grey of Wilton, who, always spoiling for a fight, begged leave of absence from his command at Guisnes for more active service under Philip's command. Thomas Percy was restored to the family earldom of Northumberland, forfeit for twenty years, in May 1557 and made Warden of the East March against Scotland. Francis Russell, earl of Bedford, a committed Protestant, none the less returned from exile in 1557, took part in the St Quentin expedition, and commanded the West Country forces against the threat of invasion in 1558.

The extent to which the war helped those involved in sedition and rebellion to make their peace with the government was remarkable. The three surviving sons of John Dudley, duke of Northumberland, fought at St Quentin: one, Harry, was killed; the other two, Ambrose and Robert, went on to distinguished military careers with Elizabeth. Lord Braye was also fatally injured in the campaign, shortly after release from imprisonment for taking part in the Dudley conspiracy of 1556. Cuthbert Vaughan, reprieved after sentence of death for his part in the Wyatt rebellion of 1554, commanded a company of arquebusiers in the Scottish war. Sir James Croft and Sir Peter Carew, leaders in the 1554 conspiracy, both held important commands in the war. Their fellow conspirator William Winter retained his office as Surveyor of the Navy, adding to it that of Master of Naval Ordnance in 1557, and commanded at sea as Vice-Admiral. Peter Killigrew, captured sailing a French royal ship, the *Sacrette*, as a privateer, turns up a few months later as captain of the Queen's ship *Jerfalcon*. These are by no means the only examples: indeed, Holinshed's list of captains at Berwick reads like a roll-call of ex-rebels.[6] This was partly because soldiers and sailors had been drawn into an opposition stance, through their association with the duke of Northumberland's regime, which had a strongly military colouring. Moreover, as Dr Loades observes, many of the conspirators were small gentlemen or younger sons whose only hope of a career lay with the sword – if necessary, in French service, but preferably in that of their Queen.[7] On its side, Mary's government could not afford to waste military talent and experience. The war provided an opportunity, therefore, to reunite a deeply divided ruling class.

The English army was a somewhat archaic force compared with the highly professional troops of France and Spain, hardened as they were by years of service and stiffened with large contingents of German mercenaries. Foreign observers and English patriots lamented the shortage of arquebus and pike, the English reliance on bill and bow, the lack of discipline in the English levies and their reluctance to undergo hardship; above all, their endemic amateurishness. The almost uninterrupted war of the 1540s had produced a group of English professional officers, but, except for garrison service at Berwick and Calais, opportunities for them had been few in Marian England; even Ireland, that refuge for captains in Elizabeth's reign, offered only limited employment under Mary. Philip evidently believed that England's most useful contribution to his armies lay in pioneers and miners for siege operations.[8]

Much more important was the navy. Built up on an impressive scale in the 1540s, it too had suffered from the subsequent economy drive. In Northumberland's time old ships were sold off but no new ones built; and little money, apparently, was spent on repairs. This situation changed in Mary's reign, probably inspired by Philip himself, who had resented the failure of the combined Anglo-Flemish fleets to sweep the Channel clean of French privateers in 1554. Rebuilding began in earnest in 1555. Two large new ships, the *Philip and Mary* and the *Mary Rose*, were ready by the beginning of 1557, and others were under construction. Naval administration was put on a regular footing in January 1557, with £14,000 allocated as a peacetime 'ordinary' – rather less, in fact, than had been spent in the two previous years (some £20,000 for the fifteen months September 1554 to December 1555, and £18,000 during 1556), but with the definite intention of making good arrears of rebuilding for such ships as needed it. The whole operation was to be under the direction of the efficient and experienced Lord Treasurer, William Paulet, marquis of Winchester. When war was declared, Lord Admiral Howard put to sea with some twenty ships, which, in association with a Flemish fleet under Caravajal, sacked Cherbourg, swept the Channel of French privateers, and, most important of all, made possible the transport of silver from Spain to pay the mammoth army Philip was fitting out in the Netherlands.[9]

The war was going well for Philip. Paul IV and Guise tried and failed to mount an invasion of Naples in May 1557. Forced back on the defensive, bad blood soon developed between them; in August the duke was recalled to northern Italy, leaving Paul IV to make terms with the Spaniards. Meanwhile Philip was assembling an army of some 60,000–80,000 men in the Netherlands too; on 2 August, under the command of Emmanuel Philibert, the exiled duke of Savoy, it crossed the border to France and laid siege to the town of St Quentin.

A small English force had crossed the Channel in July to take part in this expedition. Some 1200 horse, 4000 foot, 1500 pioneers and 200 miners, it was commanded by the earl of Pembroke. The army itself was, at least on paper, meticulously organised. Each company of 100 men had its captain and lieutenant, its ensign, sergeant, surgeon, chaplain, drum and fife. There was an artillery train commanded by Robert Dudley, a convoy of travelling mills and ovens, and a provost's department, which included two judges, two gaolers and a 'hangman with his necessaries'. There seems to be no evidence about the most important part of all, how the troops were armed, though, unusually, about half the cavalry were the heavier 'demi-lances'. Nor do we know how the troops were raised, though it seems probable that it was on the normal 'quasi-feudal' basis, the nobles and gentlemen taking part supplying troops from their servants and tenants. The English were clearly determined to put on a brave show. Philip appears to have paid for them, and to some extent it may be that he was humouring the English by allowing them to participate.[10]

The decisive moment in the siege of St Quentin came on 10 August, when the Constable of France, Anne de Montmorency, miscalculated badly while attempting to relieve the town. The battle turned into a rout in which some 3000 French troops were killed and 7000 captured, among them the Constable himself, two dukes and a marshal. The victory was Savoy's. Philip, for some reason (possibly again to humour English sensitivities), wished to arrive at the head of the English troops; and these had been delayed by the usual difficulties over transport.[11] Although they had missed the battle, there was plenty of excitement for Philip and the English when they did eventually arrive. Gaspard de Coligny was holding out fiercely in the town. Not until

27 August did it eventually fall, to a murderous assault
involving 2000 English troops, along with Germans,
Spaniards, Walloons and Burgundians. Queen Mary was told
that her troops were the first in through the breach, and
this belief, enshrined in Holinshed, forms the basis of the
continuing English belief that English troops had somehow
won St Quentin for Philip; it was somewhat crassly contra-
dicted by Philip's representative, the count of Feria, during
the bitter recriminations after the fall of Calais. The victory
was marked by the usual quarrel over the spoils – the English,
so they complained, being thrust aside by the more experienced and professional Germans.[12] Nevertheless, the English
had contributed rather more than could be expected from
their numbers, as is clearly revealed by the casualty list
kept by the conscientious treasurer:[13]

|  | Demi-lances | Light horse | Foot | Miners | Pioneers |
|---|---|---|---|---|---|
| Able | 554 | 459 | 3486 | 162 | 1168 |
| Sick | 57 | 46 | 417 | 27 | 98* |
| Hurt | 8 | 43 | 137 | 11 |  |
| Discharged through sickness | 24 | 34 | 108 | – | 289† |
| Total | 643 | 582 | 4148 | 200 | 1555 |

* Dead and slain on service.   † Discharged through sickness and wounds.

The London chroniclers show a quiet pride in English achievement in the service of the 'King our Master', while the
earl of Bedford reported that 'God prospereth the King's
Majesty in all his proceedings.' Paget's prescription of military
success as a means of reconciling Philip to his English subjects
seems to have been working.[14]

While Pembroke's troops were winning honours in France,
however, England itself faced the dangers of invasion on
its northern border. The Scots were, of course, the traditional
allies of the French: but the Scottish scene in 1557 was
quite exceptional, and provided an object lesson for the English of the dangers which they themselves might face if they
ever lowered their guard against Philip.

The Queen of Scots, the fifteen-year old Mary Stuart, had been living in France since 1548, betrothed to the Dauphin. Her mother, the Dowager Queen, Mary of Guise, was Regent. Mary of Guise (sister of the duke of Guise, commanding the French forces in Italy) had returned reluctantly to Scotland in 1551, persuaded of her duty to bring the country, as far as possible, under French control. Her daughter, after all, was destined to be Queen of France and, if all went well, Scotland seemed unlikely ever again to have a resident king or queen. The French representative in Scotland, d'Oysel, controlled French troops garrisoning key positions around Edinburgh; and the duties of the Chancellor, the earl of Huntley, were in practice exercised by his deputy, the Frenchman de Roubay. The English declaration of war on France was followed by an appeal from Henry II for Scotland to make war on England. The Scottish lords refused. Nevertheless, d'Oysel set about fortifying Eyemouth, seven miles from Berwick, possibly so as to provoke an English attack. Scottish politics were always volatile; and the English, obviously, needed to prepare for the worst. Defence arrangements were put in hand, and in May 1557 the earl of Shrewsbury, an experienced commander, was given charge of the English forces.[15]

The problem for the English was to have a force ready to repel a large-scale invasion, if one were threatened, without at the same time committing too many scarce resources – men, money, food, munitions – on any one occasion. Scottish politics were so unstable that the English were kept on their toes. The Council's policy was therefore to keep the northern counties (as far south as Derbyshire and Nottinghamshire) in a state of alert, but not to call out troops unless it was absolutely necessary. Good intelligence was therefore vital, as was judgement in its interpretation. Naturally, those commanders nearest the front line were the least sanguine. In July Lord Wharton, from Berwick, was urging the immediate call-up of the army; the earl of Westmorland, Shrewsbury's principal lieutenant, preferred to believe in the peaceful aims of the Scottish nobility. In August it was Westmorland's turn to sound the alarm, while his superior, the earl of Shrewsbury, took a cooler view. By 20 September Shrewsbury himself was convinced that an attack was imminent and summoned the army; but the Council was reluctant to approve his action and still urged caution. A Scottish attack did in fact materialise in early October, when a large army assembled at Kelso. But heavy rain, political dissension and, no doubt, the evidence of English preparation had dissuaded the nobility. The Queen Dowager raged and wept, d'Oysel accused the Scots of disloyalty, and the Scots took steps to end French power in their country.[16]

In October 1557, then, there was good news for Philip from all fronts. The Pope had made peace. No army stood between Philip and Paris; Charles V, in retirement at Yuste, looked to a triumph to surpass any of his own. Philip, however, was naturally cautious; better to consolidate St Quentin and to take a few more border fortresses than to dash for the capital and overstretch his lines of communication. Finances were in any case precarious. In June he had had to default on interest payments on his debts. The Netherlands States-General, meeting in Brussels, was awkward about the vote of taxes, demanding oversight of expenditure, and objecting to the presence of foreign troops. The Spanish treasury, too, was exhausted. Satisfied, then, with solid but limited success, Philip dismissed the bulk of his forces in November, and settled down for the usual winter respite from campaigning.

These comfortable feelings were punctured by events in France. Henry had sent urgently to bring Guise and his army back from Italy. Guise arrived by the end of October; meanwhile the Queen, Catherine de Medici, and Guise's brother, the cardinal of Lorraine, had quelled the panic in Paris and managed to secure some loans. An army of new French levies, German mercenaries, and veterans from Guise's Italian campaign was hastily raised. In spite of the hard winter, the 'honour and safety of the realm' dictated that it should be used for 'some considerable exploit'.[17] Unfortunately, from an English point of view, Henry determined on Calais as his revenge for the year's humiliations.

The recovery of Calais had been frequently mooted at the French court, especially since the return of Boulogne to France in 1550. Interest in Calais had increased during

Mary's reign. Town and garrison showed uncomfortable Protestant tendencies which might provide a lever for subversion; while many of the exiles at the French court had close connections with the Calais garrison. Lord Dudley, for instance, commander of the English fortress at Hammes in the Calais Pale, was the brother of Sir Henry Dudley, deviser of a scheme in 1556 to rob the Exchequer and depose Queen Mary. A stream of French intelligence reports – most recently that of ambassador Noailles, who returned through the town from England at the outbreak of war – drew attention to the weaknesses of the defences. In January 1557 Nicolas Denisot, one-time tutor in the family of the duke of Somerset, now serving the controller of Calais, Sir Edward Grimston, was involved in a plot to blow up the powder magazine. Sénarpont, governor of Boulogne, had for a long time taken an interest in the neighbouring fortress; and Gaspard de Coligny was said to have had a plan in his possession for an attack. On Guise's arrival in France, Henry put to him the possibility. Guise apparently was sceptical. But some time in November 1557 Sénarpont and Piero Strozzi, the brilliant Italian condottiere, suitably disguised, inspected the fortifications. Their report seems to have won Guise over.[18]

Guise's initial scepticism was understandable. Calais was more than an isolated fortress. A tract of land some twenty miles by six, it contained three major fortifications: at Calais itself, Guisnes and Hammes. All had been rebuilt between 1539 and 1542 to withstand artillery battery. In addition, there were a series of smaller forts and 'bulwarks' on the periphery of the Pale. The castle (as opposed to the town walls) had not been rebuilt, and was, according to a 1556 survey, 'so old that it ruineth daily, a place . . . more apt to give the enemy an entry to the town than to defend the town itself'. But access to the castle by an enemy was extremely difficult, since it faced the harbour; a modern fortification, the Rysbank, on the other side of the harbour, effectively kept the castle covered. Moreover, a good deal of the Pale was marsh, effectively preventing easy access by the enemy. The approach to Calais from the south was by a causeway, protected by a fortress at Newnham Bridge (Nieulay to the French). To the north Calais bordered on

Philip's territories; there was a Spanish garrison at Gravelines, ten miles from the town. Any attempt on Calais must have seemed suicidal. It was desperation that was driving Henry on.[19]

The garrison had been reinforced during the summer of 1557, but thereafter heavily reduced. By December it was at or near the normal peacetime establishment of about 600 men; there may have been 800 at Guisnes, and a handful at Hammes. In addition there were about 200 auxiliaries from the inhabitants of Calais.[20] In December the government was actually on the point of ordering further reductions. The reduction to peacetime strength in midwinter was not unusual, and no attack had in fact ever taken place in December or January. Nevertheless, we can see with hindsight that economy had triumphed over prudence – even while recognising that no Tudor government could have provided the 4000 men which would have made the town, in Henry II's view, impregnable.[21]

There were, inevitably, complaints about shortage of food. In the event, however, Calais collapsed so fast that this could not have affected the outcome.[22] The commanders also complained about shortages of guns and munition; the Master of the Ordnance later asserted (in his own defence) that a shortfall of gunpowder had prevented his guns from battering the French artillery positions.[23] Against this is the evidence that the French were impressed by the weapons and provisions they found in the town after taking it.[24] The fortifications had not been neglected, either during the economy drive of Northumberland's regime or in Mary's reign; with the fatal exception of the castle, there is no suggestion that they were weak. In short, the state of Calais left a good deal to be desired; but the belief that a negligent government had left the town indefensible cannot be sustained.[25]

'The which enterprise was begun and ended in less than eight days, to the great marvel of the world, that a town of such strength, and so well funished of all things as that was, should so suddenly be taken and conquered; but most specially in the winter season in what time all the country about, being marsh ground, is commonly overflown with

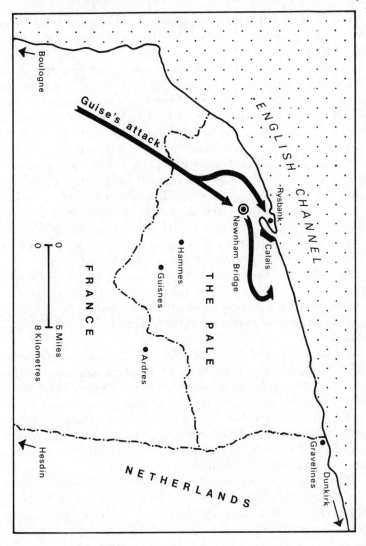

water.'[26] The fall itself is quickly told. Guise's army, some 27,000 men, appeared before Newnham Bridge, in the Pale, on 1 January 1558.[27] The marshes were frozen, enabling one part of the army to double round and proceed along the dunes to Rysbank, the fortress on the spit between the harbour and the sea-coast. Rysbank capitulated almost immediately, on 2 January; with that, the French were able to control the harbour, and also bombard the castle, the weakest part of the defences of Calais itself. Newnham Bridge surrendered on the 4th. The French took Calais castle on 7 January; two English assaults were beaten off with large casualties, and Wentworth made terms. The French then attacked Guisnes, where Lord Grey of Wilton, a stubborn and cruel fighter, held out with the aid of a detachment of Philip's troops until 21 January – when the soldiers threatened to fling Grey over the walls, because 'for his vain glory they would not sell their lives'. On the news of the surrender Lord Dudley abandoned the third fortress, Hammes. During all this time no reinforcements had arrived from England; and, except for the reinforcement of Guisnes, very little from Philip.[28]

Where does the blame lie? With the English government? With the commanders on the spot, in particular Lord Wentworth, as the responsible officer? With Philip? The heart of the matter lies in the failure of reinforcements to arrive at Calais, and that in turn raises two questions: whether there was culpable delay in sending warning of the French attack; and whether Wentworth could have held out longer, until reinforcements arrived.

The Venetian ambassador at the French court named Calais as the objective of the French army as early as 6 December. This was not based on definite information, but was an intelligent diplomat's deduction; only four days before he had thought that Guise's army would be sent to attack Luxemburg.[29] The next piece of information seems to be that of a spy who reported to Noyelle, Philip's governor at Hesdin, on 18 December, the likelihood of an attack on Calais; Noyelle passed it on to Bugnicourt (Vandeville), commanding at Gravelines, to the duke of Savoy, and to Wentworth at Calais.[30] If Wentworth ever received this, he evidently took no notice. Through Vandeville this news also reached Grey at Guisnes on 22 December; he promptly passed it on to the English government. The Council received it on the 24th, and immediately cancelled an order for the futher reduction of the garrison.[31] On the 26th Wentworth himself wrote, now convinced of an attack; this led to a Council order on 29 December to alert the ships in the Narrow Seas and to send over the earl of Rutland with two experienced captains and a small number of troops.[32] On the 29th Wentworth wrote to say that Hesdin, not Calais, was the French objective. 'I having presently no other news I cease further to trouble your Highness.'[33] The government relaxed, rescinded the order for Rutland's despatch on 31 December – the day on which Wentworth again changed his mind, and appealed to Philip for help.[34] The very next day, French forces appeared before Newnham Bridge.

In the sequence of events, there seems considerable complacency on Wentworth's part (in lowering his guard on the 29th) and on the Council's (in the inadequacy of its response, and its readiness to clutch at the straw of Hesdin). Its response is at least partially explicable in the light of the Scottish campaign; it was its business to prevent forces being dissipitated, and it would expect commanders to take an alarmist view. Neither the Council nor Wentworth thought that the situation was as critical as it was: to judge by the tone of other letters, both seemed to believe that, even if Guise were to attack, no more than a raid on the Pale need be feared.

New Year's Day changed the situation. The Council commanded Rutland to Calais once more, and ordered 500 Kentishmen to be at Dover by 5 January.[35] Rutland tried to cross on 3 January, but his sailors, hearing of the fall of Rysbank, refused to enter Calais harbour. On the same day Vandeville sent from Gravelines a relief force of 300 arquebusiers, which was beaten back by the French.[36] Calais itself was now under attack and its relief demanded a very much larger expeditionary force, one which would land at Gravelines or Dunkirk and fight its way into the besieged citadel; or, after Calais itself had surrendered, on 7 January, would be able to retake it before the French could consolidate their hold. Between 5 and 10 January, orders were issued for mass levies and the impressment of shipping.[37] (It may not be a coincidence that 5 January was the first day of the crisis on which leading peers – Arundel, Shrewsbury, Pembroke, the Lord Admiral – were present at the Council; before that decisions were being taken by clerics and administrators.) These preparations were in turn frustrated by the violent storm which blew up on the night of 9–10 January ('the Devil was raised up and become French') and put the English fleet out of action. The levies were therefore disbanded on 12 January.[38]

Guisnes, however, still held out. Under prompting from Philip, and with the promise of a Flemish fleet, the Council gave orders for a second expeditionary force on 17 January; but, since the troops were not to report until the end of the month, there seems to have been little sense of urgency.[39] Guisnes clearly mattered to Philip, if only for the defence of the Flemish frontier; but was of little interest to the English Council, in spite of the valour of Lord Grey. The fall of Guisnes and the threat of invasion of England itself led to the cancellation of these orders.[40]

Given that serious preparations did not start until 1 January, no Tudor government could have got reinforcements to Calais before Rysbank fell on 2 January, or assembled an expeditionary force to fight its way into the town before 7 January. The critical factor at this stage was therefore the speed of collapse; and that focuses attention on Lord Wentworth and on his subordinates: in particular Nicholas Alexander, commanding Newnham Bridge, and John Harleston at Rysbank.

The charges are essentially four: first, Wentworth's reluctance till 2 January to open the sluices and flood the marshes with sea water – all the more necessary since the hard frost meant that the French could cross the normally impassable marshes; secondly, the rapidity with which Rysbank and Newnham Bridge were abandoned; thirdly, Wentworth's abandonment of the castle at Calais when it was attacked; and, fourthly, his surrender of the town so quickly after the castle was taken. Explanations can be offered for all these. Wentworth believed that, in the event of a long siege, letting in sea water would make it impossible to brew beer in the town.[41] Rysbank and Newnham Bridge were certainly undermanned. (The establishment amounted to only some seventeen and thirteen men respectively.) Nevertheless, their collapse surprised the French, who found both forts well stocked with arms and were clearly at a loss to explain why Alexander (with Wentworth's consent) abandoned his post at the first or second volley; while Highfield was scathing about Harleston's behaviour at Rysbank.[42] As to the castle, Wentworth regarded it as a booby-trap: he would let the French in, then detonate a mine. Not surprisingly, it failed to go off.[43] Once the castle had fallen, the cost of further resistance would have been appalling in human terms. Coligny had expelled women and children as 'useless mouths' during his defence of St Quentin; Grey, a mere month earlier had put a French garrison to the sword for, or so he alleged, senseless resistance. Nevertheless, it was Wentworth's duty, albeit a cruel one, to hold out as long as possible; until relief arrived, or until the rigours of the winter campaign began to tell on the French.[44] (Henry II thought afterwards that the French would have been compelled to withdraw a day or two later by the storm which destroyed the English fleet).[45] That duty he failed to carry out.

The immediate reaction in London and Brussels was to look for treason. The Spaniards, particularly, pointed to Wentworth's Protestant sympathies as explanation of the collapse.[46] They also arrested Highfield, the Master of the Ordnance – under suspicion because he had been given honourable escort to the Flemish lines by his French counterpart, rather than taken prisoner for ransom. Highfield was sent to England, where he wrote a self-exculpatory account of events, but his fate is unknown.[47] Wentworth himself, Edward Grimston (the comptroller), Ralph Chamberlain (lieutenant of the castle), John Harleston (captain of Rysbank) and Nicholas Alexander (captain of Newnham Bridge) were all subsequently indicted for treason; charged with having secretly contacted Guise on 26 December, then having merely feigned resistance. The trials took place in 1559, after the principals had returned from captivity. Wentworth and Grimston were acquitted; Chamberlain and Harleston were found guilty but subsequently pardoned. Nothing is known of the fate of Alexander, who may have died in prison in France. Grimston said that the Queen had promised him a pardon if he were found guilty. It looks as if the charges were not pressed very hard at the beginning of the new reign, and in the form they were made are barely credible: 'feigned resistance' hardly fits the fury of the English assault on Calais castle after the French had first taken it.[48] Nevertheless, there was evidently a massive failure of nerve, culpable if understandable; and the chance of treason somewhere among the officers cannot be ruled out.

It is sometimes said that Philip deliberately stood idly by during the crisis – indeed, that he welcomed the fall of Calais. Philip's agent in Scotland, d'Assonleville, is reported to have said that the loss of Calais was all to the good, since Philip would now be able to reconquer it for himself.[49] Ambassadors, however, were always bound to put the best face on things in public; d'Assonleville was rebutting the jeers of the francophile party at the Scottish court. It is certainly true that Philip was more sensitive to the feelings of his Flemish than of his English subjects: they were, after all, shouldering a much greater share of the war effort, and Philip was engaged in particularly delicate negotiations with the States–General in Brussels. So, on the advice (ironically enough, in the light of later events) of Egmont, Horn and William of Orange, he refused to declare a state of war between Scotland and the Netherlands, and even allowed Flemish merchants to supply provisions for Calais after its fall.[50] Nevertheless, even from a purely Flemish point of view (the walls of Gravelines were far weaker than those of Calais), the loss of Calais was a serious blow which had to be kept secret from Charles V in his retirement in case the news damaged his health. Philip was clearly furious; and he worked hard in February 1558 to persuade a reluctant English Council to try to recapture the town.[51]

The charge against Philip is based on what Lord Grey told Henry II: that he and Wentworth had appealed five times to Philip for help before the arrival of Guise's army, and had had no reply.[52] Philip, on the other hand, maintained that he had warned Wentworth several times, but that no notice had been taken; worse, that Wentworth had spurned Spanish help.[53] As we saw, Noyelle may have sent Wentworth warning as early as 18 December. There is no trace of any request by Wentworth for help from Philip until 31 December; and then only in vague and non-specific terms.[54] On 2 January he asked for three or four hundred arquebusiers, repeating the request more desperately next day, and also asking for Flemish ships.[55] The arquebusiers were in fact sent on 3 January but were beaten back, while Caravajal, Philip's admiral, tried and, because of French possession of Rysbank, failed to land troops.[56] Spanish troops were certainly sent to Guisnes, where they played a vital role in Grey's defence.

Why was Wentworth so slow in asking for help? Equally, why did Philip not back up his warnings with aid, even uninvited? Clearly, Philip, Wentworth and the English Council all believed that a full-scale attack was unthinkable; the French could only be thinking of a raid, and a few burnt farms would be the end of the affair. In spite of the warning of 18 December, Philip was still disbanding his army on the 23rd, and, when help was asked for, could supply only a detachment from the Gravelines garrison rather than a full-scale army.[57] Moreover, the mistrust between Philip and the English plays its part here. Philip was bound, under the terms of the 1554 treaty, not to introduce his troops into English garrisons. The allegations that he meant to do so, in order to take over England (like the French in Scotland) was a staple of opposition propaganda which Wentworth, given his religious views, may well have been inclined to believe.[58] The introduction of Spanish or Flemish troops could have been contemplated only as a last resort.

'On the sea, Calais was lost and won.' This is true in a limited sense: Guise's attack depended on support from the sea; French men-of-war played a vital part in transporting supplies and especially the heavy guns with which Guise was to batter Rysbank and the castle from the coast.[59] It is not true, as is often implied, that this was because the English had no fleet at sea at all during December: a respectable squadron, though inferior to the French 'flying squadron', was in fact in the Narrow Seas on 29 December.[60] Nor did the French fleet sever communications between Dover and Calais; English and Flemish ships sailed back and forth between Dover and Gravelines with impunity. It was the capture of Rysbank, not the French fleet, which prevented communication with Calais; and, had the troops been ready at Dover, there seems no doubt they could have been brought over to Gravelines at any time up to the famous storm of 9–10 January. How far the Council or the naval officers can be blamed for this failure to stop French coastal movements is impossible to say in the absence of any firm evidence of what the English squadron was doing. No doubt it could have been more successful had it been alerted earlier. But 'control of the Channel', in the sense of denying use of the sea to the enemy, was not really possible under existing conditions of shipbuilding and navigational techniques.

The English Council, Philip and the authorities at Calais were all over-confident. Guise's movements were ambiguous; there could be no certainty that they were aimed at Calais. Nevertheless, the size of his army should have indicated that something more than a border-raid, whether into English or Flemish territory, was intended. All three parties seem to have been reluctant to believe the worst. Yet their incredulity, their inability to believe that the French could be so foolhardy as to besiege a fortress as powerful as Calais in deep winter, is understandable. Guise's organisation, the detailed planning (down to wattle rafts covered with pitch as a support for guns on marshy and sandy ground) was impeccable; the rough Gascon soldier, Blaise de Monluc, joked that Guise would have made a good 'clerk of the Parlement of Paris'.[61] The French were lucky too that the weather was exceptionally cold and dry, so that they were able to cross the marshes, attack Rysbank and cut off communications with Gravelines.[62] Even then, more determined resistance could have spelt ruin. Henry and Guise had gambled against heavy odds, and won.

While England was mourning the loss of Calais, Scotland seemed to be sinking deeper into French control. The long-deferred marriage of Mary Stuart and the Dauphin took place in April 1558, adding to the triumph of the duke of Guise, Mary's uncle. In November the Scottish Parliament granted the 'crown matrimonial' to the Dauphin. Scotland in fact remained a major threat to the English: some 9000 troops were involved in the summer of 1558, and the cost, of £15,000 a month, was about equal to that being spent on the Navy.[63] (Queen Elizabeth was insistent in 1559 on the need, because of the expense of war, for peace with Scotland.[64]) At one stage the English negotiated for 3000 German mercenaries to be sent to the border, only to be overruled by Philip, who, as always, would not take Scottish affairs seriously and wanted the troops for his own army.[65] The fall of Calais stirred fears that Berwick would soon follow; and the setting in train from August 1558 of the rebuilding (already mooted in 1557) made it the only town in the British Isles to be equipped with a complete set of the new-style angle-bastioned walls to withstand modern artillery.[66]

In general 1558 was a dismal year for the English. In February the Council gave a reasoned refusal to Philip's demand for an immediate force to retake Calais. It would need, they argued, 20,000 men. The Queen's revenue would not support it. English soldiers were 'inapt and unwonted to lie abroad' in winter. In any case, false hopes of recovery should not be raised, given the number of Englishmen 'ready against their duties to make uproars and stirs among ourselves',[67] 'One would like to see more spirit, more resentment about Calais, and more memory of the ancient virtues of their forbears', commented Philip's minister Granvelle.[68]

Thomas Smith's remark about men hanging their heads in shame at the musters is borne out by a good deal of recorded evidence.[69] Sir Thomas Cheyne resigned as Warden of the Cinque Ports, evidently exasperated by the contradictory orders on assembling troops for Calais. Robert Cockrell was hanged at Canterbury for saying 'he would serve the French King before he would serve the Queen's Majesty'. John Colby was reported to the Council for refusing to lead a company of East Anglian levies. Cuthbert Vaughan's arquebusiers deserted *en route* for the borders, while a disgruntled band of Calais veterans demonstrated for back pay. Proclamations were issued against deserting sailors; and desertion from the army was made felony at the insistence of the lords in Parliament.[70]

The financial strain was considerable. A forced loan had

been levied in the summer of 1557, and the Council records are full of orders to deal with reluctant lenders. Nevertheless, some £109,000 was raised – not dissimilar to the £112,000 raised by Henry VIII in 1542 or the £120,000 of 1545.[71] A parliament met in January 1558, in the immediate aftermath of the Calais disaster. It chafed at a government demand for a subsidy of 8s. in the pound on land, and 5s. 4d. on goods, some four times the normal rate, and for two 'fifteenths-and-tenths'. This would have raised £300,000 spread over two years. But the eventual rate of subsidy (4s. and 2s. 8d.) to be paid immediately (£140,000), and a 'fifteenth-and-tenth' payable in November (£28,000), produced as much as the government had wished to raise in 1558. Parliamentary objections were rather to committing the country in advance to taxation in 1559. Members preferred to meet again in November 1558 to reconsider the situation. This was very far from a 'taxpayer's strike': £168,000 in a year was as much as had ever been granted to Henry VIII.[72]

Nor does ill-will explain the various excuses put forward by county authorities in 1558 for not producing their quotas of armed men. The country was very hard hit by a shortage of labour. The famine of 1555–7 had already produced very high mortality – not so much, presumably, directly from starvation (though there is some evidence of this) as through malnutrition, lowering resistance to disease. Over the five years 1556–60 the death-rate was two to three times the usual level, and the total population was reduced by some 20 per cent. The peak came in 1558 with the 'sweating sickness' (apparently a virulent form of influenza). In Leicestershire the evidence of wills shows about seven times as many people dying as in a normal year. Many more were seriously ill for a time; the fleet which put in to Portsmouth in August 1558 had about half its men sick, including Lord Admiral Clinton. Not surprisingly, county authorities were reluctant to take scarce labour away from the harvest for the army.[73]

Apart from the Scottish war, the main activity in 1558 was at sea. In January, Howard was replaced as Admiral by Clinton, who had held the post in Edward's reign; the change was at Philip's instigation.[74] Clinton and Paget supported Philip's plan for a great effort to recapture Calais.

Once it was clear that the Council would not agree, the navy became (always with further promises of pioneers and miners) England's most useful contribution to the war effort, as far as Philip was concerned. In June a squadron of English ships, firing broadsides from the sea, helped Egmont to victory over a French army which had set out from Calais to take Gravelines. The English and Flemish fleets then mounted a large-scale attack on Brest, presumably as a bargaining counter for the return of Calais; 140 English ships, mostly of course merchantmen, and thirty Flemish ones were involved.[75] The campaign awaits its historian, but it was clearly badly planned; there are no intelligence reports or position papers in the archives. Brest itself was too well defended; instead Clinton confined himself to doing considerable damage to the neighbouring fishing port of le Conquêt and the surrounding countryside before being beaten off by an army of Breton peasants. The operation was a disaster and the Council seems to have been contemplating taking action against Clinton; but the political crisis which blew up as the Queen lay dying intervened.[76]

Peace negotiations had begun in May 1558. Philip and Henry had fought each other to a stalemate, and had exhausted their financial credit. With Calais to set against St Quentin, neither was too humiliated to treat; and this equilibrium was underlined in May–June 1558 with Egmont's victory for Philip at Gravelines and Guise's victory at Thionville, on France's north-eastern frontier. Gravelines may have helped Philip decide that Calais was, after all, dispensable; at any rate, in the peace negotiations he evidently regarded the demand for the return of Calais as an irritation to which he was constrained by the English. Since Henry showed himself obdurate on the issue, pressure was brought to bear on the English Council to give way; and it seems to have been preparing to do so when Queen Mary died.[77] When the talks resumed in the new year, Elizabeth was ready, as a last resort, to sacrifice Calais, provided that a face-saving formula was devised (Calais to be returned to England after eight years, on payment of an indemnity, if the English refrained from attacking France in that time), and peace with Scotland was included.[78]

On a European scale the war had been momentous. The French presence in Italy had collapsed ignominiously; for the next 150 years Italy was to be dominated by Spain. On the other hand, the French gains of 1552, of the three bishoprics of Metz, Toul and Verdun, in Lorraine, were retained, inaugurating that push towards a Rhine frontier which was to be characteristic of French policy in the seventeenth century. Calais, too, was retained, while Mary of Guise continued to rule in Scotland on behalf of a daughter who was much more a princess of France than Queen of Scots, with the prospect that Scotland would remain forever attached to the French Crown, and the possibility that England would take the same road if Elizabeth died childless. But, if the war had ostensibly strengthened the French position in Scotland, it had also stimulated a reaction against it. Helped by English arms and money, the Lords of the Congregation were, in 1559–60, to bring about the formal withdrawal of Scotland from papal obedience, and the official introduction of a Reformed church which was to move Scotland decisively, though not yet irreversibly, into the English orbit.

The most striking political effect of the war in England was the modernisation of the army. The navy, whatever mistakes had been made in handling it, was not in bad condition. Henry VIII had left it superior to any in Atlantic waters and, although its efficiency had suffered since, improvement began before the outbreak of war. The defects of the army lay deeper. The call-up of the county levies for the relief of Calais and the subsequent preparations to resist invasion showed up the deficiencies of the militia system. Assembling a force took time, and when troops appeared they were badly equipped. There had been confusion between two methods of recruitment: that by which noblemen and gentlemen supplied specified numbers of their tenants and servants; and the militia system, the obligation on all able-bodied men to turn out, properly equipped, for defence.[79] Since 1544 the division between the two functions had become blurred, as the militia came to be called upon (as in January 1558) to provide troops for foreign service. Commissioners for Musters found landlords trying to hold back their tenants from service against the day on which they would have to provide their own band. The provision of weapons was based on the 1285 Statute of Westminster, under which the modestly better-off (£10 a year in lands, or owning goods worth £13 6s. 8d.) were to provide a complete set of armour and weapons for themselves, and the poor were supposed to be fitted out from communal stores provided by each parish. The non-fulfilment of these obligations had been a scandal for some time. Out of a levy of a thousand men who arrived at Dover in January 1558, fewer than 200 were properly equipped, and this was not untypical; nor could their deficiencies be made up elsewhere, the resources of the great lords adding only a small amount of extra equipment, while that provided from government armouries was 'so evil as the soldiers utterly refuse to wear them'.[80]

The parliament which met in January 1558 made modernisation of defence its first priority after taxation. One bill tightened up the system for musters, imposing penalties for absence and for giving or accepting bribes. Another reformed the law for weapons and equipment, introducing a graduated income scale which made provision for modern weapons such as pikes and arquebuses, and also improved the supervision of parish armouries. The measure originated in the Lords and produced misgivings in the Commons, mainly about its cost to individuals and to local communities; nevertheless, with some concessions the bills were enacted to form the basis of the Elizabethan militia system.[81]

A general militia obligation, however, could not produce an army which could measure up to European professional standards; skill was needed to use pikes and firearms at all, and discipline and training to use them effectively. This problem had exercised a number of thinkers, most notably Thomas Wyatt, who had presented a scheme to Protector Somerset for a standing cadre of highly trained men in each county under the command of a paid professional. A rather similar scheme was drawn up about 1560 by Richard Barkhede, who was scathing about the military abilities of his compatriots. 'What tenderlings the great part of our young gentlemen are, preferring fine clothes to lusty horsemanship'; how feeble were the foot; how little trouble was taken about weapons, so that when troops turned up at Dover for Calais, they 'were constrained to tarry till armourers were sent for to London to leather, buckle, and fit their arms'. 12,000 trained soldiers, boasted Colonel Lazarus Schwendi, Philip's colonel of foot, could easily conquer England. What was needed was a skilled, select militia, officered by professional captains; a scheme which, in a modified way, was to be put into effect with the Elizabethan 'trained band' system.[82]

The war had produced its share of horrors, for the most part untraceable but occasionally breaking to the surface of events: the master-gunner of Newnham Bridge having his head shot off; Lord Grey's son clambering over 'naked and new slain carcases, some of them yet . . . groaning under our feet' on his way to parley at Guisnes; Foxe's story of the stout Calais Protestants, John Thorp and his wife, wandering helplessly through the Pale, their young child 'carried away of the soldiers' but miraculously rediscovered in an inn in England.[83] Readers with a taste for heroics have to look among the savage skirmishes along the Scottish border, at the resistance of Lord Grey at Guisnes, or at the battle of the *Mary Rose* against overpowering odds in the Channel.[84] No notable commanders emerged, and the belief that Philip might endear himself to his multifarious subjects by prowess in the field was dashed by his evident dislike of military life.

Mary's most distinguished councillor, Cardinal Pole, disapproved of the war, writing dignified remonstrances to Paul IV and withdrawing from an active role in the conduct of affairs; one result of the war was, of course, the Pope's depriving Pole of his legateship, although his failure to restore the cardinal when peace was made with Philip in September 1557 was owing to theological suspicions and old personal animosities. The churchmen and administrators who formed the working core of the Council were, except for Paget, always half-hearted about the war, and concerned to prevent a repetition of the financial disasters of the 1540s. Their reluctance to commit more than a bare minimum of resources succeeded on the Scottish front and failed disastrously at Calais. There is no doubt that more could have been spent on Calais, that the castle could have been modernised, that the garrison, even in winter, should have been at more than peacetime strength. The fall of Calais led to a sudden flush of military expenditure: equipping Clinton's fleet, fortifying Berwick, commissioning Gresham to buy in large supplies of arms and ammunition in the Netherlands, even recruiting German professional soldiers. The Council's reluctance to embark again on inflationary policies is understandable. Nevertheless, it had some leeway, even in 1558, when the Antwerp debt was only a fifth of that run up by Elizabeth two years later.[85] With hindsight we can see that pennies spent in 1557 might have been worth shillings a year later.

On 9 January 1558 the Queen's instruction to Vice-Admiral Woodhouse suggested that it might 'please God to give you the rule of the Narrow Seas'. Next day she knew Calais had fallen: 'now pleased Almighty God to dispose otherwise'.[86] Historians are less keen than Queen Mary and her opponents to invoke divine interference as an explanation of events. Lack of enthusiasm for the war, lack of inspiration on Philip's part, bad leadership by the Council, bad morale, or worse, among the defenders of Calais, go a long way towards explaining the sorry results of the French war. But, in the sense that these do not provide a sufficient explanation, contemporaries were surely right: factors outside human control played their part. In modern terms, luck ran against the Queen.

# List of Abbreviations

| | |
|---|---|
| *APC* | *Acts of the Privy Council*, new series J. R. Dasent (ed.), I–VII (London, 1890–1907) |
| *Agric. HR* | *Agricultural History Review* |
| *BIHR* | *Bulletin of the Institute of Historical Research* |
| BL | British Library |
| BL Add. | British Library, Additional Manuscripts |
| BL Harl. | British Library, Harleian Manuscripts |
| BL Lansd. | British Library, Lansdowne Manuscripts |
| BL Vesp. | British Library, Cotton Manuscript, Vespasian |
| *CJ* | *Commons' Journals* T. Vardon and T. E. May (eds), I (London, 1852) |
| *CPR* | *Calendar of Patent Rolls*, Edward VI, Mary, Elizabeth (London, 1924–39) |
| *CSP Dom.* | *Calendar of State Papers, Domestic Series*, I (London, 1856) |
| *CSP For.* | *Calendar of State Papers, Foreign Series*, Edward VI and Mary, W. Turnbull (ed) (London, 1861) |
| *CSP Sp.* | *Calendar of State Papers, Spanish*, XI–XIII, Royal Tyler (ed.) (London, 1916–54) |
| *CSP Ven.* | *Calendar of State Papers, Venetian*, IV–VI, R. Brown, C. Bentinck and H. Brown (eds) (London, 1864–98) |
| *DNB* | *Dictionary of National Biography* |
| *EcHR* | *Economic History Review* |
| *EHR* | *English Historical Review* |
| HLRO | House of Lords Records Office |
| HMC | Historical Manuscripts Commission |
| LCRO | London Corporation Record Office |
| *LJ* | *Lords' Journals*, I (London, 1846) |
| *L & P* | *Letters and Papers, Foreign and Domestic, of the Reign of Henry VIII*, J. S. Brewer, J. Gairdner and R. H. Brodie (eds) (London, 1864–1932) |
| NRO | Northampton Record Office |
| PRO | Public Record Office |
| *Proc. Br. Acad.* | *Proceedings of the British Academy* |
| SP | State Papers |
| *STC* | *A Short Title Catalogue . . .*, ed. A. W. Pollard and G. R. Redgrave (Bibliographical Soc., 1926) |
| *TRHS* | *Transactions of the Royal Historical Society* |
| *VCH* | *Victoria County History* |

# Notes on Further Reading

*Note.* For abbreviations, see List of Abbreviations. Place of publication is London unless otherwise stated.

## 1. CONSERVATISM AND CONSENT IN PARLIAMENT, 1547–59

The *Lords' Journals* (1846) and the *Commons' Journals* (1852) are essential reading. The Lords Journal for the first Marian parliament is missing, and that for Elizabeth's first parliament needs to be supplemented by E. Jeffries Davis, 'An Unpublished Manuscript for the Lords' Journals for April and May 1559', *EHR*, XXVIII (1913) 531–42.

There is a great dearth of secondary material for the parliaments of Edward and Mary, although the projected early-Tudor volumes of the History of Parliament will obviously fill the gap. The only general survey is a simple study by R. K. Gilkes, *The Tudor Parliament* (1969). W. K. Jordan's volumes *Edward VI: The Young King* (1968) and *Edward VI: The Threshold of Power* (1970) provide a narrative account of events in Edward's parliaments, but the statistics and some of the assertions about the origins of bills need to be treated with great caution. The only in-print study of a Marian parliament is difficult to obtain: M. A. R. Graves, 'The House of Lords and the Politics of Opposition, April–May 1554', in *W. P. Morrell: A Tribute*, ed. G. A. Wood and P. S. O'Connor (Dunedin, 1973), pp. 1–20.

The parliament of 1559 has been described by J. E. Neale in *Elizabeth I and Her Parliaments, 1559–1581*, vol. 1 (1953); see also his important article 'The Elizabethan Acts of Supremacy and Uniformity', in *EHR*, LXV (1950) 304–32.

Since the completion of this chapter there has appeared a significant article by Professor G. R. Elton, entitled 'Parliament in the Sixteenth Century: Functions and Fortunes' in *Historical Journal*, 22 (1979), pp. 255–78.

## 2. REHABILITATING THE DUKE OF NORTHUMBERLAND: POLITICS AND POLITICAL CONTROL, 1549–53

In terms of printed sources, remains of Northumberland's official correspondence with Cecil (1551–3) lie scattered among the State Papers Domestic in the Public Record Office, London, and are therefore inaccessible to all but the specialist. In any case, such materials reveal very little of Northumberland's political designs. Printed contemporary sources provide greater detail about his career, but create their own special problems of interpretation. For example, the official version of the *coup d'état* of 1549, in the *Acts of the Privy Council of England*, ed. J. R. Dasent, vols II–IV (1891–2), was written up weeks after the fact by Northumberland's triumphant faction. The diplomatic dispatches of François van der Delft and Jehan Scheyfve, the Imperial ambassadors, constitute indispensable eyewitness accounts of comings and goings at Edward VI's court. Even so, the envoys' explanations of the duke's moves, published in *Calendar of Letters, Despatches, and State Papers, Relating to the Negotiations between England and Spain, Preserved in the Archives at Vienna, Simancas, and Elsewhere*, ed. R. Tyler, vols IX–XI (1912–16), often merely repeat rumours or Northumberland's authorised version of events. Although *The Chronicle and Political Papers of Edward VI*, ed. W. K. Jordan (1966), also contains some material dictated by Northumberland's men in the King's Household, it adds unwitting evidence of the Council's management of state business. For the royal proclamations issued during Northumberland's presidency, see *Tudor Royal Proclamations*, ed. P. L. Hughes and J. F. Larkin, vol. I (New Haven, Conn., and London, 1964). A few of Paget's letters to Northumberland, including the plan for the reform of the Council's work, are printed in *The Letters of William, Lord Paget of Beaudesert, 1547–1563*, ed. Barrett L. Beer and Sybil M. Jack (Camden Society, 4th ser., XIII, 1974), pp. 1–141.

In terms of secondary material, Northumberland is the subject of two biographies, neither of which adequately comprehends his career after 1549. One may ignore Philip Lindsay's *The Queenmaker: A Portrait of John Dudley, Viscount Lisle, Earl of Warwick, and Duke of Northumberland, 1502–1553* (1951), a factually outdated popular life. Barrett Beer's professional, archivally based study *Northumberland* (Kent, Ohio, 1973) unaccountably ignores too much of what its subtitle advertises as *The Political Career of John Dudley, Earl of Warwick and Duke of Northumberland*. However, by following the guide provided by the index to D. E. Hoak, *The King's Council in the Reign of Edward VI* (Cambridge, 1976), the serious student can fill in the gaps for the period after October 1549. The significance of Northumberland's activities as President of the Council is argued in D. E. Hoak, 'Re-writing the History of Tudor Politics and Government: The Regimes of Somerset and Northumberland', *Journal of the Rutgers University Libraries*, XL, (1978) 4–13. M. L. Bush has successfully rewritten the history of *The Government Policy of Protector Somerset* (London and Montreal, 1975). W. R. D. Jones outlines Northumberland's government policies in *The Mid-Tudor Crisis 1539–1563* (1973), but C. S. L. Davies, *Peace, Print and Protestantism 1450–1558* (St Albans, 1977), and G. R. Elton, *Reform and Reformation: England 1509–1558* (Cambridge, Mass., 1977) incorporate more recent research on this subject. In *Edward VI: The Young King* (1968) and *Edward VI: The Threshold of Power* (1970) W. K. Jordan sets out the fullest account of Northumberland's Edwardian career, but *caveat lector*: Professor Jordan has misread and misdated several key documents, and consequently has built up an unhistorical picture of some of the duke's actions. For this reason Jordan's interpretation of Northumberland's political motives is suspect. For Northumberland's use of one of Edward VI's prerogative powers, see R. W. Heinze, *The Proclamations of the Tudor Kings* (Cambridge, 1976). On the all-important subject of the duke's administration of royal finance, see the following: F. C. Dietz, *Finances of Edward VI and Mary* (Northampton, Mass., 1918); W. C. Richardson, *History of the Court of Augmentations 1536–1554* (Baton Rouge, La, 1961); A. Feavearyear, *The Pound Sterling: A History of English Money*, 2nd ed., rev. E. V. Morgan (Oxford, 1963); and C. E. Challis, *The Tudor Coinage* (New York, 1978). On Northumberland's political calculations during Edward VI's last days, see S. T. Bindoff, 'A Kingdom at Stake', *History Today*, III (1953) 642–8. For the text and a discussion of 'The Saying of John Late Duke of Northumberland upon the Scaffold, 1553', see W. K. Jordan and M. R. Gleason in *Harvard Library Bulletin*, XXIII (1975) 139–75, 324–55.

## 3. THE MARIAN COUNCIL REVISITED

There is no adequate study of the Marian Privy Council in print. An exemplary work is D. E. Hoak, *The King's Council in the Reign of Edward VI* (Cambridge, 1976). For a discussion of the problems of studying the Council, see G. R. Elton, 'Why the History of the Early Tudor Council Remains Unwritten', *Studies in Tudor and Stuart Politics and Government*, 2 vols (1974), vol. I, pp. 308ff.; and 'Tudor Government: The Points of Contact. II: The Council', *TRHS*, 5th ser., XXV (1975) 195ff. Cromwell's reforms of the Council are discussed in G. R. Elton, *The Tudor Revolution in Government* (Cambridge, 1953). Further information on the Tudor Council can be found in J. A. Guy 'Wolsey, the Council, and the Council Courts', *EHR*, XC (1976) 481ff, and *The Cardinal's Court: The Impact of Thomas Wolsey in Star Chamber* (1977); W. H. Dunham, 'Henry VIII's Whole Council and Its Parts', *Huntington Library Quarterly*, VII (1943) 7ff., and 'Wolsey's Rule of the King's Whole Council', *American Historical Review*, XLIX (1944) 644ff.; and Michael Pulman, *The Elizabethan Privy Council in the Fifteen-Seventies* (Berkeley, Calif., 1971).

The traditional view of the reign can be found not only in the works of A. F. Pollard, E. H. Harbison and D. M. Loades, but also in the biographies of the Councillors, such as J. A. Muller, *Stephen Gardiner and the Tudor Reaction* (1926); F. G. Emmison, *Tudor Secretary: Sir William Petre at Court and Home* (1961); and S. R. Gammon, *Statesman and Schemer: William, First Lord Paget – Tudor Minister* (Newton Abbot, 1973). A more positive view of the reign can be found in *A Machiavellian Treatise*, ed. Peter S. Donaldson (Cambridge, 1975); G. R. Elton, *Reform and Reformation: England 1509–1558* (Cambridge, Mass., 1977); Joel Hurstfield, 'Corruption and Reform under Edward VI and Mary: The Example of Wardship', *EHR*, LXVIII (1953) 22ff.; Peter Clark, *English Provincial Society from the*

*Reformation to the Revolution: Religion, Politics and Society in Kent, 1550–1640*
(1977); and the various articles published by the other contributors to this
volume. For faction, see E. W. Ives, 'Faction at the Court of Henry VIII:
The Fall of Anne Boleyn', *History*, LVII (1972) 169ff.; G. R. Elton,
'Thomas Cromwell's Decline and Fall', in his *Studies*, vol. I, pp. 189ff.;
Hoak, *The King's Council*; Conyers Read, 'Factions in the English Privy
Council under Elizabeth', *Annual Report of the American Historical Association*,
(1911), pp. 111ff.

The various collections of State Papers provide most of the necessary
primary information, with the exception of the dispatches of ambassador
Noailles. Although his information about faction in the Council lacks
credibility owing to his reliance on informers, his other observations are
of value. René Aubert de Vertot compiled some of his letters in the
eighteenth century, but his and C. Villaret's *Ambassades de Messieurs de
Noailles en Angleterre*, 5 vols (Leyden, 1763) is incomplete. See E. H.
Harbison, *Rival Ambassadors at the Court of Queen Mary* (Princeton, NJ,
1940) pp. 343–51, for further information on the Noailles correspondence.

## 4. THE EMERGENCE OF URBAN POLICY, 1536–58

Tudor social and economic policy has more often been approached from
the viewpoint of theory than from that of practice. W. G. Zeeveld's
*Foundations of Tudor Policy* (Cambridge, Mass., 1948; 2nd edn London,
1969) pioneered the theoretical approach, and the broad outlines of his
work left their mark in F. Caspari, *Humanism and the Social Order in Tudor
England* (Chicago, 1954); J. K. McConica, *English Humanists and Reformation
Politics under Henry VIII and Edward VI* (Oxford, 1965); A. B. Ferguson,
*The Articulate Citizen and the English Renaissance* (Durham, NC, 1965); and
W. R. D. Jones, *The Tudor Commonwealth, 1529–1559* (1970). Of contemporary writings, Starkey's *Dialogue between Reginald Pole and Thomas Lupset*,
ed. K. M. Burton (1948), and *A Discourse of the Common Weal of this
Realm of England*, ed. E. Lamond (Cambridge, 1893 and later edns),
probably written by Sir Thomas Smith, are the most significant.

The important essays by F. J. Fisher, 'Commercial Trends and Policy
in Sixteenth Century England', *EcHR*, x (1940) 95–117, and L. Stone,
'State Control in Sixteenth Century England', *EcHR*, XVIII (1947) 103–20,
discuss trade policy directly, and are implicitly valuable for consideration
of all domestic policy issues. G. R. Elton, in 'State Planning in Early-Tudor
England', *EcHR*, 2nd ser., XIII (1961) 433–9, repr. in his *Studies in Tudor
and Stuart Politics and Government*, 2 vols (Cambridge, 1974), vol. I, pp.
285–93, once questioned whether one could discuss policy in the pre-Eliza-
bethan period at all but he himself has provided two valuable attempts
to link theory with the formulation of policy initiatives: 'Reform by Statute,
Thomas Starkey's Dialogue and Thomas Cromwell's Policy', *Proc. Br.
Acad.*, LIV (1968) 165–88, repr. in his *Studies*, vol. II, pp. 236–58; and
*Reform and Renewal: Thomas Cromwell and the Common Weal* (Cambridge,
1973).

The currently intense interest in urban development in the Tudor period seems to derive its inspiration, albeit somewhat belatedly, from the work of W. G. Hoskins, whose *Provincial England* (1963) and *Local History in England* (1959 and 1972) have been most instructive for this concern. The work of Peter Clark and Paul Slack has done much to bring Hoskins's approach to more general attention, and provides a more immediate springboard for much current work. See especially their joint effort *Crisis and Order in English Towns, 1500–1700* (1972), in which the introduction is especially suggestive, and their summary *English Towns in Transition, 1500–1700* (Oxford, 1976), which is easily the best introduction. Peter Clark's *The Early Modern Town: A Reader* (1976) reprints some classic articles which place Tudor urban development in perspective, and John Patten's *English Towns, 1500–1700* (1977) is a useful discussion by an urban geographer. R. B. Dobson discusses the background for mid-Tudor urban decay in 'Urban Decline in Late Medieval England', *TRHS*, 5th ser., XXVII (1977) 1–22, and, though he probably underestimates the extent to which population began to grow before the demographic crisis of the late 1550s, Charles Phythian-Adams's essay 'Urban Decay in Late Medieval England', in *Towns in Societies*, ed. P. Abrams and E. A. Wrigley (Cambridge, 1978), is also important. I have tried to explore an important aspect of town–Crown relations in the mid-century period in 'The Incorporation of Boroughs, 1540–1558', *History*, LXII (1977) 24–42. Alan Everitt has made several signal contributions to the consideration of urban development, and his essay 'The Market Towns', in *The Agrarian History of England and Wales*, vol. IV: *1500–1640*, ed. Joan Thirsk (Cambridge, 1967), and repr. in Clark, *The Early Modern Town*, is especially stimulating.

Worthy studies of particular towns are far too numerous to catalogue here, but the following are particularly important for light they shed on town–Crown relations: A. D. Dyer, *The City of Worcester in the Sixteenth Century* (Leicester, 1973); D. M. Palliser, 'York Under the Early Tudors: The Trading Life of a Northern Capital', *Perspectives in English Urban History*, ed: A. Everitt (1973), pp. 39–59; and C. G. Parsloe, 'The Growth of a Borough Constitution, Newark-upon-Trent, 1549–1688', *TRHS*, 4th ser., XXII (1940) 171–98.

## 5. SOCIAL POLICY AND THE CONSTRAINTS OF GOVERNMENT, 1547–58

Attitudes towards social reform have attracted more historical attention than their application. W. R. D. Jones, *The Tudor Commonwealth 1529–1559* (1970), is a good general survey; and the most famous tract, Sir Thomas Smith's *A Discourse of the Common Weal* is accessible (though wrongly attributed to Hales) in E. Lamond's edition (Cambridge, 1893 and 1929). H. C. White, *Social Criticism in Popular Religious Literature of the Sixteenth Century* (New York, 1944), and A. B. Ferguson, *The Articulate Citizen and the English Renaissance* (Durham, NC, 1965), are also useful, although the latter is inclined to impose preconceived categories on the literature and to exaggerate its novel features. The social and economic background at the beginning of the period is surveyed by W. G. Hoskins, *The Age of Plunder: The England of Henry VIII, 1500–1547* (1976), and some fluctuations are described in idem, 'Harvest Fluctuations and English Economic History 1480–1619', *Agric. HR*, xii (1964) 28–46; P. Slack, 'Mortality Crises and Epidemic Disease', in *Health, Medicine and Mortality in the Sixteenth Century*, ed. C. Webster (Cambridge, 1979); and J. D. Gould, *The Great Debasement: Currency and the Economy in Mid-Tudor England* (Oxford, 1970).

As for social policy itself, some periods and problems have been more studied than others. G. R. Elton, *Reform and Renewal: Thomas Cromwell and the Common Weal* (Cambridge, 1973), authoritatively analyses part of the earlier development, and M. L. Bush, *The Government Policy of Protector Somerset* (London and Montreal, 1975), gives an admirably cogent and densely argued account of the later 1540s. The 1550s have yet to enjoy similar treatment. There is information on the period of Northumberland's ascendancy in W. K. Jordan, *Edward VI: The Threshold of Power* (1970), and clearer views of his government from particular angles in R. W. Heinze, *The Proclamations of the Tudor Kings* (Cambridge, 1976) chs 8 and 9, and D. E. Hoak, *The King's Council in the Reign of Edward VI* (Cambridge, 1976) ch. 6. Mary's reign remains uncharted territory.

Among special areas of policy, agrarian issues have fared better than most. The editor's chapter 'Enclosing and Engrossing' in *The Agrarian History of England and Wales*, iv: *1500–1640*, ed. J. Thirsk (Cambridge, 1967), is the best general account, and there is detailed material in M. Beresford, *The Lost Villages of England* (1954), and 'The Poll Tax and Census of Sheep, 1549', *Agric. HR*, i (1953) 9–15, and ii (1954) 15–29. On economic policy generally, F. J. Fisher, 'Commercial Trends and Policy in Sixteenth-Century England', *EcHR*, x (1940) 95–117, continues to stimulate, although its conclusions must be qualified now by Gould's findings (*The Great Debasement*, ch. 6). There are many insights in J. Thirsk, *Economic Policy and Projects* (Oxford, 1978). Policy towards and problems of towns are considered in R. Tittler's essay in this collection and the literature introduced in its bibliography. On the vexed problem of education and schools, see J. Simon, *Education and Society in Tudor England* (Cambridge, 1966), and N. Orme, *English Schools in the Middle Ages* (1973) ch. 10. On poor relief, the standard account remains E. M. Leonard, *The Early History of English Poor Relief* (Cambridge, 1900), a remarkable work for its date and still useful, though badly in need of revision. W. K. Jordan, *Philanthropy in England 1480–1660* (London and New York, 1959), surveys charitable achievements. C. S. L. Davies, 'Slavery and Protector Somerset: The Vagrancy Act of 1547', *EcHR*, 2nd ser., xix (1966) 533–49, analyses one important statute and clarifies much more besides.

The value of local studies can be seen in A. D. Dyer, *The City of Worcester in the Sixteenth Century* (Leicester, 1973), and W. T. MacCaffrey, *Exeter 1540–1640* (Cambridge, Mass., 1958) ch. 4. London, however, has been neglected. W. K. Jordan, *The Charities of London 1480–1660* (London and New York, 1960), and E. J. Davis, 'The Transformation of London', in *Tudor Studies*, ed. R. W. Seton-Watson (1924) pp. 257–314, fill in part of the background; the histories of individual hospitals – for instance, N. Moore, *The History of St. Bartholomew's Hospital*, 2 vols (1918), and E. G. O'Donoghue, *Bridewell Hospital*, 2 vols (1923–9) – are helpful; and there is a near-contemporary view of the hospital system (clouded perhaps by Elizabethan perspectives) in *John Howes' MS., 1582*, ed. W. Lempriere (1904), continued in *Tudor Economic Documents*, 3 vols, ed. R. H. Tawney and E. Power (1924), vol. III, pp. 421–43. But the subject needs re-examination in the light of the comparative Continental material, cited and discussed in B. Pullan, 'Catholics and the Poor in Early Modern Europe', *TRHS*, 5th ser. XXVI (1976) 15–34.

## 6. THE LEGACY OF THE SCHISM: CONFUSION, CONTINUITY AND CHANGE IN THE MARIAN CLERGY

The broad introduction to the ecclesiastical problems of the mid-Tudor period can be approached through A. G. Dickens, *The English Reformation* (1964), and Claire Cross, *Church and People, 1450–1660* (1976). A large-scale recent study of Mary's whole reign is Carolly Erickson, *Bloody Mary* (New York and London, 1978), to which H. F. M. Prescott, *A Spanish Tudor: The Life of 'Bloody Mary'*, (New York, 1940; 2nd edn 1952) can be added. On Pole himself, Dermot Fenlon, *Heresy and Obedience in Tridentine Italy* (1972), provides close analysis of his Italian experience, and W. Schenk, *Reginald Pole, Cardinal of England* (1950), is the best biography, though slight on the English mission. Then there are a number of articles on Pole: J. H. Crehan, 'The Return to Obedience: New Judgment on Cardinal Pole', *Month*, new ser., XIV (Oct 1955) 221–9, and 'St. Ignatius and Cardinal Pole', *Archivum Historicum Societatis Iesu*, XXV (1956) 72–98; J. P. Marmion, 'Cardinal Pole in Recent Studies', *Recusant History*, XIII, no. 1 (Apr 1975) 56–61; and R. H. Pogson, 'Revival and Reform in Mary Tudor's Church: A Question of Money', *Journal of Ecclesiastical History*, XXV (1974) 249–65, and 'Reginald Pole and the Priorities of Government in Mary Tudor's Church', *Historical Journal*, XVIII (1975) pp. 3–20. Examples of studies of the bishops with whom Pole worked are: A. M. Jagger, 'Bonner's Episcopal Visitation of London, 1554', *BIHR*, XLV (1972) 306–11; G. Alexander, 'Bonner and the Marian persecutions', *History*, LX (1975) 374–91; J. A. Muller, *Stephen Gardiner and the Tudor Reaction* (New York, 1926); and T. F. Shirley, *Thomas Thirlby, Tudor Bishop* (1964). The pressure on the episcopate as a whole is considered in Claire Cross, 'Churchmen and the Royal Supremacy', in *Church and Society in England: Henry VIII to James I*, ed. F. Heal and R. O'Day (1977); and their response to that pressure is considered in P. Hughes, 'A Hierarchy that Fought', *Clergy Review*, XVIII (Jan 1940) 25–39. An important article on the Marian reaction is D. M. Loades, 'The Enforcement of Reaction, 1553–1558', *Journal of Ecclesiastical History*, XVI (Apr 1965) 54–66.

The following works are of value in following up specific Marian problems. For the difficulties of the clergy. M. Bowker, *The Secular Clergy in the Diocese of Lincoln, 1495–1520* (Cambridge, 1968), and P. Heath, *The English Parish Clergy on the Eve of the Reformation* (1969), provide essential background; many themes are picked up in F. Heal, 'Economic Problems of the Clergy', in *Church and Society in England*, ed. Heal and O'Day. In the same volume, D. M. Palliser, 'Popular Reactions to the Reformation during the Years of Uncertainty, 1530–70', discusses some of the confusions of the period. On Protestantism and the martyrdoms, C. H. Garrett, *The Marian Exiles: A Study in the Origins of Elizabethan Puritanism* (Cambridge, 1938), has met criticism but remains important, and D. M. Loades, *The Oxford Martyrs* (1970), gives a wide-ranging analysis.

Among important local studies are A. G. Dickens, *Lollards and Protestants in the Diocese of York, 1509–58* (Oxford, 1959), and *The Marian Reaction in the Diocese of York* (St Anthony's Hall, XI–XII, 1957); C. Haigh, *Reformation and Resistance in Tudor Lancashire* (1975); J. E. Oxley, *The Reformation in Essex to the Death of Mary* (Manchester, 1965); and K. G. Powell, *The Marian Martyrs and the Reformation in Bristol* (Bristol, 1972). On monasticism, D. Knowles, *The Religious Orders in England* (Cambridge, 1959), gives the overall coverage; detailed aspects of the subject can be seen in G. Baskerville, 'Married Clergy and Pensioned Ex-religious in Norwich Diocese, 1555', *EHR*, XLVIII (1933) 43–64, 199–228, and in H. E. P. Grieve, 'The Deprived Married Clergy in Essex, 1553–61', *TRHS*, 4th ser., XXII (1940) 141–69. On education and the spread of ideas, J. Simon, *Education and Society in Tudor England* (Cambridge, 1966), can be supplemented by A. C. F. Beales 'Education under Mary Tudor', *Month*, new ser., XIII (1955) 342–51, and D. Cressey, 'Levels of Literacy in England, 1530–1730', *Historical Journal*, XX, no. 1 (1977) 1–23.

Among printed sources, Foxe's 'Book of Martyrs' is essential for gaining a sense of the strife of the period: *The Acts and Monuments of John Foxe*, 8 vols, ed. S. R. Cattley (1837–41). The scale of damage to church fabric can be seen in *Archdeacon Harpsfield's Visitation, 1557*, ed. L. E. Whatmore (Catholic Record Society, XLV–XLVI, 1950–1). Protestant views can be followed up in *Original Letters Relative to the English Reformation*, ed. H. Robinson, (Parker Society, 1846).

## 7.  PUBLIC OFFICE AND PRIVATE PROFIT: THE LEGAL ESTABLISHMENT IN THE REIGN OF MARY TUDOR

On the subject of lawyers and the legal system there are a number of sources, both contemporary and modern, available to most readers. Sir John Fortescue's *De Laudibus Angliae* ed. and trans. S. B. Chrimes (Cambridge, 1942), is particularly good on the fifteenth century. More modern works include material in L. W. Abbott, *Law Reporting in England, 1485–1585* (1973), esp. chs 3–6; Edward Foss, *Judges of England*

... *1066–1864*, 9 vols (1848–64), esp. vol. v; Alan Harding, *A Social History of English Law* (Harmondsworth, 1966), esp. pp. 167–215; W. S. Holdsworth, *A History of English Law*, 13 vols (1922–52), esp. vol. IV; E. W. Ives, 'Promotion in the Legal Profession', *Law Quarterly Review*, LXXV (1959) 348–63; and Sir Charles Ogilvie, *The King's Government and the Common Law* (Oxford, 1958).

Much information on specific lawyers and episodes concerning them may be gleaned from *State Trials*, 42 vols, ed. William Cobbett, T. B. Howell, *et al.* (1816–98), and *Wriothesley's Chronicle*, ed. W. D. Hamilton (Camden Society, new ser. XI, 1877). *The Calendar of State Papers, Spanish, 1554*, ed. Royall Taylor (1949), includes a valuable coverage of the passage of the 1555 Treasons Act (pp. 125–6 and 128–31). *The Chronicle of Queen Jane and of Two Years of Queen Mary*, ed. J. G. Nichols (Camden Society, XLVIII, 1850) includes episodes concerning the judges' involvement in Northumberland's succession plot and also his trial. John Foxe's *Actes and Monuments*, ed. J. Pratt, 8 vols, (1870) (1837–41) contains (vol. VIII) material on the activities of lawyers in the 1557 Heresy Commission. The first volume of Edmund Plowden's *Commentaries* (1816) contains the case of *Hales* v. *Petit* (1959), which includes the circumstances and repercussions of Justice Hales's suicide. The problem of seditious words is dealt with in *The Diary of Henry Machyn*, ed. J. G. Nichols (Camden Society, XLII, 1848), pp. 137–81, and in *Wriothesley's Chronicle* (see above).


## 8.  ENGLAND AND THE FRENCH WAR, 1557–9

There are surprisingly few modern and accessible works. The origins of the war are brilliantly explored in E. H. Harbison, *Rival Ambassadors at the Court of Queen Mary* (Princeton, NJ, 1940). D. M. Loades, *Two Tudor Conspiracies* (Cambridge, 1965), deals with the plotters against Mary's regime encouraged by Henry II. The European background is treated by L. Romier, *Les Origines politiques des guerres de religion*, 2 vols (Paris, 1913–14) for France, vol. III of H. Pirenne's massive *Histoire de Belgique*, 7 vols (Brussels, 1909–32), and, succinctly, in Geoffrey Parker, *The Dutch Revolt* (1977). For Scotland, see Gordon Donaldson's *Scotland, James V to James VII* (vol. III of the *Edinburgh History of Scotland*) (1965).

The organisation of the English army is best studied in C. G. Cruickshank, *Elizabeth's Army*, 2nd edn (Oxford, 1966), and Lindsay Boynton, *The Elizabethan Militia* (1967). See also Jeremy Goring, 'Social Change and Military Decline in Mid-Tudor England', in *History*, LX (1975) 185–97, which usefully includes a summary of the author's thesis on military recruiting. There is no accessible treatment of the fall of Calais. The best work is an (unfortunately unpublished) Oxford D.Phil. thesis of 1966 by P. T. J. Morgan, 'The Government of Calais, 1485–1558' (I must thank Dr Morgan for once again allowing me to use and cite it.) The fortifications are expertly treated by H. M. Colvin in *The History of the King's Works*, vol. III, ed. Colvin, D. R. Ransome and John Summerson (1975). The best accounts in print are the anonymous article 'The Loss of Calais' in *North British Review*, XLV (1866) (its author is convincingly shown by Dr Morgan 'Government of Calais', p. 254, to be Paul Friedmann), and G. Daumet, *Calais sous la domination anglaise* (Arras, 1902). Contemporary accounts of the fall of Calais from the English side were edited by Edward Arber for vol. IV of *An English Garner*, 8 vols (1877–96) and were reprinted by A. F. Pollard in *Tudor Tracts* (1903).

On the navy, there is a good modern survey by G. J. Marcus, *A Naval History of England*, 2 vols (1961–71), vol. I. The fundamental account remains M. Oppenheim, *The Administration of the Royal Navy, 1509–1660* (1896). Two articles by Tom Glasgow Jr argue convincingly that the process of making the navy effective after its decline under Northumberland began in Mary's reign: 'The Navy in Philip and Mary's War, 1557–8', and 'The Maturing of Naval Administration, 1556–64', in *Mariner's Mirror*, LIII (1967) and LVI (1970).

# Notes and References

(For abbreviations, see List of Abbreviations. Place of publication is London unless otherwise stated.)

INTRODUCTION  *Jennifer Loach* and *Robert Tittler*

1. A. F. Pollard, *England Under Protector Somerset* (1900), *Henry VIII* (1902), *The History of England from the Accession of Edward VI to the Death of Elizabeth* (1910), *The Evolution of Parliament* (1920) and *Wolsey* (1929).
2. Pollard, *History of England*, p. 172.
3. J. E. Neale, *Queen Elizabeth* (1934), *The Elizabethan House of Commons* (1949) and *Elizabeth I and Her Parliaments, 1559–1601*, 2 vols (1953 and 1957).
4. S. T. Bindoff, *Tudor England* (1950) p. 182.
5. Ibid., chs 4–5.
6. G. R. Elton, *The Tudor Revolution in Government* (Cambridge, 1953).
7. G. R. Elton, *Reform and Reformation: England 1509–1558* (1977) pp. 298, 341.
8. P. Williams, 'Dr. Elton's Interpretation of the Age' and 'The Tudor State', and G. L. Harriss, 'Medieval Government and Statecraft', in *Past and Present*, no. 25 (1963); P. Williams and G. L. Harriss, 'A Revolution in Tudor History?', ibid., no. 31 (1965).
9. W. K. Jordan, *Edward VI: The Threshold of Power* (1970) p. 210.
10. Ibid., p. 531.
11. R. W. Heinze, *The Proclamations of the Tudor Kings* (Cambridge, 1976) pp. 221–2.
12. D. E. Hoak, *The King's Council in the Reign of Edward VI* (Cambridge, 1976).
13. A. Weikel, 'Crown and Council: A Study of Mary Tudor and Her Privy Council' (unpublished Ph.D. dissertation, Yale, 1966); G. A. Lemasters, 'The Privy Council in the Reign of Mary I' (unpublished Ph.D. thesis, Cambridge, 1971).
14. F. J. Fisher, 'Commercial Trends and Policy in 16th Century England', *EcHR*, x (1940); C. E. Challis, 'The Debasement of the Coinage, 1542–1557', ibid., 2nd ser. xx (1967); idem, 'The Circulating Medium and the Movement of Prices in Mid-Tudor England', in *The Price Revolution in Sixteenth Century England*, ed. P. H. Ramsey (1971); idem, 'Currency and Economy in Mid-Tudor England', *Ec. HR*, 2nd ser., xxv (1972); J. D. Gould, *The Great Debasement* (Oxford, 1971).
15. C. E. Challis, *The Tudor Coinage* (Manchester, 1978) pp. 116–17.

16. *CPR*, Philip and Mary, vol. III, p. 317, and vol. IV, p. 31.

17. G. D. Ramsay, *The City of London in International Politics at the Accession of Elizabeth Tudor* (Manchester, 1975) p. 151. See also T. S. Willan, *A Tudor Book of Rates* (1962).

18. W. Notestein, *The Winning of the Initiative by the House of Commons* (1924).

19. S. E. Lehmberg, *The Reformation Parliament, 1529–1536* (Cambridge, 1970), and *The Later Parliaments of Henry VIII, 1536–1547* (Cambridge, 1977); G. R. Elton, 'Tudor Government: the Points of Contact, I: Parliament', *TRHS*, 5th ser., XXIV (1974) 183–200.

20. S. J. Loach, 'Opposition to the Crown in Parliament, 1553–1558' (unpublished D. Phil. thesis, Oxford, 1974).

21. See, among other works, R. Crowley, *The Way to Wealth* (1550).

22. Julian Cornwall, *The Revolt of the Peasantry 1549* (1978); D. Willen, 'Lord Russell and the Western Counties, 1539–1555', *Journal of British Studies*, XV (Nov 1975) 26–45.

23. J. Hurstfield, 'Corruption and Reform under Edward VI and Mary: The Example of Wardship', *EHR*, LXVIII (1953) 22–36, repr. in *Freedom, Corruption and Government in Elizabethan England* (1973) pp. 137–62; W. C. Richardson, *History of the Court of Augmentations 1536–1554* (Baton Rouge, LA, 1961).

24. C. Cross, *Church and People, 1450–1660: The Triumph of the Laity in the English Church* (1976), is a good general introduction to religious change. There are several interesting essays in *Church and State in England: Henry VIII to James I*, ed. F. Heal and R. O'Day (1977). J. Phillips, *The Reformation of Images* (1973) illustrates the impact of constant change in one area of religious life.

25. A. G. Dickens, *The English Reformation* (1964) p. 280. See also D. M. Loades, *The Oxford Martyrs* (1970) ch. 8.

26. J. Bellamy, *The Tudor Law of Treason* (1979) pp. 53, 61.

27. The lack of scholarly attention to the reign of Mary is reflected in the paucity of scholarship devoted to a biography of the Queen. The standard account of H. M. F. Prescott, *The Spanish Tudor*, was published in 1940, and reissued with a new title but few revisions in 1953. Until Carolly Ericson's *Bloody Mary* (New York, 1977) this was the best on the subject, but even Ericson makes little use of unpublished sources, and neither approaches the profundity of scholarship which may be found in at least one modern biography of every other Tudor monarch save Queen Jane.

28. W. G. Zeeveld, *Foundations of Tudor Policy* (Cambridge, Mass., 1948); J. K. McConica, *English Humanists and Reformation Politics* (Oxford, 1964); A. B. Ferguson, *The Articulate Citizen and the English Renaissance* (Durham, N.C., 1965); W. R. D. Jones, *The Tudor Commonwealth, 1529–1559* (1970); G. R. Elton, 'Reform by Statute: Thomas Starkey's Dialogue and Thomas Cromwell's Policy', *Proc. Br. Acad.*, LIV (1968) 164–88, repr. in *Studies in Tudor and Stuart Politics and Government* (Cambridge, 1974) vol. II, 236–58; idem, *Reform and Renewal; Thomas Cromwell and the Common Weal,* (1973).

29. G. R. Elton, *Policy and Police* (Cambridge, 1972) pp. 171–3.

## 1. CONSERVATISM AND CONSENT IN PARLIAMENT,
### 1547–59  *Jennifer Loach*

The author wishes to thank Alastair Parker, Paul Slack and Robert Tittler for their advice and assistance in the writing of this chapter.

(In the notes to this chapter reference is made to the date under which an entry appears in the *Lords'* and *Commons' Journals* rather than to the page of the *Journal* on which it appears. However, where the date of a bill or a vote is mentioned in the text no reference is here given to the *Lords'* or *Commons' Journals*.)

1. J. E. Neale, *Elizabeth I and Her Parliaments, 1559–1581* (1953) pp. 21–7.

2. For example, R. K. Gilkes, *The Tudor Parliament* (1969) pp. 123–4, 126–9.

3. S. E. Lehmberg, *The Later Parliaments of Henry VIII, 1536–1547* (Cambridge, 1977) pp. 200–2.

4. D. E. Hoak, *The King's Council in the Reign of Edward VI* (Cambridge, 1976) p. 169.

5. PRO SP 10/15/73.

6. Ibid., 11/6/18.

7. P. L. Hughes and J. F. Larkin, *Tudor Royal Proclamations* (New Haven, Conn., and London, 1964–9) vol. I, nos 281, 292, 390, 451, 454.

8. Ibid., no. 287.

9. Hoak, *The King's Council*, pp. 175–6, quoting NRO Fitzwilliam (Milton) MS. n. c. 21.

10. *York Civic Records*, ed. A. Raine, vol. IV, pp. 165, 166, 168; vol. V, pp. 31, 93, 135, 138; and vol. VI, p. 2 (Yorkshire Archaeological Society Record Series, CVIII [1945], CX [1945], CXII [1948]).

11. LCRO, Repertory 13, I, fos. 85, 94v., 323v.

12. See, for example, the preamble to 1 & 2 Philip and Mary, c. 14.

13. *APC*, vol. II, pp. 193–5.

14. *CJ*, 4 Apr 1552; *LJ*, 31 Mar 1552.

15. 2 & 3 Philip and Mary, c. 4.

16. The bill was passed on 3 Dec 1555. See *CSP Ven.*, vol. VI, i, p. 270.

17. The bill was rejected on 6 Dec 1555. See ibid., p. 283.

18. *Original Letters Relative to the English Reformation*, ed. Hastings Robinson (Parker Society, 1847) pp. 441–2; J. Foxe, *Acts and Monuments*, ed. S. R. Cattley, vol. VI (1841) pp. 653–4.

19. *CSP Ven.*, vol. VI, i, p. 283.

20. *The Diary of Henry Machyn*, ed. J. G. Nichols (Camden Society, XLII, 1850) p. 52; *CSP Sp.*, vol. XII, p. 297. He was a brother of Catherine Howard.

21. *Ambassades de Messieurs de Noailles en Angleterre*, ed. R. Aubert de Vertot and C. Villaret (Leyden, 1763), vol. V, p. 252.

22. E. L. Barnwell, 'Notes on the Perrot Family', *Archaeologia Cambrensis*, III, no. 11 (1865) 108–29.

23. F. Peck, *Desiderata Curiosa* (1732–5) vol. I, p. 9.

24. Ibid.

25. *Ambassades*, vol. V, p. 223.

26. PRO SP 11/8/25.

27. Ibid., 11/8/46, 11/8/52.

28. HMC, Shrewsbury MSS. in Lambeth Palace Library, p. 704.

29. *DNB*.

30. A list of 106 names of Members of the House of Commons of 1555 exists, entitled, 'All these in Queen Mary's time were in the parliament first holden against the general repeal of all treasons etc. whereby the statute of the supremacy was repealed' (Guildford Museum, Loseley MS. 1331/2). This list is probably to be linked with these bills, but the evidence is too scanty for any conclusive arguments to be advanced here.

31. *CSP Ven.*, vol. VI, i, p. 275.

32. 13 Elizabeth, c. 3. See also 14 Elizabeth, c. 6.

33. *CSP Ven.*, vol. VI, i, pp. 228–9.

34. The Privy Council had wanted a grant of one subsidy and three-fifteenths, but the grant offered was of one subsidy and only two-fifteenths.

35. *CSP Sp.*, vol. XI, p. 335. See also *Ambassades*, vol. II, p. 247 and *Epistolae Reginaldi Poli*, ed. A. M. Quirini (1744–57), vol. IV, p. 121.

36. *CSP Sp.*, vol. XIII, p. 125.

37. BL Add. 41577, fos 161–6.

38. HLRO, original act 1 & 2 Philip and Mary, c.8.

39. *Epistolae*, vol. V, p. 314. See also BL Harl. 419, fo. 132.

40. PRO SP 10/18/6, 10/18/8.

41. Ibid., 10/6/12, 10/6/11.

42. Hoak, *The King's Council*, p. 75.

43. It had only one reading in the Lords, on 21 Dec 1547.

44. *CSP Sp.*, vol. XII, pp. 151, 168, 170, 216; vol. XIII, p. 88. For a fuller discussion of this incident, see my 'Opposition to the Crown in Parliament, 1553–1558' (unpublished D.Phil. thesis, Oxford, 1974) pp. 93–111.

45. *CSP Sp.*, vol. XII, p. 238.

46. *CJ*, 1 May 1554.

47. 1 & 2 Philip and Mary, c.6.

48. *CSP Sp.*, vol. XII, p. 240.

49. Ibid., pp. 230, 251.

50. 1 & 2 Philip and Mary, c.10.

51. The following pages are based on the account given in Neale, 'The Elizabethan Acts of Supremacy and Uniformity', *EHR*, LXV (1950) 304–32, and *Elizabeth I and Her Parliaments*, vol. I, pp. 51–84, together with the Journals of both Houses and E. Jeffries Davis, 'An Unpublished Manuscript for the Lords' Journals for April and May 1559', *EHR*, XXVIII (1913) pp. 531–42.

52. *CJ*, 15 and 16 Feb 1559.

53. *CSP Ven.*, vol. VII, p. 46.

54. *CJ*, 17 and 18 Mar 1559.

55. *CSP Ven.*, vol. VII, p. 52.

56. Bodley MS., Eng. th. b., II, fo. 840v.

57. C. Read, *Mr Secretary Cecil and Queen Elizabeth* (1955) p. 110–11.

58. R. Tittler, *Nicholas Bacon: The Making of a Tudor Statesman* (1976) pp. 89–90.

59. *CJ*, 18 Apr 1559.

60. Duchy of Cornwall Record Office, Proceedings in Parliament, Elizabeth, pp. 58–9.

61. Neale, *Elizabeth I and Her Parliaments*, vol. I, p. 58.

62. *APC*, vol. II, p. 516.

63. BL Royal MS. 18, c. 24, fo. 290v. On this incident see W. K. Jordan, *Edward VI: The Threshold of Power* (1970) pp. 505–6.

64. BL Lansd. 3, fo. 36.

65. For instance, *HMC Grimsby Corporation*, vol. XIV,, p. 255.

66. PRO SP 11/12/2. See also Bodley MS. Tanner 90, fo. 211.

67. PRO C 219/23, fos 69, 95.

68. Abingdon, Banbury and Higham Ferrers.

69. For example, Aylesbury was enfranchised as a reward for its loyalty (*CPR, Philip and Mary*, vol. I, pp. 44–5).

70. *CSP Ven.*, vol. VI, 1, p. 426.

71. M. L. Bush, *The Government Policy of Protector Somerset* (1975) p. 145.

72. 3 & 4 Edward VI, c. 5: *CJ*, 9, 10, 11, 13, 16, 17, 20 and 23 Dec 1549.

73. 5 & 6 Edward VI, c. 11: *CJ*, 24, 25, 26 and 28 Feb, 14 and 21 Mar, and 4, 9 and 13 Apr 1552.

74. HLRO, original acts 1 Mary 2, c. 17.

75. 1 & 2 Philip and Mary, c. 10; *CJ*, 7, 17, 20, 27 and 28 Dec 1554, and 4, 12 and 14 January 1555; *CSP Sp.*, vol. XIII, p. 125. On anxiety about Philip's coronation, see J. Bradford, *The Copye of a Letter* (n.p., n.d.) sig. C, fo. 7v.

76. HLRO, original acts 1 & 2 Philip and Mary, c. 3; *CJ*, 17, 19, 22 and 29 Dec 1554.

77. H. Miller, 'Attendance in the House of Lords during the Reign of Henry VIII', *Historical Journal*, x (1967) 325–51.

78. V. Snow, Proctorial Representation in the House of Lords during the Reign of Edward VI', *Journal of British Studies*, VIII (1969) 1–27.

79. Miller, in *Historical Journal*, x, 345.

80. W. Notestein, *The Winning of the Initiative by the House of Commons* (1924).

## 2. REHABILITATING THE DUKE OF NORTHUMBERLAND: POLITICS AND POLITICAL CONTROL, 1549–53 *Dale Hoak*

1. C. S. L. Davies, *Peace, Print and Protestantism 1450–1558* (St Albans, 1977) pp. 386–387.

2. Quoted in W. K. Jordan and M. R. Gleason, 'The Saying of John Late Duke of Northumberland upon the Scaffold, 1553', *Harvard Library Bulletin*, XXIII (1975) 338–9.

3. R. B. Wernham, *Before the Armada: The Growth of English Foreign Policy 1485–1588* (1966) p. 193.

4. W. G. Hoskins, *The Age of Plunder: The England of Henry VIII, 1500–1547* (1976) p. 233.

5. Barrett Beer's *Northumberland: The Political Career of John Dudley, Earl of Warwick and Duke of Northumberland* (Kent, Ohio, 1973) was written before the discovery of some of the evidence presented in this essay.

6. M. L. Bush, *The Government Policy of Protector Somerset* (1975) pp. 38–9, 98–9.

7. See *The Letters of William, Lord Paget of Beaudesert, 1547–1563*, B. L. Beer and S. M. Jack (Camden Society, 4th ser., XIII, 1974), pp. 14–78, for Paget's letters to Somerset and the Council, 1548–9.

8. D. E. Hoak, *The King's Council in the Reign of Edward VI* (Cambridge, 1976) pp. 15–23, 101–4, 114–15.

9. J. Cornwall, *Revolt of the Peasantry 1549* (1977) pp. 227–9.

10. Hoak, *The King's Council*, pp. 167–90.

11. Ibid., pp. 241–58.

12. BL Lansd. MSS 160, fos 264–7; Hoak, *The King's Council*, pp. 96–7, 301 (note 26).

13. Davies, *Peace*, pp. 281–2.

14. G. R. Elton, 'Tudor Government: The Points of Contact. II: The Council', *TRHS*, 5th ser., XXV (1975) 204–5.

15. PRO, SP 10/15/137–8, from Chelsea, 7 Dec 1552.

16. *Calendar of Letters, Despatches, and State Papers, Relating to the Negotiations between England and Spain, Preserved in the Archives at Vienna, Simancas, and Elsewhere*, ed. R. Tyler, vol. x, (1914) 610–11.

17. Hoak, *The King's Council*, pp. 91–164.

18. Ibid., pp. 166, 203–12, for the outline of Northumberland's financial programme.

19. Hatfield House, Cecil Papers, 151, fos 7–8, 16 June 1551; G. L. Harriss, 'Thomas Cromwell's "New Principle" of Taxation', *EHR*, XCIII (1978) 730–1.

20. F. C. Dietz, *Finances of Edward VI and Mary* (Northampton, Mass.: Smith College Studies in History, 1918) p. 91, note 9; PRO, SP 10/13/24; *A Collection of State Papers*, ed. S. A. Haynes (1740) p. 119; W. C. Richardson, *History of the Court of Augmentations 1536–1554* (Baton Rouge, La, 1961) pp. 361–5; S. E. Lehmberg, *Sir Walter Mildmay and Tudor Government* (Austin, Tex, 1964) pp. 28–39; A. Feavearyear, *The Pound Sterling: A History of English Money*, 2nd edn, rev. E. V. Morgan (Oxford, 1963), p. 71.

21. Ibid., pp. 70–1.

22. W. K. Jordan, *Edward VI: The Threshold of Power* (1970) pp. 402–27, 440–55.

23. Hoak, *The King's Council*, pp. 118–23.

24. Ibid., pp. 27, 151.

25. Bibliothèque Nationale, Paris, MS. Ancien Saint-Germain Français 15888, fos 214–15.

26. Ibid.

27. PRO, SP 10/14/137–8, from Chelsea, 7 Dec 1552.

28. Beer, *Northumberland*, p. 162.

29. Ibid., pp. 167–71, 177–94, for Northumberland's aquisition of property, 1547–53, and esp. pp. 191–2, where Professor Beer cautiously compares Northumberland's income with that of Somerset and some other early-Tudor peers.

30. PRO, SP 10/14/127–8, from Chelsea, 3 Dec 1552; ibid., fo. 141, 9 Dec 1552; SP 10/18/3, 3 Jan 1553.

31. BL Add. MS. 48126, fo. 15a.

32. According to a French eyewitness, Northumberland confessed in 1553 that 'nothing had pressed so injuriously upon his conscience as the fraudulent scheme against the Duke of Somerset'—Bibliothèque Nationale, Paris, MS. Ancien Saint-Germain Français 15888, fo. 212a.

33. Ibid., fo. 215a.

34. Ibid. This French observer, probably a member of the embassy of René de Montmorency-Laval, seigneur de Boisdauphin, said that Gates had been 'one of the principals who induced the King to make out his will to the prejudice of the Lady Mary'.

3. THE MARIAN COUNCIL REVISITED   *Ann Weikel*

1. A. F. Pollard, *The History of England from the Accession of Edward VI to the Death of Elizabeth* (1910); E. H. Harbison, *Rival Ambassadors at the Court of Queen Mary* (1940); G. R. Elton, *The Tudor Revolution in Government* (Cambridge, 1953); D. E. Hoak, *The King's Council in the Reign of Edward VI* (Cambridge, 1976); G. A. Lemasters, 'The Privy Council in the Reign of Mary I' (unpublished Ph.D. dissertation, Cambridge, 1971); G. R. Elton, 'Tudor Government: The Points of Contact. II: The Council', *TRHS*, 5th ser., xxv (1975) 195–211; idem, *Reform and Reformation: England 1509–1558* (1977); D. M. Loades, *Politics and the Nation 1450–1660* (1974).

2. Pollard, *History of England*, pp. 113–15; Harbison, *Rival Ambassadors*, pp. 61–2.

3. *A Machiavellian Treatise*, ed. P. S. Donaldson (Cambridge, 1975) pp. 26, 33, 35, 37; PRO SP 11/6/62.

4. S. R. Gammon, *Statesman and Schemer: William, First Lord Paget – Tudor Minister* (Newton Abbott, 1973); *The Letters of William, Lord Paget of Beaudesert, 1547–1563*, ed. B. L. Beer and S. M. Jack (Camden Society, 4th ser., xiii, 1974), pp. 1–141.

5. PRO SP 11/1/3, 5; *APC*, vol. xiv, pp. 337–60.

6. *CSP Sp.*, vol. xi, pp. 236, 312–13, 319–24.

7. Ibid., pp. 363–5.

8. Ibid., pp. 412, 414–16, 432–3, 435–6; *Ambassades de Messieurs de Noailles en Angleterre*, ed. R. Aubert de Vertot and C. Villaret (5 vols, Leyden, 1763), vol. ii, pp. 239–48.

9. CSP Sp., vol. XI, pp. 332–6, 372, 381–3; vol. XII, pp. 2–3. PRO SP 11/1/20.

10. *CSP Sp.*, vol. XI, p. 411.

11. Ibid., pp. 415–16, 425, 431, 443–5, 470; PRO SP 46/14/213.

12. D. M. Loades, *Two Tudor Conspiracies* (Cambridge, 1965) pp. 8–13, 41–3, 52–8, 63–4. See P. Clark, *English Provincial Society from the Reformation to the Revolution* (1977) pp. 87–98, for a criticism of Loades's analysis of the situation in Kent and rebel motivation.

13. *APC*, vol. IV, p. 382; PRO SP 11/2/2, 5–8; *CSP Sp.*, vol. XII, pp. 10–14, 16, 20, 22–4, 31–4, 38–42.

14. PRO SP 11/2/10, 19–20, 25, 29; *CSP Sp.*, vol. XII, pp. 51–6; *The Chronicle of Queen Jane and of Two Years of Queen Mary*, ed. J. G. Nichols (Camden Society, XLVIII, 1850) pp. 36–7.

15. PRO SP 11/2/26; *CSP Sp.*, vol. XII, pp. 53–6, 64.

16. *CSP Sp.*, vol. XII, pp. 70, 78.

17. The following account is based on ibid., XII, 53–6, 63–6, 76–82, 85–8.

18. The captured French letter enclosed with the dispatch might be interpreted as corroboration of Renard's view, but it has enough errors to cast doubt on its reliability. Gardiner tried to conceal Courtenay's name which further aroused Renard's suspicions.

19. *CSP Sp.*, vol. XII, pp. 166–8.

20. Ibid., pp. 168–9.

21. Ibid., pp. 197–203, 220–2, 230, 238–9, 240; *Ambassades*, vol. III pp. 153, 167, 174.

22. Ibid., pp. 250–1, 258–9, 261–2, 276, 290.

23. *CSP Sp.*, vol. XI, pp. 270, 320, 327, 343, 349, 412; vol. XII, pp. 220, 251; *Ambassades*, vol. II, pp. 245–6; vol. III, p. 225; For the dispute over the war with France (1557), when Petre disagreed with Paget, see Harbison, *Rival Ambassadors*, pp. 322–7; *Affaires Etrangères*, XII, fos 182–3, 186, 188, 191–2.

24. *CSP Sp.*, vol. XII, pp. 321, 251; vol. XIII, p. 101.

25. Ibid., vol. XII, p. 290; A. H. Anderson, 'Henry, Lord Stafford (1501–1563) in Local and Central Government', *EHR*, LXXVIII (1963) 225–42.

26. *CSP Sp.*, vol. XIII, pp. 87–90.

27. A. Weikel, 'Crown and Council: A Study of Mary Tudor and Her Privy Council' (unpublished Ph.D dissertation, Yale, 1966) pp. 54–118.

28. Ibid., pp. 118–71; *CSP Sp.*, vol. XI, p. 216; *CSP Ven.*, vol. VI, ii, p. 1004; *APC*, vol. IV, pp. 397–8.

## 4.  THE EMERGENCE OF URBAN POLICY, 1536–58
### Robert Tittler

1. G. R. Elton, *Reform and Renewal: Thomas Cromwell and the Common Weal* (Cambridge, 1973) esp. pp. 106–9.

2. The best recent treatments of the state of towns in the pre-Tudor period are R. B. Dobson, 'Urban Decline in late Medieval England',

*TRHS*, 5th ser. xxvii (1977) 1–22, and C. Phythian-Adams, 'Urban Decay in Late Medieval England', in *Towns in Societies* ed. P. Abrams and E. A. Wrigley (Cambridge, 1978) pp. 159–86. I should like to thank Dr Paul Slack for his discussion of these issues with me, though he should bear no responsibility for the views expressed here.

3. For instance, 7 Henry VII, c. 11; 12 Henry VII, cc. 12 and 13. Cambridge, for example, paid a reduced rate of tenths and fifteenths by Edward IV.

4. 3 Henry VIII, c. 22, followed what had by then become a well established pattern of exemptions, but 5 Henry VIII, c. 17, and 6 Henry VIII, c. 26, for example, omitted the remission for poor towns.

5. PRO SP 10/5/20, repr. in *A Discourse of the Common Weal of this Realm of England*, ed. E. Lamond (Cambridge, 1954 edn), pp. xlii–xlv.

6. 3 & 4 Edward VI, c. 18.

7. 4 Henry VII, c. 19; 6 Henry VIII, c. 5; 7 Henry VIII, c. 1.

8. *APC*, vol. ii, pp. 294–6; cited in Blanchard, 'Population Change, Enclosure, and the Early Tudor Economy', *EcHR*, 2nd ser., xxiii (1970) 427–45, esp. 439; repr. in *English Economic History: Selected Documents*, ed. A. E. Bland, P. A. Brown, and R. H. Tawney (1919) pp. 266–8.

9. SP 10/15/109, Mayor and Burgesses of Boston to Cecil, 27 Nov 1552.

10. W. G. Hoskins, 'The Rebuilding of Rural England, 1570–1640', *Past and Present*, no. 4 (1953) 44–59; repr. in *Provincial England; Essays in Social and Economic History* (1963). The indication of government support for rebuilding both strengthens Hoskins' view and allows one to question the recent assault made upon it in R. Machin, 'The Great Rebuilding: A Reassessment', *Past and Present*, no. 77 (1977) 33–56.

11. Elton, *Reform and Renewal*, pp. 106–9.

12. T. Starkey, *A Dialogue between Reginald Pole and Thomas Lupset*, ed. K. M. Burton (1948), p. 27.

13. Ibid., pp. 27–8.

14. Ibid., p. 92.

15. Ibid., pp. 161, 144–5.

16. Ibid., p. 183.

17. A. Fletcher, *Tudor Rebellions* (1968) p. 10.

18. Phythian-Adams, *Towns in Societies*, pp. 174–7.

19. 21 Henry VIII, c. 12; 21 Henry VIII, c. 21; 22 Henry VIII, c. 20; 25 Henry VIII, c. 18.

20. The best summaries of these difficulties are W. R. D. Jones, *The Mid-Tudor Crisis* (1973), and W. G. Hoskins, *The Age of Plunder: The England of Henry VIII, 1500–1547* (1976).

21. F. J. Fisher, 'Commercial Trends and Policy in Sixteenth Century England', *EcHR*, x (1940) 95–117.

22. Cf., for example, Phythian-Adams, in *Towns in Societies*.

23. G. R. Elton, 'Parliamentary Drafts, 1529–1540', *BIHR*, xxv (1952) esp. 112–3; *L & P*, vol. vii, p. 67, and vol. xiv, i, p. 409.

24. A. Everitt, 'The Marketing of Agricultural Produce', in *Agrarian History of England and Wales*, vol. iv: *1500–1640*, ed. J. Thirsk (Cambridge, 1967), pp. 502–6; Tittler, 'The Incorporation of Boroughs, 1540–1558',

*History* (Feb 1977) pp. 24–42, esp. p. 28.

25. R. Tittler, 'Incorporation and Politics in Sixteenth Century Thaxted', *Essex Archaeology and History: Transactions of the Essex Archaeological Society*, VIII (1976; issued 1978) 224–33.

26. *A Discourse of the Common Weal*, p. 130.

27. Ibid., pp. 125–31.

28. 27 Henry VIII, c. 25 (1536); 1 Edward VI, c. 3 (1547); 3 & 4 Edward VI, c. 16 (1549–50); 5 & 6 Edward VI, c. 2 (1551–2); 2 & 3 Philip and Mary, c. 5 (1555).

29. 39 Elizabeth, cc. 2–4; 43 Elizabeth, c. 2.

30. J. J. Goring, 'The Military Obligations of the English People, 1511–1558' (unpublished Ph.D thesis, London, 1955) *passim*, and 'Social Change and Military Decline in Mid-Tudor England', *History*, LX, 185–97.

31. J. Cornwall, *The Revolt of the Peasantry, 1549* (1977) chs 3–5.

32. Goring, 'Military Obligations', pp. 194–7.

33. *APC*, vol. I, p. 192 (Privy Council to sheriff of Cambridgeshire, 10 June 1545).

34. Ibid., vol. I, p. 327 (same to Mayor of Portsmouth, 30 Jan 1546).

35. Cornwall, *Revolt*, pp. 90–3, 240.

36. For example, *APC*, vol. v, p. 8 (Privy Council to bishop of Salisbury and other commissioners of muster in Wiltshire, 7 Apr 1554).

37. Cf. charters incorporating the boroughs of Lichfield in 1553, *CPR*, Mary, vol. I, pp. 50–2; Worcester in 1555, PRO C 66/844/m. 3; Launceston in 1556, C 66/903/m. 13; and Brecon in 1556, C 66/899/m. 36.

38. Goring, 'Military Obligations', pp. 286–7; A. H. Smith, *County and Court: Government and Politics in Elizabethan Norfolk, 1558–1603* (Oxford, 1974) p. 290.

39. See my 'Incorporation of Boroughs', *History*, LXII (1977) 24–42.

40. I should like to thank the Editor of *History* for permission to reprint this list from the essay cited in note 39. Cf. also *Crisis and Order in English Towns, 1500–1700*, ed. P. Clark and P. Slack (1972) p. 22.

41. *Reports from the Commissioners Appointed to Inquire into Municipal Corporations in England and Wales*, Report I, app. (1834) *passim*.

42. Using the table of incorporations in M. Weinbaum, *The Incorporation of Boroughs* (Manchester, 1936), a table which is at least sufficiently accurate for this purpose, one may compute the following rates of borough incorporation per year during the period 1509–1603: Henry VIII, 0·4 per year; Edward VI, 2·0 per year; Mary, 4·5 per year; Elizabeth, 1·35 per year.

43. *APC*, vol. v, p. 218 (Privy Council to Mayor and Aldermen of Coventry, 7 Jan. 1556); vol. vi, pp. 55 and 111–12 (same to the Mayor, Jurats and Commonality of Rye, 15 Aug 1556 and 29 June 1557).

5. SOCIAL POLICY AND THE CONSTRAINTS OF
GOVERNMENT, 1547–58    *Paul Slack*

1. G. R. Elton, *Reform and Renewal: Thomas Cromwell and the Common Weal* (Cambridge, 1973); J. Thirsk, *Economic Policy and Projects* (Oxford, 1978) ch. 2.

2. W. G. Hoskins, 'Harvest Fluctuations and English Economic History

1480–1619', *Agric. HR*, XII (1964) 35–6; *Agrarian History of England and Wales*, IV: *1500–1640*, ed. J. Thirsk (Cambridge, 1967), pp. 831, 836, 842–3. Cf. M. L. Bush, *The Government Policy of Protector Somerset* (1975) pp. 41–2.

3. Cf. C. Phythian-Adams, 'Urban Decay in Late Medieval England', in *Towns in Societies*, ed. P. Abrams and E. A. Wrigley (Cambridge, 1978), pp. 159–85; R. Tittler, above, pp. 79–80.

4. For instance, *The Ledger of John Smythe 1538–50*, ed. J. Vanes (Bristol Record Society, XXVIII, 1974) p. 23; *Tudor Economic Documents*, 3 vols, ed. R. H. Tawney and E. Power (1924), vol. I, pp. 45, 52–3; *York Civic Records*, ed. A. Raine, vol. V (Yorkshire Archaeological Society Record Series, CX, 1946) p. 23.

5. *A Discourse of the Common Weal of this Realm of England*, ed. E. Lamond (Cambridge, 1929 edn), pp. xlvi–xlvii.

6. P. Slack, 'Mortality Crises and Epidemic Disease in England 1485–1603', in *Health, Medicine and Mortality in the Sixteenth Century*, ed. C. Webster (Cambridge, 1979).

7. *Tudor Royal Proclamations*, ed. P. L. Hughes and J. F. Larkin (New Haven, Conn., and London, 1964–9), vol. I, no. 336, p. 465.

8. *The Works of John Caius*, ed. E. S. Roberts (Cambridge, 1912), 'A boke . . . against . . . the sweate', pp. 18–19; PRO SP 10/13/30.

9. 5 & 6 Edward VI, c. 25; *Tudor Economic Documents*, vol. I, pp. 330–1. Cf. *Middlesex County Records*, 4 vols, ed. J. C. Jeafferson (1886–92), vol. I, pp. 10–11.

10. 5 & 6 Edward VI, c. 20; *LJ*, vol. I, pp. 398–9; *CJ*, vol. I, p. 17; *The Chronicle and Political Papers of King Edward VI*, ed. W. K. Jordan (1966), p. 165.

11. *CJ*, vol. I, pp. 30, 34; *CPR*, 1548–9, Edward VI, II, pp. 9–10. Cf. HMC, *Salisbury (Cecil) MSS.*, vol. I, pp. 133–4, for a project for a public bank.

12. Cf. B. Pullan, 'Catholics and the Poor in Early Modern Europe', *TRHS*, 5th ser., XXVI (1976) 15–34.

13. *Tudor Economic Documents*, vol. III, p. 312. Cf. 'Vox Populi, Vox Dei', ibid., p. 39.

14. *Records of the Borough of Nottingham*, IV: *1547–1625*, ed. W. H. Stevenson (1889) pp. 15–27; P. Clark, *English Provincial Society from the Reformation to the Revolution* (1977) pp. 84–5; *York Civic Records*, vol. V, pp. 87, 93.

15. Bush, *Government Policy*, pp. 52–3, 81. Cf. *York Civic Records*, vol. V, pp. 140, 142–3.

16. *CJ*, vol. I, pp. 13, 17, 29.

17. Cf. Elton, *Reform and Renewal*, ch. 4. The following paragraphs are based on my own reading of the journals and statutes. For a detailed account of the legislative process from a different perspective, see C. G. Ericson, 'Parliament as a Legislative Institution in the Reigns of Edward VI and Mary' (unpublished Ph.D thesis, London, 1974).

18. Bush, *Government Policy*, pp. 49–51; *Discourse of the Common Weal*, pp. lxii–lxiii.

19. *Chronicle and Papers of Edward VI*, p. 165 (dated 1551 by the editor, more probably 1552); PRO SP 10/14/4, 10/18/13 (misdated in the Calendar).

20. 2 & 3 Philip and Mary, cc. 5, 2, 3; *CJ*, vol. I, pp. 43–4.

21. 1 & 2 Philip and Mary, c. 2; *CJ*, vol. I, pp. 20, 25, 33, 41; *LJ*, vol. I, pp. 439, 462, 490; Bush, *Government Policy*, pp. 77 and 82, note 189; 3 & 4 Edward VI, cc. 19, 21; 5 & 6 Edward VI, c. 14; *LJ*, vol. I, pp. 381, 402, 406, 424.

22. *Agrarian History*, vol. IV, pp. 214–28; *LJ*, vol. I, p. 295.

23. *Agrarian History*, vol. IV, p. 215; Elton, *Reform and Renewal*, pp. 101–6; *Discourse of the Common Weal*, pp. xlvii–xlviii; Bush, *Government Policy*, pp. 77–8, 80–1; *CJ*, vol. I, pp. 16–19, 38; *LJ*, vol. I, pp. 404, 410, 412, 418.

24. 3 & 4 Edward VI, c. 3; *CJ*, vol. I, pp. 13–14, 16; *LJ*, vol. I, pp. 385–6; 2 & 3 Philip and Mary, c. 3; PRO SP 10/2/21.

25. 5 & 6 Edward VI, c. 5; 2 & 3 Philip and Mary, c. 2; *Tudor Economic Documents*, vol. I, p. 326; 5 Elizabeth, c. 2.

26. G. R. Elton, 'An Early Tudor Poor Law', *EcHR*, 2nd ser., VI (1953) 55–67. Cf. S. E. Lehmberg, *The Later Parliaments of Henry VIII, 1536–1547* (Cambridge, 1977) p. 18.

27. 1 Edward VI, c. 3; C. S. L. Davies, 'Slavery and Protector Somerset: The Vagrancy Act of 1547', *EcHR*, 2nd ser., XIX (1966) 533–49.

28. 3 & 4 Edward VI, c. 16; 14 Elizabeth, c. 5.

29. 5 & 6 Edward VI, c. 2; *LJ*, vol. I, pp. 408, 414, 419–20; *CJ*, vol. I, p. 22.

30. 1 & 2 Philip and Mary, c. 16; 2 & 3 Philip and Mary, c. 5; *CJ*, vol. I, 43–4; *LJ*, vol. I, pp. 503, 505.

31. 5 Elizabeth, c. 3, sect. x.

32. *Tudor Royal Proclamations*, vol. II, no. 420; Norfolk and Norwich Record Office, Norwich Court Book 1555–6, p. 122; HMC, *Various Collections*, vol. II, pp. 89–92 (Wombwell MSS.); *York Civic Records*, vol. v, pp. 154–8; G. Burnet, *History of the Reformation of the Church of England* (Oxford, 1829) vol. II, ii, p. 399. Cf. the savage Marian act against gypsies: 1 & 2 Philip and Mary, c. 4.

33. See Sir Thomas Smith's comments: P. F Tytler, *England under the Reigns of Edward VI and Mary* (1839), vol. I, pp. 186–7.

34. J. J. Scarisbrick, 'Cardinal Wolsey and the Common Weal', in *Wealth and Power in Tudor England*, ed. E. W. Ives, R. J. Knecht and J. J. Scarisbrick (1978), pp. 45–67; Bush, *Government Policy*, pp. 44–8; *Tudor Economic Documents*, vol. I, p. 41; 5 & 6 Edward VI, c. 5, sect. ii; 2 & 3 Philip and Mary, c. 2, sect. iii.

35. On 1527 see R. W. Heinze, *The Proclamations of the Tudor Kings* (Cambridge, 1976) pp. 99–102.

36. PRO, SP 10/9/55, 10/10/40–3, 10/11/5; *Tudor Royal Proclamations*, vol. I, no. 365, p. 502; *CPR*, 1550–3, pp. 140–2; HMC, *Salisbury (Cecil) MSS.*, vol. I, p. 81; *York Civic Records*, vol. v, pp. 44–7; HMC, *15th Report*, app. x, p. 49; *Tudor Economic Documents*, vol. I, p. 148; Lincolnshire Record Office, Lincoln Entries of Common Council 1541–64, fo. 79.

37. N. S. B. Gras, *The Evolution of the English Corn Market* (Cambridge, Mass., 1926) pp. 448–9; Norfolk and Norwich Record Office, PRA 652, 382 × 8. Cf. *CPR*, Philip and Mary, III, 1555–7, p. 369; and *Tudor Royal*

*Proclamations*, vol. II, no. 430, an incomplete draft of a proclamation which may, like no. 366, have included search provisions.

38. *Tudor Royal Proclamations*, vol. I, nos 365, 366; PRO SP 10/11/11, 15; *Tudor Economic Documents*, vol. III, p. 188; Heinze, *Proclamations*, pp. 226–33.

39. F. A. Youngs, *The Proclamations of the Tudor Queens* (Cambridge, 1976) pp. 114–16.

40. *The Records of the City of Norwich*, ed W. Hudson and J. C. Tingey (Norwich and London, 1906–10), vol. II, p. 126; Exeter City Muniments, Act Book 2, fo. 95r.; *The Coventry Leet Book Part III*, ed. M. D. Harris (Early English Text Society, CXXXVIII, 1909), pp. 783–4; A. D. Dyer, *The City of Worcester in the Sixteenth Century* (Leicester, 1973) pp. 166–7. Cf. N. Bacon, *The Annalls of Ipswich 1654*, ed. W. H. Richardson (Ipswich, 1880) p. 235; J. W. F. Hill, *Tudor and Stuart Lincoln* (Cambridge, 1956) pp. 66–7; W. E. Stephens, 'Great Yarmouth under Queen Mary', *Norfolk Archaeology*, XXIX (1946) 147, 149.

41. *York Civic Records*, vol. V, pp. 25–76; D. M. Palliser, 'Epidemics in Tudor York', *Northern History*, VIII (1973) 49–51.

42. For instance, B. Pullan, *Rich and Poor in Renaissance Venice* (Oxford, 1971) pp. 216 *et seq.*; N. Z. Davis, *Society and Culture in Early Modern France* (1975) ch. 2; H. Heller, 'Famine, Revolt and Heresy at Meaux 1521–5', *Archiv für Reformationsgeschichte*, LXVIII (1977) 144–57.

43. 'The Ordre of the Hospital of S. Bartholomewes', in Thomas Vicary, *The Anatomie of the Bodie of Man*, ed. F. J. and P. Furnivall (Early English Text Society, extra ser., LIII, 1888) pp. 293, 294, 296, 313; *Tudor Economic Documents*, vol. III, pp. 416, 421, 437.

44. W. K. Jordan, *The Charities of London 1480–1660* (1960) pp. 187–91, 423; T. S., *A Psalme of Thanksgiving, to be Sung by the Children of Christ's Hospitall* (1610).

45. *Tudor Economic Documents*, vol. II, 305–6.

46. R. M. Kingdon, 'Social Welfare in Calvin's Geneva', *American Historical Review*, LXXVI (1971) 50–69; Davis, *Society and Culture*, ch. 2.

47. The aldermen's activities are recorded in LCRO, Rep., *passim*, and their careers described in A. B. Beaven, *The Aldermen of the City of London*, 2 vols (1908).

48. J. A. Kingdon, *Richard Grafton, Citizen and Grocer of London* (1901); Beaven, *Aldermen*, vol. II, p. 29; LCRO, Rep. 11, fos 445v.–446r.; C. E. Challis, *The Tudor Coinage* (Manchester, 1978) pp. 31, 81–2. Another printer involved in the early stages was Thomas Berthelet: LCRO, Journal 15, fo. 213v.

49. LCRO, Rep. 10, fos 79v., 81v.; Rep. 11, fos 254v., 346. *Parliamentary Papers*, 1840, XIX (1) (Reports of Charity Commissioners) 1–4, 472–3.

50. Ibid., pp. 74–86, 614–6; LCRO, Rep. 12, fos 51v., 57v., 59v., 312v., 331v., 510v.

51. LCRO, Rep. 13, fo. 6or.; *CPR*, 1533, pp. 283–5; *Parliamentary Papers*, 1840, XIX (1) 387–8; *Tudor Economic Documents*, vol. II, pp. 306–12.

52. E. G. O'Donoghue, *Bridewell Hospital, Palace, Prison, Schools*, vol. I (1923) p. 154; LCRO, Rep. 13, fos 442r., 448v., 544r.

53. *John Howes' MS., 1582*, ed. W. Lempriere (1904) pp. 66–70.
54. W. Schenk, *Reginald Pole, Cardinal of England* (1950) p. 147; *John Howes' MS.*, pp. 66–8; *Visitation Articles and Injunctions of the Period of the Reformation*, ed. W. H. Frere and W. M. Kennedy (Alcuin Club, XIV–XVI, 1910), vol. II, pp. 368, 425–6. See PRO SP 11/14/12, fo. 35, for a memorial, touching on poor relief, presented to Philip.
55. *Some Early Tracts on Poor Relief*, ed. F. R. Salter (1926) pp. 76–8.
56. *CPR*, 1555–7, pp. 543–4; PRO SP 11/9/8; *John Howes' MS.*, pp. 71–2; *Visitation Articles*, vol. II, p. 351; LCRO, Rep. 13, fos 442r., 453r., 456v. and 478v., and Repertory 14, fo. 24v.
57. Vicary, *Anatomie of the Bodie of Man*, pp. 292–3.
58. LCRO, Rep. 11, fo. 511v.; Reportary 12, fo. 50; Rep. 13, fo. 459v. St. Bartholomew's Hospital Treasurers' Ledger 1547–61, *passim*.
59. *Tudor Economic Documents*, vol. III, p. 418; *Parliamentary Papers*, 1840, XIX (1) 75.
60. LCRO, Rep. 11, fos 353r., 358v.; Guildhall Library, MS. 12819/1, Christ's Hospital Treasurers' Accounts 1552–8, fo. 33 and *passim*.
61. See V. Pearl, 'Puritans and Poor Relief: The London Workhouse 1649–60', in *Puritans and Revolutionaries. Essays in Seventeenth-Century History presented to Christopher Hill*, ed. D. Pennington and K. Thomas (Oxford, 1978) pp. 206–32.
62. Cf. Thirsk, *Economic Policy and Projects*, p. 43.
63. W. K. Jordan, *Philanthropy in England 1480–1660* (1959); C. Carlton, *The Court of Orphans* (Leicester, 1974).
64. The phrase is J. P. Cooper's: *Times Literary Supplement*, 16 June 1978, p. 674.

# 6. THE LEGACY OF THE SCHISM: CONFUSION, CONTINUITY AND CHANGE IN THE MARIAN CLERGY *Rex H. Pogson*

1. Pole's legatine register is the major source for day-to-day administration during his mission. The original is in Douai Municipal Library, but there are microfilm copies in Lambeth Palace Library and at Ampleforth Abbey, Yorkshire. It is a detailed list of dispensations, absolutions, grants, letters, and so on, amounting to 854 folios, but, owing to some strange gaps in the record, incomplete.
2. *The Acts and Monuments of John Foxe*, ed. S. R. Cattley (1837–41), vol. VI, p. 592.
3. BL Cotton MS. Cleopatra E vi, fo. 359 (Pole to Tunstall in 1536); *Epistolae Reginaldi Poli*, ed. A. M. Quirini (Brescia, 1744–57), vol. v, p. 297.
4. BL Harl. 417, fo. 70 (Pole to Cranmer).
5. There is detailed treatment of this theme in C. Cross, 'Churchmen and the Royal Supremacy', in *Church and Society in England: Henry VIII to James I*, ed. F. Heal and R. O'Day (1977), pp. 17–24; and in D. M. Loades, *The Oxford Martyrs* (1970) pp. 37–69. See also J. A. Muller, *Stephen Gardiner and the Tudor Reaction* (New York, 1926), and, for changes

in Cranmer's doctrinal position, P. Brooks, *Thomas Cranmer's Doctrine of the Eucharist* (1965).

6. BL Stowe 141, MS. fo. 63, 30 May 1553.

7. Pole's difficulties over Church lands are discussed in R. H. Pogson, 'Revival and Reform in Mary Tudor's Church: A Question of Money', *Journal of Ecclesiastical History*, xxv (1974) 252–4. It took the whole summer of 1554 to convince Pole and Rome of the concessions which they had to make.

8. Foxe, *Acts and Monuments*, vol. vii, p. 407.

9. Ibid., p. 288.

10. The extraordinary findings of John Hooper, Edwardian bishop of Gloucester, on clerical ignorance, are outlined in A. G. Dickens, *The English Reformation* (1964) p. 243, citing F. D. Price, 'Gloucester Diocese under Bishop Hooper', *Transactions of Bristol and Gloucester Archaeological Society*, lx (1939) 51–151.

11. D. M. Loades, *Two Tudor Conspiracies* (Cambridge, 1965) pp. 4–6.

12. *CSP Sp.*, vol. xi, p. 228 (Renard to the bishop of Arras, 9 Sep 1553).

13. Archivio Segreto Vaticano, Rome: Nunziatore Diverse 145, fo. 126 (a conversation of 19 Sep 1554 between Mary and one of Pole's agents, Henry Penning).

14. D. B. Fenlon, *Heresy and Obedience in Tridentine Italy* (Cambridge, 1972), gives a detailed account of Pole's Italian experiences and his troubles at Trent.

15. He had expressed this view at great length and with bitterness in a letter to Edward VI: *Epistolarum Reginaldi Poli*, vol. iv, pp. 309, 322, 335, 349, etc.

16. Pole put this view in a heated Council debate on 21 Dec 1554, soon after his arrival in England: BL Add. 41577, fo. 161.

17. Pole's refusal of Jesuit help is discussed by J. H. Crehan, 'St. Ignatius and Cardinal Pole', *Archivium Historicum Societatis Iesu*, xxv (1956) 72–98. Pole made it clear that he deliberately avoided preaching campaigns until he could feel that Roman discipline had been restored (*Epistolarum Reginaldi Poli*, vol. v, p. 73).

18. BL Add. 41577, fo. xx 161.

19. *CSP Sp.*, vol. xi, p. 202; PRO SP 11/7/15; ibid., 69/11/119 (Carne to Mary from Rome, 11 Dec 1557).

20. Ibid., 11/13/114 and 15/8/120, for letters of Tunstall and Thirlby to Pole; Bonner's register (Guildhall Library, London, MS. 9531/12) gives ample evidence of his enforcement of Pole's plans.

21. The decrees of the synod were printed in Rome in 1562 as *Reformatio Angliae*, and reprinted in facsimile in 1962. The sixth decree is on p. 17.

22. The bulls of August 1553 are printed in C. Dodd, *The Church History of England from 1500 to the year 1688*, ed. M. A. Tierney (1839–43), vol. ii, pp. cx–cxvii; the amplification of the powers of March 1554 is in Archivio Segreto Vaticano, Rome, as are Paul IV's additions. For detail, see R. H. Pogson, 'Cardinal Pole – Papal Legate to England in Mary Tudor's Reign' (unpublished Ph.D. thesis, Cambridge, 1972) pp. 325–8.

23. Various opinions can be found in W. H. Frere, *The Marian Reaction in Relation to the Clergy* (Church History Society, XVIII, 1896); E. C. Messenger, *The Reformation, the Mass, and the Priesthood*, 2 vols (1936–7); J. J. Hughes, *Stewards of the Lord, a Reappraisal of Anglican Orders* (1970).

24. For example, Messenger, *Reformation*, vol. II, pp. 128–9, cites instances of reordination of those with Edwardian orders; one such reference coincides with an entry in the legatine register.

25. Cf. P. Hughes, 'A Hierarchy that Fought', *Clergy Review*, XVIII (Jan 1940) 25–39. Biographical works on some of the leading bishops are to be found in the Notes on Further Reading. The *DNB* gives details of many of their careers.

26. Pole's archiepiscopal register, Lambeth Palace Library, fos 61–2.

27. BL Add. 12529, fo. 5: by December 1556 Pole's agents and friends were wearying of the battle to reason with Paul IV.

28. BL Cotton MS., Vespasian F iii, fo. 28 (Pole to Elizabeth, 14 Nov 1558).

29. *Reformatio Angliae*, pp. 11, 15, 21.

30. 21 Henry VIII, c. 13. M. Bowker, *The Secular Clergy in the Diocese of Lincoln, 1495–1520* (Cambridge, 1968), and P. Heath, *The English Parish Clergy on the Eve of the Reformation* (1969), provide detailed studies of the abuses and problems of the early sixteenth-century Church.

31. H. E. P. Grieve, 'The Deprived Married Clergy in Essex, 1553–61', *TRHS*, 4th ser., XXII (1940) 141–69.

32. *Reformatio Angliae*, p. 23.

33. A. C. F. Beales, 'Education under Mary Tudor', *Month*, new ser., XIII (1955) 342–51; D. M. Loades, 'The Press Under the Early Tudors: A Study in Censorship and Sedition', *Cambridge Bibliographical Society Transactions*, IV, i (1964) 29–50; J. Simon, *Education and Society in Tudor England* (Cambridge, 1966).

34. Foxe, *Acts and Monuments*, p. 258.

35. *Concilia Magnae Britanniae et Hiberniae*, ed. D. Wilkins (1737), vol. IV, p. 166; Simon, *Education and Society*, p. 303; *VCH; Lincolnshire*, vol II, p. 431; the information on Wells is from a paper by Dr R. Dunning to the colloquium on ecclesiastical history at Cambridge, 1972.

36. *VCH: Worcestershire*, vol. IV, p. 479; *VCH: Warwickshire*, vol. II, p. 324.

37. Detailed discussion of the links between various attempts at educational reform in the Church can be found in J. A. O'Donohoe, *Tridentine Seminary Legislation, its Sources and Formation* (Louvain, 1957); 'The Seminary Legislation of the Council of Trent', *Il Concilio de Trento e la riforma tridentina* (Rome, 1965).

38. Foxe, *Acts and Monuments*, vol. VII, p. 91.

39. Beales, in *Month*, new ser., XIII, 346; BL Add. 5807, fo. 143.

40. BM Harl. 416, fo. 71, for the speech of welcome to Pole's visitors to Oxford; Pole's archiepiscopal register, Lambeth, fos 78–80, for the All Souls' episode.

41. J. E. Oxley, *The Reformation in Essex to the Death of Mary* (Manchester, 1965) p. 187.

42. Foxe, *Acts and Monuments*, vol. VII, p. 435.
43. *Visitation Articles and Injunctions of the Period of the Reformation*, ed. W. H. Frere and W. P. M. Kennedy (Alcuin Club, XIV–XVI, 1908), vol. II, p. 412; Lambeth Palace Library, VC III/1/2; Harpsfield's visitation in *Archdeacon Harpsfield's Visitation, 1557*, ed. L. E. Whatmore (Catholic Record Society, XLV–XLVI, 1950–1); Somerset County record Office, Taunton, D/D/Ca. 27.
44. D. Knowles, *The Religious Orders in England* (Cambridge, 1959) vol. III, pp. 421–43.
45. Ibid., p. 438.
46. Ibid., p. 425.
47. Ibid., p. 431.
48. *VCH: Somerset*, vol. II, p. 38; *VCH: City of York*, p. 149.

7. PUBLIC OFFICE AND PRIVATE PROFIT: THE LEGAL ESTABLISHMENT IN THE REIGN OF MARY TUDOR
*Lewis Abbott*

1. *Harleian Miscellany*, ed. J. Malham (1808–11), vol. I, p. 326.
2. See S. T. Bindoff, 'A Kingdom at Stake, 1553', *History Today*, III (1953) 642–8.
3. *CSP Sp.*, 1553, XI pp. 49–50, 52, 55, 57; T. Fuller, *Church History of Britain* (Oxford, 1845) vol. IV, pp. 137–45.
4. See most recently W. K. Jordan, *Edward VI: The Threshold of Power* (1970) pp. 516–20.
5. Fuller, *Church History*, vol. IV, pp. 140–2.
6. HMC, *16th Report: Montagu of Beaulieu*, pp. 4–5.
7. *CSP Sp.*, 1553, XI, p. 57.
8. Fuller, *Church History*, vol. IV, pp. 142–3.
9. *The Chronicle of Queen Jane and of Two Years of Queen Mary*, ed. J. G. Nichols (Camden Society, XLVIII, 1850) p. 93.
10. W. S. Holdsworth, *History of English Law*, 3rd edn (1922) vol. II, pp. 504–12.
11. *Holinshed's Chronicles*, ed. H. Ellis (1807–8), vol. III, p. 826.
12. J. Strype, *Memorials of Thomas Cranmer* (1840) vol. II, p. 920.
13. *Letters of Stephen Gardiner*, ed. J. A. Muller (Cambridge, 1933), pp. 390, 393, 444; cited in W. H. Dunham, 'Regal Power and the Rule of Law', *Journal of British Studies*, III, (1963) 25.
14. Cf. *Letters of Gardiner*, pp. 268–9, 393, 493–4.
15. HMC, *16th Report: Montagu of Beaulieu*, p. 6; *Wriothesley's Chronicle*, ed. W. D. Hamilton (Camden Society, new ser., XX, 1877) vol. II, p. 91.
16. *Chronicle of Queen Jane*, pp. 99–100; *Wriothesley's Chronicle*, p. 91.
17. G. Burnet, *History of the Reformation* (1865) vol. II, p. 399.
18. *CPR*, 1553–4, Philip and Mary, I, p. 71.
19. *Chronicle of Queen Jane*, pp. 99–100.
20. *Harleian Miscellany*, vol. I, pp. 326–7; *Letters of Gardiner*, pp. 228–30.
21. *APC*, 1553, IV, pp. 331, 426; 1554, pp. 103, 180, 363.

22. See *CJ*, vol. i, p. 26; *CPR*, 1553–4, Philip and Mary, i, p. 162.

23. *LJ*, vol. i, pp. 474, 480–1, 489; *CJ*, vol. i, p. 40.

24. *CPR*, 1555–7, Philip and Mary, iii, p. 363; E. Foss, *Judges of England* (1848–64) vol. v, pp. 390–2.

25. *CPR*, 1557–8, Philip and Mary, iv, p. 457.

26. J. Foxe, *Actes and Monuments*, ed. S. R. Cattley (1870 edn) vol. viii, pp. 304–5; *DNB*, *vide* Bendlowes; *CSP Sp.*, 1558–67, p. 224.

27. Cf. C. Russell, *Crisis of Parliaments* (1971) pp. 133–4; C. H. Williams, *The Making of the Tudor Despotism* (1967) pp. 232–4; W. R. D. Jones, *The Tudor Commonwealth* (1967) pp. 43–64.

28. G. R. Elton, *Policy and Police* (Cambridge, 1972) *passim*; cf. D. M. Loades, *Two Tudor Conspiracies* (Cambridge, 1965) p. 147.

29. *CPR*, 1556–7, Philip and Mary, iii, pp. 281–2; J. E. Oxley, *The Reformation in Essex* (1965) *passim*.

30. H. F. M. Prescott, *Mary Tudor* (1952) p. 295.

31. Foxe, *Acts and Monuments*, vol. viii, pp. 304–5; Oxley, *Reformation in Essex*, pp. 226–7.

32. J. Strype, *Ecclesiastical Memorials* (1822) vol. iii, p. 440; cf. A. Hassel Smith, *County and Court* (1974) pp. 178–9.

33. *APC*, 1554–6, pp. 30, 104, 135, 165: Foxe, *Acts and Monuments*, vol. vii, p. 86.

34. 1 Mary, st. 1, c. 2.

35. Elton, *Policy and Police*, pp. 80–2; *Wriothesley's Chronicle*, pp. 101–41; *The Diary of Henry Machyn*, ed. J. G. Nichols (Camden Society, xlii, 1848), pp. 137–81.

36. *Tudor Royal Proclamations*, ed. P. L. Hughes and J. F. Larkin (1964–69), vol. ii, p. 4.

37. J. Loach, 'Pamphlets and Politics', *BIHR*, xlviii (1975) 31–44.

38. Elton, *Policy and Police*, p. 82.

39. 1 & 2 Philip and Mary, c. 6; *LJ*, vol. i, pp. 477–8; *CJ*, vol. i, p. 39; See Loach, in *BIHR*, xlviii.

40. *Official Returns* (1878) vol. i, pp. 389–91. I also wish to thank Professor S. T. Bindoff and the History of Parliament Trust for granting access to biographies of certain lawyer MPs.

41. *CJ*, vol. i, pp. 37–41; *LJ*, vol. i, pp. 465–91.

42. *Papiers d'Etat du Cardinal de Granvelle*, ed. C. Weiss (Paris, 1841–52), vol. iv, p. 346; cf. E. F. Rice, *Foundations of Early Modern Europe* (1970).

43. *Papiers d'État*, p. 346; E. H. Harbison, *Rival Ambassadors at the Court of Queen Mary* (1940) p. 217; *CSP Sp.*, 1554, p. 130.

44. BL Lansd. 1057, fo. 5v.

45. J. A. Froude, *History of England: The Reign of Mary Tudor* (1924) p. 179.

46. *CJ*, vol. i, pp. 39–40; 1 & 2 Philip and Mary, c. 8., sect. xiii.

47. *CSP Ven.*, 1555–6, p. 226; *LJ*, vol. i, p. 504; *Cj*, vol. i, p. 43.

48. Dunham, in *Journal of British Studies*, iii, 42.

49. *The Tudor Constitution*, ed. G. R. Elton (1960), p. 60.

50. *LJ*, vol. i, p. 474; *CSP Sp.*, 1554, xii, p. 126.

51. *CJ*, vol. I, p. 39; *Official Returns*, p. 390; *Papiers d'État*, p. 347.

52. Ibid., p. 347.

53. *Official Returns*, vol. I, p. 389; cf. Harbison, *Rival Ambassadors*, p. 347.

54. J. E. Neale, *The Elizabethan House of Commons*, (1949) pp. 199, 273; *Official Returns*, vol. I, pp. 390, 393, 395.

55. *CSP Sp.*, 1554, XII, pp. 128–31; *Papiers d'État*, p. 357.

56. *CJ*, vol. I, p. 41; *LJ*, vol. I, pp. 489–91; I & 2 Philip and Mary, c. 10.

57. See L. M. Hill, 'The Two Witness Rule in English Treason Trials', *American Journal of Legal History*, XII (1968) 103–6.

58. *CJ*, vol. I, p. 37; Foxe, *Acts and Monuments*, vol. VIII, pp. 356–9.

59. *LJ*, vol. I, p. 470; *CJ*, vol. I, p. 38.

60. *LJ*, vol. I, pp. 472, 474.

61. Ibid., pp. 475, 477; *CJ*, vol. I, p. 39; I & 2 Philip and Mary, c. 3.

62. I & 2 Philip and Mary, c. 3, and I Elizabeth, c. 6.

63. See T. F. T. Plucknett, *A Concise History of the Common Law*, 5th edn (1956) pp. 485–7.

64. Ibid., p. 486.

65. See L. W. Abbott, *Law Reporting in England 1485–1585* (1973) pp. 73–6.

66. See *Deputy Keeper of the Public records*, 4th Report (1843) app. II, pp. 232–59.

67. Holdsworth, *History of English Law*, vol. IV, pp. 492–9.

68. *CSP Sp.*, 1553, XI, p. 185; *Chronicle of Queen Jane*, p. 17.

69. Ibid., pp. 186–7.

70. Ibid., pp. 184–5.

71. *State Trials*, ed. W. Cobbett, T. B. Howell, *et al.* (1816–98) vol. I, p. 872.

72. *CSP Sp.*, 1554, p. 221; cf. Loades, *Two Tudor Conspiracies*, pp. 97–8.

73. *CPR*, 1553–4, pp. 18–19.

74. Ibid., pp. 20–2, 24.

75. Loach, in *BIHR*, XLVIII, 32–3.

76. *APC*, 1554–6, pp. 135, 141; Foxe, *Acts and Monuments*, vol. VII, p. 86; cf. Prescott, *Mary Tudor*, p. 305.

77. Strype, *Memorials*, vol. III, p. 586; but cf. A. G. Dickens, *The English Reformation* (1964) p. 267.

78. *CPR*, 1555–7, p. 281; Foxe, *Acts and Monuments*, vol. VIII, pp. 304–5.

79. Ibid., pp. 301–3.

80. Froude, *History of England*, pp. 280–1.

81. Oxley, *Reformation in Essex*, p. 123.

82. Ibid., pp. 158–60, 170–5.

83. *APC*, 1552–4, pp. 305, 308, 338, 415, 422.

84. Ibid., 1554–6, p. 63.

85. Ibid., p. 147; 1556–8, p. 354.

86. *CPR*, 1553–4, p. 71; 1557–8, pp. 65, 459. *APC*, 1556–8, p. 211.

87. *CPR*, 1557–8, pp. 50, 331.

88. Ibid., 1553–4, p. 327; 1554–5, p. 214; 1556–7, p. 59.

89. Foss, *Judges of England*, vol v, p. 511. *CPR*, 1557–8, p. 459; 1558–60, pp. 64–5.

90. Abbott, *Law Reporting*, pp. 74–5.

91. See Foss, *Judges of England*, vol. v, pp. 277–552.

92. *CPR*, 1557–8, p. 457; 1558–60, p. 65. Strype, *Memorials*, vol. III, pp. 262–4.

93. *The Mirror for Magistrates*, ed. L. B. Campbell (1938) p. 73.

94. Foss, *Judges of England*, vol. v pp. 340–7; *CPR*, 1558–60, pp. 18, 58, 104.

95. Foss, *Judges of England*, vol. v, pp. 410–11; cf. J. E. Neale, *The Elizabethan House of Commons* (1949) pp. 309–11.

96. See the case of Skrogges v. *Coleshill* (1559), printed in J. Dyer's *Reports* (1794) vol. II, pp. 175a–b; cf. Margaret Hastings, *The Court of Common Pleas in Fifteenth Century England* (1947) pp. 101–2.

97. M. Axton, 'The Influence of Edmund Plowden's Succession Treatise', *Huntington Library Quarterly*, XXXVII (1973) 209–26.

98. A. Wood, *Athenae Oxonienses* (1813–20) vol. I, pp. 356–8, 405.

99. *DNB*, vide Browne.

## 8.    ENGLAND AND THE FRENCH WAR, 1557–9
### C. S. L. Davies

1. L. Pastor, *History of the Popes*, Eng. trans. (1891–1940) vol XIV, pp. 129–39. See *CSP Ven.*, 1556–7, VI, ii, no. 746, for a choice piece of papal invective.

2. E. H. Harbison, *Rival Ambassadors at the Court of Queen Mary* (1940) pp. 320–8. For the treaty, see the statute 1 Mary, st. 3, c. 2.

3. Although it is impossible to be certain of the yield until a harvest is safely in the barn, some indications of what a harvest may be like are often available from April; if the prognosis is good, farmers and dealers storing grain during a high-price year will release it immediately and so cause a sudden drop in prices. See P. J. Bowden, in *Agrarian History of England and Wales*, vol. IV: *1500–1640*, ed. J. Thirsk (Cambridge, 1967) p. 620.

4. W. G. Hoskins, 'Harvest Fluctuations and English Economic History, 1480–1619', in *Essays in Agrarian History*, ed. W. E. Minchinton (Newton Abbot, 1965), vol. I; F. J. Fisher, 'Influenza and Inflation in Tudor England', in *Ec. HR*, 2nd ser., XVIII (1965); A. Friis, 'The Two Crises in the Netherlands, 1557', in *Scandinavian Ec. HR*, vol. I (1953); LCRO, Rep. 13 pt ii, fos 370, 476 and 490 (French grain), 501 and 503 (glut); Stow, *Annales* (1631 edn) p. 631.

5. S. R. Gammon, *Statesman and Schemer: William, First Lord Paget* (Newton Abbot, 1973) pp. 212–3; *CSP, Scotland* (1898), vol. I, no. 416.

6. For these two paragraphs see *DNB*, and G. E. Cokayne, *Complete Peerage*, 13 vols (revised edn, 1910–49), as appropriate; C. H. Garrett, *The Marian Exiles* (Cambridge, 1938); D. M. Loades, *Two Tudor Conspiracies* (Cambridge, 1965); R. Holinshed, *Chronicles* (1577) vol. I, p. 487.

7. Loades, *Two Tudor Conspiracies*, pp. 154, 204.

8. *CSP Ven*, 1556–7, VI, ii, no. 884, pp. 1046 ff., for a perceptive Venetian view; *CSP For.*, 1559–60, p. 168, for sneers by Philip's minister Granvelle; and BL Harl 68, fos 1–7, for an English view.

9. M. Oppenheim, *History of the Administration of the Royal Navy* (1896) p. 112, and Tom Glasgow in *Mariner's Mirror*, LIII and LVI (see Notes on Further Reading); Harbison, *Rival Ambassadors*, pp. 187, 255; BL Cotton MSS., Otho Eix, fo. 88 (orders of September 1555); PRO E 351/2195, 2196; *CSP Sp.*, 1554–8, XIII nos 313–4, 334, for silver transport.

10. The best of several copies of the accounts is BL Stowe 571, fos 88 ff.

11. *CSP Sp.*, 1554–8, XIII nos 321–3.

12. *CSP Sp.*, 1554–8, XIII nos 339, 413; Holinshed, *Chronicles*, vol. 1, p. 1768.

13. BL Stowe 571, fo. 95.

14. *State Papers*, ed. S. Haynes (1740), p. 205; *Wriothesley's Chronicle*, ed. W. D. Hamilton (Camden Society, new ser., XI vol. II 1877), p. 148; *The Diary of Henry Machyn* (Camden Society, XLII, 1848), pp. 147–150.

15. For Scottish politics generally see G. Donaldson, *Scotland, James V to James VII* (1965) ch. 5. For detailed events of 1557 from the Scottish side, see J. Leslie, *History of Scotland* (Scottish Text Society, 1884–9) vol. 11, pp. 367ff.; from the English side, G. W. Bernard, 'The Fourth and Fifth Earls of Shrewsbury. A Study in the Power of the Early Tudor Nobility' (unpublished D Phil. thesis, Oxford, 1978) ch. 7.

16. E. Lodge, *Illustrations of English History* (1838 edn) vol. 1, documents 29–60 J. Strype, *Ecclesiastical Memorials* (1824 edn) vol. III, pt ii, documents 75–7; *CSP Dom (Add)*, 1547–64, pp. 450–9.

17. Jacques de Thou, *History of His Own Time*, Eng. trans. (1729) vol. I, p. 239.

18. P. T. J. Morgan, 'The Government of Calais, 1485–1558' (unpublished D Phil. thesis, Oxford, 1966) ch. 10; L. Romier, *Origines Politiques des Guerres de Religion* (Paris, 1913–14) vol. II, pp. 215–6; C. Jugé, *Nicolas Denisot du Mans* (Le Mans, 1907) pp. 121–2.

19. See Morgan, 'Government of Calais'; and H. M. Colvin, in *The History of the King's Works*, vol. III, ed. Colvin, D. R. Ransome and J. Summerson (1975), pp. 337–75. The 1556 survey is in *APC*, 1554–6, V, pp. 340–2.

20. For the establishment (other than Guisnes) see the 'Calais Act', 27 Henry VIII, c. 63; and cf. Ferrers in E. Arber, *An English Garner* (1877–98) vol. IV, p. 177. Guisnes may have had 800 English troops (Morgan, 'Government of Calais', p. 266) though this number seems to be arrived at by subtracting the 500 reinforcements sent by Philip from the 1300 reported by Churchyard to be holding Guisnes (Arber, *An English Garner*, vol. IV, p. 207).

21. *CSP For.*, 1553–8, Mary no. 696, for cancellation of orders for further reductions; *CSP Ven.*, 1557–8, VI, iii, no. 1161, for Henry's views.

22. Wentworth's and Grey's letter to the Council, 27 Dec 1557 (Arber, *An English Garner*, vol. IV, pp. 187–9); *CSP For.*, 1553–8, II nos 615, 631, 633.

23. Arber, *An English Garner*, vol. IV, p. 198. Philip acknowledged (*CSP Sp.*, 1554-8, XIII no. 367) that reports of lack of men and supplies had encouraged the French to attack.

24. François de Rabutin, repr. in B. Zeller (ed.), *Henri II*, (Paris, 1890), vol. III, p. 141.

25. Colvin, in *History of the King's Works*, vol. III, p. 358.

26. Ferrers, in Arber, *An English Garner*, vol. IV, p. 177.

27. Morgan, 'Government of Calais', p. 256.

28. See the accounts of Ferrers in Arber, *An English Garner*, vol. IV, pp. 173-85, and of Highfield, ibid, pp. 196-201. On Guisnes, see Churchyard, ibid., pp. 205-14, and Grey, *Commentary on the Services . . . of William Lord Grey of Wilton* (Camden Society, 1847) XL, pp. 18-39; on the French side, de Rabutin, in *Henri II*, vol. III, pp. 129-52.

29. *CSP Ven.*, 1557-8, nos 1089, 1098.

30. Quoted from the Royal Archives in Brussels in 'The Loss of Calais', *North British Review*, XLV (1866) 446. I have not been able to check the document, but the warning seems to be the one referred to in Granvelle's summary of events (*CSP Sp.*, 1554-8, no. 365), which formed the basis of the 'official' Spanish version.

31. PRO SP 69/11/695-6 (*CSP For.*, 1553-8). Holinshed's *Chronicles*, vol. I, p. 1773, states that Highfield and Ralph Chamberlain were sent by Wentworth to warn the English government, which failed to respond 'either by wilful negligence' or disbelief of the news. There is no evidence of Chamberlain's mission. Highfield was summoned to London on routine business on 18 December; had he taken a warning with him he would surely have mentioned it in his defence. (Aber, *An English Garner*, vol. IV, p. 196: *APC*, 1556-8, p. 217.)

32. PRO SP 69/11/697, 699 (*CSP For.*, 1553-8). The last document is a draft – the addition of Rutland seems to be an afterthought.

33. PRO SP 69/11/700 (*CSP For.*, 1553-8).

34. PRO SP 69/11/701-3 (*CSP For.*, 1553-8); *CSP Sp.*, 1554-8, no. 346.

35. *APC*, 1556-8, p. 225. Next day, orders were given for more troops, apparently up to 2000, to be ready at Dover by 7 Jan. PRO SP 11/12/3, 11; *APC*, 1556-8, p. 230.

36. PRO SP 69/11/712, 715 (*CSP For.*, 1553-8); Arber, *An English Garner*, vol. IV, p. 198.

37. *APC*, 1556-8, pp. 230, 233-4; PRO SP 11/12/8-12, 16.

38. Arber, *An English Garner*, vol. IV, p. 178; PRO SP 11/12/18, 20; *APC*, 1556-8, p. 238.

39. PRO SP 11/12/22.

40. Ibid. 11/12/35. The English government offered to hand over Guisnes to Philip (*CSP Sp.*, 1554-8, p. 384).

41. Arber, *An English Garner*, vol. IV, p. 193.

42. Ibid., p. 197; de Rabutin, in *Henri II*, vol. III, p. 136: 27 Henry VIII, c. 63.

43. Arber, *An English Garner*, vol. IV, p. 199.

44. E. Lavisse, *Histoire de France* (Paris, 1900-11) vol. V, ii, p. 170, for Coligny; *CSP For.*, 1553-8, no. 689, for Grey.

45. *CSP Ven.*, 1557–8, no. 1161.

46. *CSP Sp.*, 1554–8, nos 392–3, 399.

47. *CSP For.*, 1553–8, 735; Arber, *An English Garner*, vol. IV, pp. 196ff.

48. *Deputy Keeper of the Public Records*, *4th Report* (1843) app. ii, pp. 259–62. *CPR*, 1558–60, pp. 331, 462; HMC, *Earl of Verulam* (1906) pp. 13–14. For the ferocity of the English attack on the castle, see Ferrers and Highfield in Arber, *An English Garner*, and on the French side, de Rabutin in *Henri II*, vol. III, p. 146, and de la Chastie in *Collection Complète des Mémoires*, ed. C. B. Petitot (Paris, 1819–29), vol. XXXII, pp. 490–1.

49. The most influential 'anti-Philip' account is that in A. F. Pollard, *The Political History of England, 1547–1603* (1910) pp. 167–70. Pollard makes much of d'Assonleville's remark, and of Venetian reports derived from what Grey told Henry II. Pollard fails to mention the evidence of Wentworth's ignoring Spanish warnings, although he had mentioned it in his earlier article on Wentworth in *DNB*. For d'Assonleville's remark, see *Relations Politiques des Pays-Bas et de l'Angleterre*, ed. de Lettenhove (Brussels, 1882–1900), vol. I, p. 133.

50. *CSP Sp.*, 1554–8, nos 353, 409 *Relations Politiques*, vol. I, pp. 96–103.

51. M. Gachard, *Retraite et Mort de Charles-Quint* (Brussels, 1854–5) vol. I, p. 253; *CSP Sp.*, 1554–8, nos 353, 397, 403, 423.

52. *CSP Ven.*, 1557–8, no. 1165.

53. *CSP Sp.*, 1554–8, nos 365, 367.

54. Ibid., no. 346.

55. Ibid, no. 348.

56. PRO SP 69/12/715; Arber, *An English Garner*, vol. IV, p. 198; *CSP Sp.*, 1554–8, XIII no. 350.

57. Ibid., p. 367; the absence of a field army presumably accounts for Vendeville's cry of warning. 'The English ask the King for help. I believe that, unless it comes soon, we shall hear an evil song' *Relations Politiques*, vol. I, p. 166).

58. For instance, John Bradforth's *Copye of a Lettre* (*STC*, no. 3480), printed in Strype, *Memorials*, vol. III, ii, pp. 339ff.; and R. P., *An Admonition to the towne of Callays* (1557; *STC*, no. 19078).

59. Pollard, *History of England*, p. 168; C. de la Roncière, *Histoire de la Marine Française* (Paris, 1899–1932) vol. III, pp. 552–64.

60. PRO SP 11/11/65. Five English ships with 400 men, compared to the French 'flying squadron' (de la Roncière, *Histoire*, vol. III, p. 557) of eight ships, with 850 men. All the ships were small or medium-sized; large warships were left in port in midwinter.

61. De Rabutin, in *Henri II*, vol. III, p. 136; Blaise de Monluc, *Commentaries*, ed. Ian Roy (1971), p. 177.

62. De la Roncière, *Histoire*, p. 557, quoting Brantôme's account of frozen rivers.

63. PRO SP 11/13/28.

64. *CSP For.*, 1553–8, II no. 335.

65. *CSP For.*, 1553–8, II no. 736; *CSP SP.*, 1554–8, XIII no. 450.

66. I. MacIvor, 'The Elizabethan Fortification of Berwick-on-Tweed', *Antiquaries Journal*, XLV (1965), pp. 64–96.

67. Printed in Strype, *Memorials*, vol. III, pt ii, pp. 101–3.

68. *CSP Sp.*, 1554–8, no. 423.

69. J. Strype, *The Life of . . . Sir Thomas Smith* (1820 edn) p. 146.

70. PRO SP 11/12/46; P. Clark, *English Provincial Society . . . Kent 1500–1640* (1977) pp. 104–5; *APC*, 1556–8, pp. 249, 257, 284, 296; *Tudor Royal Proclamations*, ed. P. H. Hughes and J. F. Larkin (New Haven, Conn., and London, 1964–9) vol. II, nos 438, 442; 4 & 5 Philip and Mary, c. 3.

71. See references in Pollard, *History of England*, p. 166. PRO SP 11/13/28 for the amount raised; cf. F. C. Dietz, *English Government Finance 1485—1558* (Urbana, Ill., 1920) pp. 164, 166. This point was made by the late J. P. Cooper.

72. PRO SP 11/13/28: S. J. Loach, 'Opposition to the Crown in Parliament, 1553–58' (unpublished D Phil. thesis, Oxford 1974) ch. 6.

73. See work cited in note 4, above; PRO SP 11/13/64; BL Add. 25079, fo. 8, for the reluctance of the Northamptonshire authorities to take men away from the harvest.

74. *CSP Sp.*, 1554–8, no. 397. Philip had been dissatisfied with Howard in 1557 (ibid., no. 338).

75. De la Roncière, *Histoire*, vol. III, p. 564.

76. Cf. Winter's very defensive account of what happened, and the compilation of a set of abstracts of Clinton's letters for July and August (PRO SP 11/13/60, 64).

77. *CSP Sp.*, 1554–8, no. 472; *CSP For.*, 1553–8, nos 829, 849, 856.

78. *CSP For.*, 1558–9, no. 335.

79. See J. Goring, 'Social Change and Military Decline in Mid-Tudor England', in *History*, LX (1975) 185–97.

80. SP 11/12/33–4.

81. Loach, 'Opposition to the Crown', ch. 6; 4 & 5 Philip and Mary, cc. 2–3.

82. D. M. Loades (ed.), *The Papers of George Wyatt*, (Camden Soc., 4th ser., V, 1968); BL Lansd, MSS. 1225, fos 41ff.; L. Boynton, *The Elizabethan Militia* (1965) pp. 90–125; BL Harl. MS 68 fo. 3. (Harl. 68 is a plea for a militia written at the beginning of Elizabeth's reign by Richard Barkhede. Another version, BL Lansd. 1225, fos 41–51, is intriguingly headed 'Project for a Land Militia Addressed to King Philip 1558'. But that document is a very inaccurate seventeenth-century copy. The copyist has inserted 'King' when the Harleian version has 'Queen' but the frequent references to the Siege of Leith make it clear that the copyist had before him a work composed, at the earliest, in 1560.) Schwendi was notable both as a German mercenary leader and as a military theorist.

83. Arber, *An English Garner*, vol. IV, pp. 175; Grey, *Commentary on the Services of Lord Grey of Wilton*, p. 33; John Foxe, *Acts and Monuments*, ed. J. Pratt (1870) vol. VIII, pp. 560–1.

84. *Diary of Henry Machyn*, pp. 152–3.

85. The Council estimated the foreign debt in June 1558 at £57,000 (PRO SP 11/13/28); in 1560 it was £279,000; R. B. Outhwaite, 'The Trials of Foreign Borrowing' in *EcHR*, 2nd ser., XIX (1966) 290.

86. PRO SP 11/12/12, 16.

# Notes on Contributors

LEWIS ABBOTT received his early education in Montreal and Ottawa. He read for his doctoral degree at the University of London, and now teaches history at the University of Guelph, Ontario. His field of research is English legal history, and he is the author of *Law Reporting in England, 1485–1585* (1973).

C. S. L. DAVIES, Fellow and Tutor in Modern History, Wadham College, Oxford, was educated at St Paul's School and at Wadham, and formerly taught at Glasgow University. He is author of *Peace, Print and Protestantism, 1450–1558* (1976), and articles on political and social history.

DALE HOAK is Associate Professor of History at the College of William and Mary, Virginia. He completed his doctoral thesis under the direction of G. R. Elton at Cambridge, and is the author of *The King's Council in the Reign of Edward VI* (Cambridge, 1976).

JENNIFER LOACH, Fellow and Tutor in Modern History, Somerville College, Oxford, was an undergraduate at St Hilda's College, Oxford. She is the author of a thesis on opposition in the parliaments of Mary's reign and of 'Pamphlets and Politics', *BIHR*, 1975.

REX H. POGSON is Head of History at Hymers College, Hull. He received his MA and Ph. D from Cambridge University. He has conducted research into Cardinal Pole's legatine mission to England, and has written two articles on Marian ecclesiastical administration.

PAUL SLACK, Fellow and Tutor in Modern History at Exeter College, Oxford, studied at St John's and Balliol colleges, Oxford, and has taught at the University of York. He was co-editor, with Peter Clark, of *Crisis and Order in English Towns, 1500–1700* (1972), and co-author, also with Peter Clark, of *English Towns in Transition, 1500–1700* (1976). He has written several articles, on social issues in the sixteenth and seventeenth centuries.

ROBERT TITTLER, Associate Professor of History at Concordia University of Montreal, was educated at Oberlin College and New York University. He has written *Nicholas Bacon: The Making of a Tudor Statesman* (1976), and edited *Accounts of the Roberts Family of Boarzell, Sussex, 1568–1582* (Sussex Record Society, LXXI, 1979).

ANN WEIKEL, Associate Professor of History at Portland State University, wrote a doctoral dissertation on the Marian Privy Council (Yale, 1966), and is currently editing a volume of the Wakefield Manor Court Rolls (1583–85) for the Yorkshire Archaeological Society.

# Index